The
Perfectionist's
Guide to
Losing Control

The Perfectionist's Guide to Losing Control

A Path to Peace and Power

KATHERINE MORGAN SCHAFLER

PORTFOLIO | PENGUIN

Portfolio / Penguin
An imprint of Penguin Random House LLC
penguinrandomhouse.com

Most Portfolio books are available at a discount when purchased in quantity for sales promotions or
corporate use. Special editions, which include personalized covers, excerpts, and corporate imprints,
can be created when purchased in large quantities. For more information, please call (212) 572-2232
or e-mail specialmarkets@penguinrandomhouse.com. Your local bookstore can also assist with
discounted bulk purchases using the Penguin Random House corporate Business-to-Business
program. For assistance in locating a participating retailer, e-mail B2B@penguinrandomhouse.com.

Library of Congress Cataloging-in-Publication Data
Names: Schafler, Katherine Morgan, author.
Title: The perfectionist's guide to losing control :
a path to peace and power / Katherine Morgan Schafler.
Identifiers: LCCN 2022034965 | ISBN 9780593329528 (hardcover) |
ISBN 9780593329535 (ebook) | ISBN 9780593544006 (international edition)
Subjects: LCSH: Perfectionism (Personality trait)
Classification: LCC BF698.35.P47 S33 2023 | DDC 155.2/32—dc23/eng/20220914
LC record available at https://lccn.loc.gov/2022034965

Printed in the United States of America
1st Printing

BOOK DESIGN BY CHRIS WELCH

Dedicated to Michael

The client vignettes in this book are fictional. All names, backgrounds, and story details have been materially altered; they are amalgamations of amalgamations. The session depictions in the pages that follow are storied around specific feelings, thoughts, and connections I encountered in the room, in the work, in the person. That core emotional accuracy is what I endeavored to express, not a recounting of anything else. I remain indescribably grateful to every person with whom I have had the privilege of working. To my former and current clients: your stories belong to you, and I will never share them.

She is what she is and she is whole.

DR. CLARISSA PINKOLA ESTÉS

CONTENTS

Perfectionism
Is a Power

The night before our wedding, my husband and I decided to sleep separately, so that each of us could spend the evening in the most relaxing way possible before our big day. I returned home from the rehearsal dinner at around 10:30 p.m., walked my dogs while responding to emails, and then worked out.

After working out, I took an amazing shower, rewrapped the gifts I was giving to my bridesmaids the following day (the gift wrap from the store graffitied the paper with so much tape, and it was all too kitschy in the first place), filed some clinical notes, edited my vows in bed for about twenty minutes, checked my emails again, and then drifted off to sleep a touch after 2:00 a.m. It was, by all accounts, the perfect night.

Perfectionists are not balanced people, and that's okay. Subscribing to prepackaged notions of balance and generic wellness when they don't fit who you are isn't being healthy, it's being obedient. I wrote this book for the women* who are done being "good." I wrote this book for the women who are ready to set themselves free.

If you were sitting across from me on my therapist couch right now, we could share confidential eye rolls over how you've been told ad nauseam that perfectionists set themselves free by getting rid of their perfectionism. I'm telling you right now that that will never work.

Writing "I will not be a perfectionist" one thousand times on the proverbial chalkboard is a complete waste of your time. So how *do* you set yourself free, or even begin to understand what freedom looks like for you? You start by being honest with yourself about who you are.

You admit that you'd never be satisfied with an average life—you long to excel, and you know it. You acknowledge just how much you thrive by being pushed—you need a challenge or your boredom risks tipping over into a depressive episode. And you stop playing small and denying your gifts—you were born to shine, and you can feel it.

Until now, you've resisted your perfectionistic tendencies in response to our collective portrayal of perfectionism, which is deeply skewed and highly selective. It leads with the negative (which is true but not holistic) to demonstrate how perfectionism is bad, abruptly concluding that perfectionists are unhealthy and need to be fixed.

Interestingly (read: predictably), the push to curb perfectionism and be "perfectly imperfect" is directed towards women. Have you ever heard a man refer to himself as a "recovering perfectionist"? When Steve Jobs or Gordon Ramsay or James Cameron demand perfection, they're exalted as geniuses in their respective fields. Where are the celebrated female perfectionists?

You could argue that Martha Stewart built an empire on her perfectionism and is perhaps the most celebrated female perfectionist of our time, but notice what her company, Martha Stewart Living Omnimedia,

---

* *Women* here and throughout this book refers to all those who identify some or all of the time as women and all those who others perceive to be women.

centers itself on: brunch recipes in a pinch, all things holiday entertaining, paint palettes that pop, weddings. These are archetypal homemaker interests. Martha Stewart wears her perfectionism on her sleeve to roaring acclamation instead of being told to "be more balanced" (i.e., temper her powerful drive) because her interests stay within the realm of what is acceptable for women to be publicly ambitious about. None of this is a coincidence.

Part of the urging to stamp out perfectionism in women arises because perfectionism is a powerful energy. Like every kind of power (the power of wealth, words, beauty, love, etc.), perfectionism—if you don't understand how to harness it correctly—will corrupt your life. Perfectionism makes an excellent servant and a terrible master; let's also be honest about *that*.

Can we just say it?

We both know that in the past, your perfectionism has tortured you in every arena of life: professionally, romantically, artistically, physically, spiritually. That's because you didn't understand it as a power and a gift, you didn't respect it, you tried to deny it, and you reduced it to a proclivity for tidiness and punctuality, though real perfectionism has little to do with either. The more you pushed your perfectionism away, the harder it pushed back. You couldn't get rid of your perfectionism if you tried (and try you did) because it's a fundamental component of who you are.

Lucky for you, the deepest, most powerful parts of who you are never abandon you. Whatever you did to numb out or downplay or otherwise mute the powerful energy inside you that you didn't know what to do with, *I did it, too*. It's okay; none of it worked. Thankfully, your perfectionism is still intact, and now you have a real solution to your problem.

Your problem is not that you're a perfectionist. Some of the most joyful, extraordinary, fulfilled people in the world are perfectionists. Your problem is that you're not being your full self.

Women receive an eternal fountain of directives every day about how to be less. How to weigh less, how to want less, how to be less emotional, how to say yes less, certainly how to be less of a perfectionist. This is a book about more. About how to get more of what you want by being more of who you are.

I've been working with perfectionists for years in my private practice in New York City. This book is based on that work, as well as my clinical experience in a broad range of settings, including being an on-site therapist at Google, working in residential treatment, and counseling in an addiction rehab center.

Long obsessed with exploring the ways we struggle, grow, and thrive, I received my undergraduate degree in psychology from the University of California, Berkeley, before completing my graduate work and clinical training at Columbia University. Additionally, I completed my postgraduate certification at the Association for Spirituality and Psychotherapy in New York City. My research experience at the Institute of Human Development and UCLA's Hammen Lab sparked questions that I've been turning over in my mind for the past twenty years. While the depth of my curiosity about the way human beings connect to one another assures that I'll always have more questions than answers, I've worked to fill this book with the answers I've collected thus far.

Here's one question I've been asking myself for a long time: What do people mean when they say, "I'm a perfectionist"?

The colloquial definition of what it means to be a perfectionist is reduced to the following: a perfectionist is someone who wants everything to be perfect all the time and who gets upset when things aren't perfect.

It's not that simple.

When people say, "I'm a perfectionist," they're not saying that they expect themselves to be perfect, others to be perfect, the weather to be perfect, all events that unfold in life to be perfect.

Perfectionists are intelligent people who understand that everything can't work out perfectly all the time. What they sometimes have trouble with is understanding why they still feel so disappointed by imperfection in the face of that intellectual concession. What they sometimes wonder about is why they feel so compelled to endlessly strive. What they're sometimes confused by is what they're striving for in the first place. What they often question is why they can't just enjoy relaxing "like a normal person." What they want to know is who they are outside of what they accomplish.

Every human being encounters versions of these existential curiosities at some point. Perfectionists think about them all the time.

I've identified five types of perfectionists; by identifying which type you are, you'll unlock your gifts. You'll also gain a deeper understanding of your intense drive to excel, you'll stop squandering your willpower trying to force yourself to not be a perfectionist, and then you'll exploit all that freshly liberated energy in service of your most authentic self.

The first half of this book dismantles perfectionism to better understand its parts. Chapter 1 introduces you to the five types of perfectionists. Chapter 2 invites you to connect to adaptive perfectionism, an advantageous dimension of perfectionism well known to the research community but scarcely discussed in the world of commercial wellness. Chapter 3 explores perfectionism from a feminist perspective. In addition to showing you the difference between control and power, chapter 4 peels back the layers of perfectionism to offer an in-depth understanding of what perfectionism is, when it's healthy, and when it's not.

The second half of this book shows you how to restructure your perfectionism in a way that works *for* you, not against you. In chapter 5, you'll learn about the number one mistake perfectionists make, and in chapter 6, you'll learn what to do instead. Chapter 7 offers ten key perspective shifts to catapult you into the healthiest mindset possible. Chapter 8 presents eight behavioral strategies each type of perfectionist can implement to sustain their progress and unlock long-term growth. The final chapter of this book answers a question every perfectionist must face: *I know I'm technically free to do what I want, so why do I still feel so trapped?*

Ultimately, this book will teach you how to make the single greatest trade you'll ever make in your life, which is to exchange superficial control for real power.

If you're looking for a book to instruct you on how to deal with the parts of yourself that are broken, you'll have to continue your journey elsewhere. This book explores the possibility that (even with those self-destructive habits of yours that we'll be addressing in chapter 5) *there's nothing wrong with you.*

This is a phrase I've learned people do not like to hear in therapy. Excluding narcissists, no one comes to therapy to hear that they're okay, good, extraordinary in fact.

Most people harbor a private suspicion that they're worse off than even they themselves know. Like, *it's bad.* And going to therapy represents their readiness to hear just how bad it really is. Basically, people want to know how broken they are via professional consultation and in clinical speak. They'd also like help navigating the world with all their jagged defectiveness.

No.

Investing in a pathologized version of who you are is a profoundly unnecessary use of your energy. It's also an excuse for you to avoid healing. I'm not here for either. I'm here to shift the focus of the conversation from weakness to strength. From correction to connection. From pathology to phenomenology. From fear to curiosity. From reactivity to proactivity. From eradication to integration. From treatment to healing.

Perfectionism does not have to be a struggle. You do not have to stop being a perfectionist to be healthy.

If at any point you wish to return to the notion that you need to be corrected instead of seen, stop reading. We all sway in our readiness to step into our power—you're allowed to sway, too. It's okay to need more time or flatly refuse to grow. I'd add that it's also okay to not want to grow in the first place, but that point would be moot for you. You're a perfectionist. You cannot shut off your desire to ascend. You can't help but test the limits. You can't help but poke the bear.

Here's another question I've spent years exploring: *What if your perfectionism exists to help you?*

Some gifts feel like a burden until you understand how they can serve you. Let me show you how your perfectionism is a gift to you, and how you are a gift to the world.

Which Type of Perfectionist Are You?

After each question that follows, circle the answer that best describes you. Each answer corresponds with a letter (A, B, C, D, E). When you finish answering all the questions, use the perfectionist profile key at the end of the quiz to determine which type of perfectionist you are.

1. **Have you ever displayed an angry outburst at work, such as shouting, banging your desk, or slamming doors?**

   A) Yes. When I'm frustrated with myself or others, it often shows.

   B) Never. I'm composed and extremely professional at all times.

   C) No. It's important to me that people feel I'm easy to connect with, so I try my best to avoid behaviors that may be off-putting to others.

D) No. I *want* to express a lot but I'm waiting for the right time and figuring out the right way to express it.

E) No. I don't struggle with managing anger but I can struggle with impulse control. For example, I'll share a series of new ideas in a meeting without thinking them through.

2. **Which of the below is most likely to bother you?**

A) Observing that the people around you aren't performing at the highest standard possible.

B) Going on a vacation with no itinerary.

C) When you know someone doesn't like you.

D) You've decided you want to paint your living room. You're given a color wheel with fifty paint options and told you need to pick a color in the next ten minutes.

E) Being told you can only focus on one goal for the next six months.

3. **Which statement best describes you?**

A) I impose extremely high standards on those around me. I can be punitive with others when they don't meet my standards.

B) I'm reliable, highly organized, and I love planning. I sometimes get the sense that other people experience me as "uptight."

C) I get frustrated that other people's opinions and feelings towards me matter to me. I often feel needy because I want the deepest connections possible.

D) I get frustrated with my indecisiveness. I wish I could allow myself to be a little more impulsive about taking clear action towards my goals.

E) I love the rush of momentum at the start of a new project—I feel unstoppable in the beginning! But I struggle to stay focused when I get distracted by other passions.

4. **If someone were giving you praise, they'd be most likely to say that you're great at . . .**

A) Being direct and keeping razor-sharp focus on the goal at hand.

B) Doing exactly what you say you'll do, exactly when you say you'll do it, in the exact way you're expected to do it.

C) Engendering meaningful connections with others.

D) Preparing, asking smart questions, and considering alternative scenarios.

E) Imagining possibilities, getting inspired, and generating ideas.

5. **Which statement best describes you?**

A) I get frustrated by others' inefficiency and lack of focus. I don't care if other people like me, I want to get the job done.

B) I consider it somewhat offensive when people make adjustments to the structure and timeline of anything (a meeting, a dinner, a vacation, etc.). We should be able to make one plan and stick to it.

C) I spend more energy than I want wondering what people think of me.

D) I know I have a lot more to offer (in my relationships, at work, in my community, etc.) but I can't unleash my full potential until I take care of a few things first.

E) I'm always resisting the urge to do things like purchase domain names for businesses I want to start. I have more ideas than I could ever know what to do with.

6. **I've received feedback about:**

A) Being mean, "intense," or intimidating.

B) Not being spontaneous enough or being too rigid.

C) Being too much of a people pleaser.

D) Not taking enough risks and being too indecisive.

E) Being disorganized, scatterbrained, or poor at following through on commitments.

7. **It's most meaningful to me . . .**

A) When someone follows through on what they said they were going to do, when they said they were going to do it, and to the level of quality I expect.

B) That I'm able to offer myself and others stability through routine, structure, and predictability.

C) When another person works to understand who I am as a person and why what matters to me matters to me.

D) That I enter into new opportunities (relationships, jobs, everyday decisions) as prepared and as sure of my decisions as possible. I don't want to commit unless I'm highly confident it's the right choice.

E) That I lead a passionate life where I entertain as many opportunities as possible to create new projects, develop new skills, travel, grow, and continue exploring.

PERFECTIONIST PROFILE KEY:

Whichever letter predominates, that's your perfectionist type.

A) **Intense perfectionists** are effortlessly direct and maintain razor-sharp focus on achieving their goal. Left unchecked, their standards can go from high to impossible, and they can be punitive with others and themselves for not achieving impossible standards.

B) **Classic perfectionists** are highly reliable, consistent, and detail-oriented, and they add stability to their environment. Left unchecked, they struggle to adapt to spontaneity or a change in routine, and they can experience difficulty connecting meaningfully with others.

C) **Parisian perfectionists** possess a live-wire understanding of the power of interpersonal connection and hold a strong capacity for empathy. Left unchecked, their desire to connect to others can metastasize into toxic people-pleasing.

D) **Procrastinator perfectionists** excel at preparing, can see opportunities from a 360-degree perspective, and have good impulse control. Left unchecked, their preparative measures hit a point of diminishing returns, resulting in indecisiveness and inaction.

E) **Messy perfectionists** effortlessly push through the anxiety of new beginnings, are superstar idea generators, adapt to spontaneity well, and are naturally enthusiastic. Left unchecked, they struggle to stay focused on their goals, ultimately spreading their energy too thin to follow through on their commitments.

Note: You can also rank your results to discover your broader perfectionist profile. For example, if you score highest in the Parisian perfectionist category but you scored almost as high in the messy perfectionist category, then you're a Parisian perfectionist with a significant tilt towards messy perfectionism. If you score an equal amount in two or more categories, then you're equal parts of those perfectionist types.

In tandem with the deeper descriptions within the book—as well as your own intuition about which type best describes you—your answers will guide you to a clearer understanding of how to appreciate and manage your unique perfectionist profile.

A digital version of this quiz is available here:

1

Expect to Be Graded on This

When an inner situation is not made
conscious, it happens outside as fate.

C. G. JUNG

A procrastinator perfectionist would experience immense difficulty writing this sentence because it comes at the beginning of a book about perfectionism and, accordingly, *needs* to be perfect (and there's no better first sentence than the one a procrastinator perfectionist imagines in her head but never actually writes down).

A classic perfectionist writes the first sentence, hates it, tries her best to forget it ever existed, but is inevitably haunted by it for a minimum of eight years.

An intense perfectionist writes it, hates it, and then channels her frustration into aggression about something entirely unrelated.

A Parisian perfectionist pretends not to notice she wrote a first sentence, affecting an air of, "Oh yeah, I guess I did. Huh." Then she secretly, desperately hopes everyone loves it and, as a result, loves her. *Who wrote that first sentence? I must be friends with her immediately!*

A messy perfectionist writes the first sentence, loves it, and then writes seventeen other, very different versions of the first sentence and loves each one of those and couldn't possibly pick just one because you can't have a favorite child, and those are all her sentence babies.

One thing they all have in common: they might not even know they're perfectionists, nor appreciate all the ways perfectionism can hold them back or allow them to soar, depending on how it's managed.

In the most basic sense, managing your perfectionism looks like becoming aware of the core impulse all perfectionists reflexively experience: noticing room for improvement—*Hmm, this could be better*—and then consciously responding to that reflex instead of unconsciously reacting to it. Perfectionists are people who consistently notice the difference between an ideal and a reality, and who strive to maintain a high degree of personal accountability. This results in the perfectionist experiencing, more often than not, a compulsion to bridge the gulf between reality and an ideal themselves.

When left unchallenged, the perfectionist mindset hooks itself on the motive to perfect (as opposed to improve upon or accept) that which could be made better. This impulse to enhance evolves into a belief that urgently wallpapers itself on all sides of the perfectionist's mind, including the ceiling and floor: "I need something to be different about this moment before I can be satisfied."

Perfectionism is the invisible language your mind thinks in, the type of perfectionism that shows up in your everyday life based on your personality is just the accent.

I built my private practice around perfectionism because I so enjoy the energy of the perfectionist. Always pushing limits, forever poking the bear, unafraid to travel to the depth of their anger or desire, eternally seeking a connection to something bigger, to more.

Acknowledging that you want more is an act of boldness, and every perfectionist (when they're being honest, which people generally are in therapy) flaunts a bold streak I'm magnetically drawn towards.

I work mostly with women who can present well, who can seem

completely put together when they want to seem that way, and whose problems aren't immediately apparent to others. This is exceedingly nuanced work because, as I suspect you know all too well, no one can hide their suffering better than the highly functioning person. I thrive on the constant challenge because, as I realized during one of the most disorienting moments of my life, I'm a perfectionist myself.

The cliché of it all bothers me still—I never realized how attached I was to control until I started to lose so much of it. In the exact moment that my personal and professional life began skyrocketing, I was diagnosed with cancer. I lost a pregnancy and had no opportunity to freeze my eggs before chemotherapy. I lost an extraordinary amount of time to the busyness of being sick. I lost my pretty brown hair. I lost confidence in my brand-new marriage. I lost professional opportunities I had spent years working towards. I lost control over the life I had painstakingly, perfectly constructed.

One moment I was riding the rapids, then the next it was as if something yanked me by the stomach into the still, quiet, and unseen place behind the waterfall. I was looking at what I'd always been looking at (perfectionism) but from a different vantage point. Why was I in a different position? Because in a misguided effort to be more balanced and healthy, I was resisting my own perfectionism.

I was sick, so of course I should've been relaxing, doing the bare minimum. It all made sense on paper. So I tried, I really did. And it was terrible, it really was. I was plopping pink bath bombs into my tub and sitting there watching them fizz away, bored out of my fucking mind, when I would've much rather been working, pushing, doing. Not pushing from a compensatory or avoidant place, not pushing to the extent that it disrupted my healing, but pushing because I enjoy being intensely engaged in my work and in my life.

The energy my perfectionist clients brought into the room presented in stark contrast to what I had started to feel in my private life. Their energy was charged, magnetic, brimming with infinite potentialities, destructive and constructive all at once. In noticing the burgeoning differences between myself and my clients, I simultaneously recognized the similarities that had been there the whole time.

I saw perfectionism for the power that it is, a strength I wanted to reclaim. It was a dynamic energy I had been helping my clients harness and exploit to their advantage for years, without having the language I have now for what I was doing. It wasn't until I tried to suppress the drive of my own perfectionism that I realized what I had in it.

I also realized that if I could be a perfectionist, *me*, the woman who could never find her phone and who extolled the work of social scientist extraordinaire Dr. Brené Brown to people behind her in line at the grocery store, then anybody could be a perfectionist and not even know it. What exactly was happening here?

I started to reverse engineer perfectionism, turn it inside out. In examining my own perfectionism and diving into the years I spent working with perfectionists, clear patterns emerged—five distinct presentations of one core concept, the five types of perfectionists.

Because perfectionism operates on a continuum, all perfectionists can embody aspects of each type within them. Though one type is usually dominant, it's also possible to experience contextually specific manifestations of perfectionism. For example, you can be a messy perfectionist when it comes to dating but a classic perfectionist during the holidays. Since I'm not a procrastinator perfectionist and can easily pick an entry point, let's start our discussion of the five types at the beginning: classic perfectionists.

The Five Types of Perfectionism

Tuesday, 10:58 a.m.

I opened the door for my 11:00 a.m. session. Claire was standing in the waiting room, hovering around four empty chairs, finishing an email on her phone. "And, done," she said as she efficiently gathered her small army of belongings to bring into my office: a jacket, two phones, a laptop bag, an indiscriminately labeled commuter bag for her heels, a not indiscriminately labeled Prada bag, and two grande, unsweetened, iced passion teas from Starbucks.

"We talked about this," I said after noticing the extra drink. "Can I help you with any of that?"

"I got it," she replied, modern-day juggling act in motion.

Claire entered my office seamlessly, swaying through the door like a red velvet curtain at showtime on opening night; gloriously on cue. As is the case with classic perfectionists, there was something ceremonious about Claire, who at twenty-two had legally changed her name because the original spelling didn't include the *e* at the end, a detail that irked her intolerably. As she described to me, "From second grade on, every single time I wrote my name, I died a little on the inside. Cumulatively, I'm sure it's taken two years off my life, but it's fixed now."

She pulled some kind of highly absorbent towelette out of her bag and wiped the water beads off the sides and bottom of her clear plastic Starbucks cup before setting it on the coaster. "I love these coasters; I don't want them getting wet," she explained (in fairness, they were really pretty coasters).

Claire repeated the water-bead sweep with the cup she had brought me before setting it down on my desk and saying, "I know we talked about it." Switching her tone to a perky whisper and with a half wink, she added, "But I also know you'll drink it after I leave." Then she sat in the exact same place on the couch that she sat in every week, but that's not a classic perfectionist thing; everyone does that.

The difference between putting your phone down next to you and *setting* your phone down next to you, that *is* a classic perfectionist thing. Classic perfectionists tend to be extremely deliberate about the way they handle physical objects; for example, they might *set* their phones down— meaning they take both hands, lay the phone down, and then take half a second to just kind of tilt it a bit, officially designating its otherwise arbitrary placement on the couch. This micro-ritual that so many classic perfectionists perform always looked to me like tucking the phone into an invisible little bed with no covers. In a way that never got old, noticing the idiosyncrasy gave me a sweet dot of private joy.

Claire set her two phones next to her on the couch, only to flip them over midsentence thirty seconds later when they started lighting up. I closed the door after Claire ("with an *e*," as she loved to say) left. My iced passion tea was watered down by the past forty-five minutes but still as refreshing as ever.

CLASSIC PERFECTIONISTS

Classic perfectionists, not surprisingly, present in a classic way, and Claire with an *e* was no exception. Everything about her was so clean and crisp, as if she'd purchased all her belongings earlier that morning and started a brand-new pop-up life. I think she made my couch cleaner just by sitting on it.

I had seen on Pinterest that if you run a lint roller along the bottom of your purse, you can easily pick up all the crumbs and bits accrued at the bottom. I hadn't checked, but I imagined that Claire didn't have any crumbs and bits, not at the bottom of her purse at least. But she was honest in our conversations together; she opened up to me about the invisible crumbs and bits in her life, the kinds of problems Pinterest hacks unfortunately can't solve for.

Only because Claire chose to let me in did I have any inkling that there was turmoil under the surface. Highly self-disciplined, classic perfectionists are adept at presenting in a uniform way, making it difficult to take their emotional temperature. Are they thrilled? Enraged? Having the best orgasm of their life? Who knows. They're either stoic or smiling as if they're about to have their picture taken. While it's easy to interpret this engagement style as inauthentic or closed off, it's anything but.

Classic perfectionists can be experienced by others as unapproachable or haughty, but the order this type builds around themselves is about reverence, not creating a wall. Classic perfectionists aren't trying to be impressive or distance themselves as much as they're trying to offer to others what they most value themselves: structure, consistency, predictability, an understanding of all the options so as to make an informed choice, high standards, objectivity, clarity through organization.

The opposite of inauthentic, classic perfectionists operate with incredible transparency about their particular set of preferences. Classic perfectionists also constantly broadcast their perfectionistic tendencies (here's my impeccable spreadsheet about restaurant options for vacation; here's my haircut that somehow perpetually looks like I just got a trim).

Reliable and predictable, classic perfectionists make it clear that they don't like disorder. For example, a classic perfectionist might say, "I don't like drinking because I don't like feeling out of control." Classic perfectionists take pride in their perfectionism. It's an *ego-syntonic* aspect of self (a feature they like) as opposed to an identity feature that's *ego-dystonic* (a feature they don't like).

Boasting a solid work ethic and patience to match, classic perfectionists can't help but be the teensiest bit smug about their style of control, which you can't really fault them for. (If I had zero crumbs and bits at the bottom of my bag, I would be beyond smug about it.)

In the cons corner, classic perfectionists have difficulty adjusting to schedule changes, big or small, and they tend to experience spontaneity as stressful. An itinerary-centered existence doesn't lend itself to discovering new and unexpected pleasures, and creating formulaic systems for dealing with family, work, friends, and more—with little room for organic expansion or any margin for error—can rob these perfectionists of the opportunity to grow in a way that isn't planned or goal-oriented.

Interpersonally, this type can be hard for others to connect with because of classic perfectionists' perceived lack of vulnerability. We tend to conflate external reliability with inner strength; that's a mistake. Classic perfectionists are as reliable in their darkest hour as they are in their brightest; just because they can always show up, that doesn't mean they're invincible or that they feel strong on the inside.

Also, the systematic way of operating that classic perfectionists default to doesn't encourage a spirit of collaboration, flexibility, or openness to external influence—qualities that help us build connections. The risk of this interpersonal style is that it can unintentionally generate relationships that veer towards the superficial and transactional. In turn, classic perfectionists can be left feeling excluded, misunderstood, and underappreciated for all that they do.

PARISIAN PERFECTIONISTS

Lauren texted me ten minutes before our session was set to begin: "running 10 late. sorry, worst day." Tall and beautiful (and caught in the rain), she came in soaked, looking like a Barbie doll that had been unceremoniously left in the backyard during a storm. I took her coat, and in between the time I took it and turned around to hang it, she started crying while apologizing for crying.

We discussed a meeting she'd had earlier that morning, which she perceived to have gone disastrously. When pressed, she acknowledged that the idea she presented dominated the conversation, and the team chose to spotlight her work at an upcoming conference.

I waited for her to finish before I said, "Help me understand the problem."

Lauren blurted her response out in exasperation: "Because I can tell she doesn't like me, and I hate it!"

I knew she was referring to her direct manager, who appeared to value Lauren's work, was never uncivil to Lauren, even prompted her recent raise—but who didn't seem to like her all that much.

On an intellectual level, Lauren understood that not everyone likes everyone, and it's nothing personal. Still, it bothered Lauren that her manager was disinterested in connecting with her outside of transactional work matters; she couldn't let it go.

Parisian perfectionists want to be perfectly liked, an "achievement" other types of perfectionists don't prize. Even when everything else is going exactly the way they'd choose, when a Parisian perfectionist is experiencing difficulty connecting to someone with whom they want to connect, it can all feel for naught.

The perception or reality that others don't like them gets under the skin of this type of perfectionist, eclipsing their perspective and creating a loathsome experience of self-infantilization wherein the perfectionist feels like a needy child vying for attention and approval.

As we'll discuss more later in the book, this type of perfectionism is about being liked by others on a surface level. On a deeper level, Parisian perfectionism is about wanting ideal connections. The trademark perfectionistic impulse to keep achieving and excelling manifests interpersonally for Parisian perfectionists; they want ideal relationships with their partners, with themselves, with their colleagues, with everyone.

Unlike classic perfectionists, Parisian perfectionists hide their perfectionism; they want to appear effortless. Parisian perfectionists care very much about how well they perform and what others think of them, but they feel a peculiar sense of embarrassment about how much they care. This is because they carry within them a heightened sense of the ever popular "Who do you think you are?" insecurity chip.

Revealing how much they're invested is a vulnerable act for this type of perfectionist, who cannot help but be emotionally influenced by others' perception of them and, whether they admit it or not, hold a strong desire to please others. If they want to start a business, for example, Parisian perfectionists will take many steps towards that goal without the slightest utterance to anyone about what they're doing. What if they fall on their face? Why risk sharing your dreams with people unless you're certain they'll come true?

For the same vulnerability-themed reasons, Parisian perfectionists cannot stand to look like they're trying too hard. On the outside, these types of perfectionists seem to be living in alignment with their own values and goals without any attachment to what others think, but they're secretly waiting for approval around every corner—they want the laughs at the party, the likes on their feed, and the compliments on their work.

Parisian perfectionists do broadcast their imperfections, but in a way that feels comfortable (and not actually vulnerable) for them. Named Parisian after the way that French women exude an aesthetic sense of effortlessness when it comes to beauty (but behind the scenes do a lot more work than they care to admit or want others to know about), Parisian perfectionists try to execute a deliberate message: "I'm not trying that hard because I don't need your approval and I don't care if you like me"—the subtext of the message being, "You can't hurt me." No part of the external messaging is accurate.

Parisian perfectionists invest a great deal of emotional energy into everything they do; they want a commensurate emotional return on their investment (i.e., validation and connection) and can be left hurt and angry if they don't get it.

In fact, their strategy usually backfires. They're hurt *more* often because in their efforts to get others to perfectly like them by being easy-breezy and low maintenance, Parisian perfectionists who haven't yet discovered how to manage their perfectionism fail to articulate what they need or want.

What's interesting is that their defense of irreverence is often unconscious, so much so that Parisian perfectionists can be blindsided by how much they're irked when others don't experience them in the perfect way they want. There can be a sense of "Why am I still thinking about this, I don't even care!"

Even (perhaps especially) when they most wish they weren't, Parisian perfectionists are driven by a desire to connect meaningfully with others.

Because interpersonal connection is paramount to them, Parisian perfectionists are genuinely warm people who want everyone they encounter to feel included and connected. They will, for example, go out of their way at a party to engage the person standing alone. Unlike classic perfectionists, who can unintentionally exude an air of distance and superiority, Parisian perfectionists operate in a way that celebrates and invites a myriad of different types of meaningful relationships into their lives.

Accepting and nonjudgmental, Parisian perfectionists are unstoppable when they learn to articulate just how much they care, implement boundaries, and embrace the people, places, and things that reciprocate their rich ability to connect.

PROCRASTINATOR PERFECTIONISTS

Layla was smart, kind, capable, driven, and confident. She came to see me because she couldn't bring herself to leave the job she absolutely hated.

Layla planned extensively for her departure from work. She saved money. She read every book on career transitions she could find. She identified multiple other professional paths she could see herself pivoting towards. For reasons unclear to her, Layla also regularly attended networking events that she got nothing out of.

I could so easily imagine her standing in an awful sports bar in midtown, surrounded by seven-too-many TVs, smiling, and waiting. "Layla" written in blue Sharpie on her sticker name tag. A Styrofoam tray of cubed warm cheddar next to half a sleeve of Ritz crackers that are *still in the torn-open bag*. What a waste of this brilliant person's energy.

The worst part? She knew she was squandering her time. Layla was fully aware that she'd done everything she needed to do, except choose a date to leave. She couldn't choose a date to leave because she couldn't line up the perfect start to her career pivot (all loose strings on her current projects tied up, accepted offer for her next illustrious job, four to six weeks of transition time between jobs so that she could decompress). Two years of this went by before she emailed me for our first appointment.

Procrastinator perfectionists wait for the conditions to be perfect before starting. Dwelling in hesitation, they live alongside the void that forms within you when you don't do the thing you most want to do.

Even when procrastinator perfectionists are able to get something going, they can find it difficult to continue because continuing involves restarting. While this type of perfectionist can easily start and finish smaller-scale projects to achieve short-term goals, they may abandon opportunities that require a longer runway because committing to any long-term process involves stopping and starting over several times.

Dating or getting married, joining a runner's club, switching careers, volunteering, taking the trip to Portland they've been wanting to take— the pleasure of the task they avoid is insignificant, which is always so interesting to me.

The behavior block is the same no matter what because the struggle is not in carrying out the goal, it's in beginning and returning to the endeavor while accepting that it can't be superficially perfect. To a procrastinator perfectionist, setting a date for a dinner party can be as paralyzing as submitting a letter of resignation for a major career change.

The problem for these perfectionists is that starting a process taints it—now that it's real, it can no longer be perfect. If something is perfect to them, it exists only in past memory or future ideal.

Layla was so stuck in indecision that she chose nothing (which meant that she indirectly chose to continue doing the soul-sucking work she loathed). She was living her life passively instead of actively, and the part that stung Layla the most was that she felt she was the architect of her own misery. The more self-aware a procrastinator perfectionist is, the more frustrated with themselves they are.

Until you understand how to harness your perfectionism, it's vexing to be a procrastinator perfectionist. Unlike Parisian perfectionists, who hear the internal taunt "Who do you think you are?" and initially feel embarrassed to answer the question with pride, procrastinator perfectionists have no problem answering that question with a parade of dazzling (and accurate) attributes: "I'm smart, funny, talented, hardworking—and I'm so creative!"

Procrastinator perfectionists aren't skimping on the self-esteem; they're painfully aware of their gifts. Painfully aware, that is, because procrastinator perfectionists live in the space between knowing you have a gift you want to share (romantic love, talent, a new idea, etc.) and not feeling ready to share it. They see others whom they believe don't have as much to offer shoot past them at work or with personal milestones, and it stings every time.

It's one thing to witness someone else accomplishing something you don't believe you can do; there's an awe factor within that experience. When you witness people doing the thing you know you can do, and do well? The thing you want to do the most? The awe is eclipsed by a lumpy mix of defeatism and resentment.

Disconcerted by their own paralysis, procrastinator perfectionists assume that if they had more energy or discipline, they'd be able to execute, which is not the case. Procrastinator perfectionists have plenty of discipline and aren't lazy at all. What they don't have is acceptance. Acceptance that now is the only time anyone ever starts anything, and that starting now means you're taking something that's perfect in your mind and bringing it into the real world, where it is bound to change.

Procrastinator perfectionists feel a sense of loss around starting that other types of perfectionists don't encounter. Avoiding loss is perhaps the most natural emotional reflex there is, hence why the habit of hesitation is so powerful for this type.

When the looming loss is felt on an unconscious level, procrastinator perfectionists also mistakenly attribute the avoidance of starting to a lack of desire: *I must not really want it; otherwise I would've done it by now.*

The more procrastinator perfectionists tell themselves that they're undisciplined, not passionate enough, lazy, and so on, the more they believe it. Thus begins a negative cycle of false identity, one they can't ever seem to break.

Procrastinator perfectionists who aren't managing their perfectionism become self-loathing and critical. Not just self-critical, other-critical; they're disparaging towards others who aren't constrained by the same tendencies. Procrastinator perfectionists might publicly or privately declare all the ways in which they could've done X so much better—thrown the party, written the book, built the house, organized the conference, cooked the meal. And maybe they're right. They probably could've done it better if they had tried, but they didn't allow themselves to take the risk of trying. This haunts them.

Unlike classic perfectionists, who like their perfectionism, and Parisian perfectionists, who are willing to risk failure but ride major self-esteem highs and lows as they do, procrastinator perfectionists have nothing to show for wanting to start. Salt on the wound? The things that irk procrastinator perfectionists the most are hints at the very things they would excel at themselves if they only gave it a shot.

When a procrastinator perfectionist brings awareness to the anticipatory loss fueling their hesitation, aligns themselves with support, and stops wasting energy critiquing other people who are trying, they're an absolute force. As they learn to shift from a passive to an active state, they gain access to an internal power that has thus far remained elusive for them. What happens next is a sight to behold.

My favorite thing about working with this type is bearing witness to the score of not one but two winning lottery cards waiting to be scratched off by every procrastinator perfectionist in the world:

1. It's not mere talent that rises to the top, it's persistence.

2. While change does always involve loss, not changing involves a much deeper loss.

When those lessons saturate the heart and mind of a procrastinator perfectionist, the restraint that defined them is lifted. Number one is motivating. Number two is liberating. It's a joy to have a gifted person who is liberated and motivated in your orbit. It's also a joy to be that person.

MESSY PERFECTIONISTS

I rarely give "homework" in therapy, it's not my style, but Pei-Han was an exception. I challenged her to stop watching documentaries for ninety days.

"What do you mean, what kind of documentaries?" she asked.

"All kinds, any kinds, no more documentaries." I practically begged her.

Pei-Han was a messy perfectionist through and through, so anytime she watched a documentary on anything (the hotel industry, sushi, migrant workers), she'd lunge herself full speed ahead in the direction of a new documentary-inspired goal, all the while trying to juggle the multiple other objectives she was attempting to achieve—online training for yoga-teacher certification, applying for residency at Brooklyn Arts Council, decorating her apartment in preparation to become an Airbnb Superhost, the list continued.

Pei-Han couldn't help the way her brain lit up like a fireworks show when she became newly informed about and emotionally attached to a topic she found interesting. It was something adjacent to mania, the way her mind flooded with ideas about how to improve, solve, create. The volume of possibilities she generated was astounding, even more so because for Pei-Han, it was effortless.

Messy perfectionists are in love with starting. Unlike their procrastinator perfectionist counterparts, nothing brings a messy perfectionist more joy than beginnings. Messy perfectionists are optimistic and "start happy," but they struggle to maintain momentum unless the remainder of the process feels as exciting and as energizing (i.e., as perfect) as it did in the beginning. Since that never happens, messy perfectionists who haven't yet learned how to use their perfectionism to their advantage take on a million and seven projects only to abandon them all.

I walk a fine line in my work with messy perfectionists. In what masterful therapist Dr. Irvin D. Yalom describes as being "love's executioner," I'm tasked with conveying unconditional emotional support while also being clear about the reality that enthusiasm itself will not be enough to sustain an endeavor. When my messy perfectionist clients don't want to engage that reality, I can only do my best to cushion the crash.

The crash is inevitable because messy perfectionists contending with unmanaged perfectionism disregard natural and unavoidable resource constraints (time, money, physical energy, etc.) in enthusiastic and active pursuit of their dreams.

In contrast to Parisian perfectionists, who hide what they're trying to do until they've generated enough traction to feel secure proclaiming their goal to others, messy perfectionists are unabashed about saying what they want aloud, often at the most nascent stage of their idea. And unlike classic perfectionists, messy perfectionists aren't the most disciplined bunch, which doesn't bother them in the slightest. It's as if they signed themselves up for Montessori school for adults—and good for them, because they're having the best time!

Theirs are the Instagram profiles featuring half a dozen vague and grossly unrelated job descriptions in the bio: interior decorator, chef, photographer, author, entrepreneur, guide for historic tours of downtown Boston.

Come again?

Messy perfectionists blatantly ignore limitations and don't accept the notion that while you can do anything, you can't do everything. It takes focus to bring something to completion. You have to say no to secondary opportunities so that you can concentrate on matters of primary importance. All the matters cannot hold primary importance.

Messy perfectionists reject hierarchies. They're die-hard romantics who can convince themselves that everything can work out all at once, as long as you have the heart. There's an endearing naivete surrounding messy perfectionists. They live in a bubble you almost don't want to burst.

We need messy perfectionists in the world; they are the champions of possibility. They effortlessly push through the anxiety of a new beginning. They inspire others with their enthusiasm and optimism, and the world would be a dim place without them around. Messy perfectionists possess tremendous gifts, but none of those gifts can come to fruition without focus.

It's important to note that not all messy perfectionists *want* to finish what they start. Some people love the abrupt start–abrupt abandon cycle, and there are certain jobs and lifestyles that are a perfect fit for that.

Additionally, "messy" is a misnomer. Messy perfectionists don't necessarily appear messy in their presentation or create literal messes around themselves, it's that they try to do a million things at once in a way that (at least figuratively) piles up all over the place.

Messy perfectionists do organize, but in a specific manner that only they understand. For example, their "system" for a project might include a series of saved Word documents that makes total sense to them but is impenetrable to anyone else:

"Dog Walking Business Plan"

"Dog Walking Business Plan 2"

"Dog Walking Business Plan Post-Thanksgiving Version"

"Dog Walking Business Plan New"

"Dog Walking Business Plan For Real"

"Dog Walking Business Plan Final"

"Dog Walking Business Plan Open This One"

Multiply that by everything they try to take on and you can see the problem.

I read somewhere that people who get married more than three times always feel a reassuring wash of "This is it, this is really it!" when they get remarried. I remember thinking how difficult that must be, to have your heart flooded with pure optimism and then sink like a stone. Not just once but repeatedly. That's what happens to messy perfectionists who don't manage their perfectionism. They get hooked on the intoxicating rush of a fresh start, then become disillusioned by the sobering tedium required to complete the work.

Messy perfectionists believe that they can do it all without ever having to give anything up, that they can be the humans who figure out how to exist without limits. When it becomes apparent that they can't, messy perfectionists are crushed. Like procrastinator perfectionists, messy perfectionists experience a type of loss associated with their perfectionism, just at a different stage in the process. Making matters worse, because they scatter their energy in so many different directions, they aren't able to complete even *one* thing.

This grand opening–grand closing emotional commute is a grueling ride every messy perfectionist knows all too well. Just as procrastinator perfectionists often build a false negative identity around their failure to execute, so will messy perfectionists who haven't discovered how to exploit their perfectionism.

The fall from the high messy perfectionists get when they begin something is fast and formidable. We all have blind spots, and we all crash into our blind spots, but when this type of perfectionist does it, she turns it into a story about how she's "bad" in some way. She's not persistent enough, her ideas aren't good enough, no one takes her seriously, and so on.

In some cases, the crash may result in an unexpected episode of clinical depression that stands in stark contrast to a messy perfectionist's normally upbeat, energetic outlook—very scary for her and those closest to her.

Messy perfectionists take over the world when they learn how to channel their enthusiasm into single, intentional missions they can execute in dynamic ways. Entrepreneur extraordinaire Marie Forleo is a great example of a messy perfectionist getting it right.

Forleo is all heart and drives full speed ahead, a true romantic who believes she can change the world and who has more incredible ideas to get it done than she knows what to do with. Except that she does know what to do with them. The open secret to Forleo's success is that she's taught herself how to focus on one thing at a time, and she subscribes to a professional approach by continuing the work when she's not in the mood—all without ever abandoning her high standards at any point in the process. These are skills that can be learned.

INTENSE PERFECTIONISTS

On the corner of Broadway and Liberty Street in Manhattan's financial district stands a classic 1960s building where I once had an office. Like several buildings in the city, the security at 140 Broadway requires you to confirm your identification at the concierge desk in the lobby so that you can receive a badge to enter the electronically guarded elevator bank.

Dawn spent the first five minutes of her session explaining to me why the security system was "inefficient and idiotic." The more she spoke, the more her annoyance morphed into antagonism. She was, as my neighbor calls it, "lathering." The antagonism wasn't directed towards me, or herself, or the security personnel downstairs. It was an antagonism against the void. She was fighting with the sky.

The antagonistic energy behind intense perfectionism isn't always existential; intense perfectionists can be provocative. I interrupted Dawn as we passed the five-minute mark: "You've been talking about the check-in system since you sat down. I understand it annoys you; it's annoying. Is there anything else you're feeling, alongside your frustration with the building's security protocol?"

Dawn collected all that floating antagonism and aimed it right at the middle of my forehead, "Well, I pay you to listen, so this is what I want to talk about."

Dawn was unaware that I started my career working with fifteen-year-old girls who were mandated to counseling; there was no level of resistance or combativeness that she could deliver to rival my experience. "What you pay me to do is to be helpful. Rumination without reflection isn't helpful."

Intense perfectionists want a perfect outcome. While some intense perfectionists focus on a grand vision, others' vision can be pedestrian. For example, an intense perfectionist may focus on the goal of boarding a flight perfectly. Their desired outcome is to get to their seat as quickly as possible with everything they need to have a comfortable flight readily available to them (headphones, water, blanket, quiet, etc.). A classic perfectionist may share a similar goal, but the difference is that classic perfectionists understand that it's not reasonable to impose their expectations on the people and environment around them.

Accordingly, classic perfectionists don't experience the shock and near rage that intense types might encounter when things don't go their way. Immediately sensing the first break in efficiency, intense perfectionists break, too. Sometimes they'll direct their anger outwardly, but most often, they turn it inward—the woman in seat 11A whose blood pressure rises with the plane, sitting stiffly in a quiet hell, only able to see everything that's not going the way she wants it to go.

A quality that often works to their advantage professionally and to their detriment personally, intense perfectionists don't care about being liked. While everyone else in the meeting is in a highly unproductive politeness contest—"Yes, Remi, I love that idea! I'm just wondering if maybe it would be better if we switched X to Y, not that Y is better than your original approach. It's just that . . ."—intense perfectionists cut through the fat and get right to the point: "That won't work. What's the next idea?" It's a wonderful strength; intense perfectionists are effortlessly direct and transparent.

Unlike classic perfectionists, who consistently present in a uniform manner, intense perfectionists are wild cards; some demonstrate extreme self-control, while others are reckless (temper tantrums at work, making impulsive decisions out of anger, etc.). Their off-the-charts work

ethic is more like a work mandate and can take a steep toll on their physical and emotional well-being, as well as the quality of their interpersonal
relationships.

People around intense perfectionists who haven't yet learned how to
manage their perfectionism are susceptible to becoming collateral emotional casualties. In the same way that a joyful person can contagiously
lift the mood of a room, intense perfectionists can exude a powerfully
dense energy for people in their orbit. Because this type projects their
perfectionistic standards onto others, it takes a lot to resist the downward
gravitational pull of true intense perfectionists who are not managing
their perfectionism. Most healthy people who come across the more extreme examples (either professionally or personally) ultimately hit a breaking point and leave.

To be clear, anger isn't dysfunctional. Anger is a powerful, healthy,
necessary, and motivating force. Dysfunction arises when you use your
anger to hurt yourself or others, which intense perfectionists tend to do
(consciously or not).

More than any other type, intense perfectionists rely on the outcome
of a process to define their sense of success. If an intense perfectionist
sets a goal that isn't reached, or isn't reached in the perfect manner they
envisioned, they consider the entire endeavor a failure. Intense perfectionists see nothing redemptive in the process, such as what they learned
along the way. Unless they hit their goal, it was all for nothing. Others
may try to help them gain perspective: *I'm sorry you lost the bid, but at least
you got to make new connections that could lead to more projects later, right?*
Intense perfectionists will have none of it. They have a simple answer to
all those well-intended, rhetorical questions: a frustrated, sometimes furious, always unequivocal "No."

Say, for example, that an intense perfectionist racks up $14,900 worth
of sales commissions, just shy of their self-imposed $15,000 goal (which
was likely an arbitrary marker in the first place) but still breaking a company record. They know they're supposed to be somewhat pleased with

the result and can objectively register the net positive, but they cannot access an emotional sense of excitement or redemptive pride in their achievement because they were short of their goal and the outcome is all that matters.

Before intense perfectionists learn to manage their perfectionism, their inability to extract value from the process can leave them feeling isolated. Other people seem to be able to connect to joy and a sense of purpose regardless of the outcome in a way intense perfectionists can't understand or relate to. They may internalize their isolation, thinking, "I know I should be happy about some of this, but I'm not. Something is wrong with me."

For intense perfectionists, the need to achieve eclipses all other priorities, such as their health and relationships. Intense perfectionists perpetually address their life from a future state: *I'll connect with my kids after I achieve X, I'll start dating after I achieve X, I'll focus on my health after I achieve X.* Renowned psychologist Dr. Alfred Adler described this unhealthy relationship to perfectionism: "All present life appears to him only a preparation."[1]

This myopic way of thinking creates a situation in which intense perfectionists cannot win. In the moments when intense perfectionists don't achieve their outcome, defeatism saturates their perspective. When intense perfectionists who don't yet know how to manage their perfectionism *do* achieve their desired outcome, it's anticlimactic. Because no introspection occurred in the process, no meaning was constructed. Meaning is what fills our experiences up. Without meaning, victories aren't weighted; they can't be felt and they're hollow. There's a ten-second victory lap and then it's on to the next goal.

This robotic relationship with external success also robs intense perfectionists of the opportunity to consider the toll (on themselves, on their team, on their company, on their friends, etc.) that treating the process as a means to an end takes. It's great that your team outperformed the rest, but how great will it be when half your team quits in the next quarter?

How wonderful it is that your kid got accepted into "the best" school that you pushed them into, but how wonderful will it be if they spend their first two years at college struggling with suicidal ideation? Depending on their level of self-awareness, intense perfectionists may minimize their role in generating the negative impacts that result from the pressure they can put on others: *Clearly this company wasn't the right fit; She'll be glad she went to that school when she's older.*

As a society, we sometimes romanticize intense perfectionists. The hard-ass visionary strivers who stay up through the night, fueling their work benders with bottomless coffee and riding everyone around them as intensely as they push themselves to achieve a breakthrough or hit an impossible goal. It's true that some intense perfectionists do generate breakthroughs. What's also true is that all kinds of different people generate breakthroughs; intense perfectionists don't have a monopoly on being visionary leaders.

What happens when intense perfectionists learn how to process and manage the intensity of their internal world?

It's nothing short of miraculous to witness an intense perfectionist do the work to replace unhealthy tendencies with healthy ones. Their intensity remains but becomes imbued with openness and vulnerability. They transform into magnetic live wires and trusted collaborators. The same qualities that once pushed people away, when managed consciously, now draw people in. Intense perfectionists managing their perfectionism constructively become high-gravitas leaders who are intoxicating and inspiring to be around.

As intense perfectionists learn to identify and connect to the process over the outcome, they experience more joy, connection, and interpersonal fulfillment—all without giving up their high standards.* There's a level of determination within every intense perfectionist that is otherworldly.

---

* If you'd like to see a consummate example of an intense perfectionist who learns how to manage perfectionism adaptively, watch the movie *Burnt*.

When their determination is aimed at succeeding through generic, external markers of success (bigger, better, faster, more), intense perfectionists lose themselves. When their determination is aimed at self-defined success, wherein their goals are aligned with their values and their process serves a conscious intention, intense perfectionists come home to themselves.

Seeing yourself and others from a new perspective invites appreciation for our respective gifts, curiosity about how we can best collaborate, and deeper empathy for the ways in which we each struggle. If you open yourself up to it, the invisible network linking the perfectionist profiles can enhance every aspect of your life. If you're a messy perfectionist entrepreneur with a brilliant idea, the smart move would be to get some intense and classic perfectionists on your team ASAP, or you'll never make it past naming the company (clearly the most fun part). If you're a procrastinator perfectionist trying to sell your home, invite a messy perfectionist over for dinner and you'll have the staging scheduled, the realtor selected, and the listing up—all before dessert is served. Just don't expect her to do an ounce of follow up.

Each profile includes a set of valuable gifts that come naturally to each type of perfectionist. When their gifts are honed into skills, perfectionists unleash their inner dynamos and free themselves to live powerful and authentic lives. Most importantly, perfectionists learn to enjoy their lives.

Joy holds tremendous power. It is impossible to live joyfully without your joy benefiting the world. You persuade joy to come out of hiding and step into the spotlight through celebration. It's not enough to simply learn to appreciate perfectionism; perfectionism is meant to be celebrated.

2

Celebrating Your Perfectionism

RECLAIMING THE GIFTS AND ADVANTAGES
BEHIND YOUR INSATIABLE DESIRE TO EXCEL

> We are taught to look at our clients, to analyze them, and to
> note their weaknesses, limitations, and pathological trends;
> less often do we look for positive healthy characteristics
> in our clients, or question our conclusions.
>
> DR. DERALD WING SUE

The following are actual titles of books and articles on perfectionism:

Killing the Perfectionist Within

Perfectionism Is a Disease

5 Ways to Cure Your Perfectionism

Recovering from Perfectionism

How to Overcome Perfectionism

How to Stop Being a Perfectionist

It's quite stunning to see the shame-inducing, emotionally charged, highly pathologized language around which the wellness industry so casually frames the concept of perfectionism. The medical-model language in particular (cure, treat, heal, affliction, etc.) cements in our psyche the association between perfectionism and disease.

When perfectionism is simplified into a one-dimensional, negative construct, it's easy to accept the simplistic notion that "perfectionism equals bad." Tagging perfectionism onto anything we don't like becomes second nature.

That throbbing inability to love your body? Perfectionism. The unexpected malaise that came out of nowhere? Perfectionism. Feeling anxious about getting there on time? Can't choose the paint color for your living room? Insomnia coming on strong? Perfectionism. Perfectionism. Perfectionism.

We reflexively implicate perfectionism both in our everyday frustrations with life and in a wide array of mental health disorders (anorexia nervosa, obsessive-compulsive disorder, etc.), and yet the field of mental health doesn't offer a standardized definition of what perfectionism is. In the absence of clinical clarity, researchers, academics, and clinicians form their own independent definitions of what it means to be a perfectionist. Some definitions overlap one another, some directly contravene one another.

None of these definitions capture the variegated, complex, kaleidoscopic force that is perfectionism. None of them claim to. It's widely acknowledged in the field of mental health that we are in the infancy of our research and understanding of this topic. The more we try to nail down what perfectionism is, the more we allow ourselves to see that perfectionism is a multidimensional and elaborate construct that unfurls itself in unique and individualized ways.

For the past few decades, researchers have been exploring the enabling factors that lead some perfectionists to thrive while other perfectionists suffer. Not without controversy, perfectionism has been split into two branches: *adaptive perfectionism* (using perfectionism to your advantage in a healthy way) and *maladaptive perfectionism* (the unhealthy manifestation of perfectionism).

Research demonstrates that, in contrast to maladaptive perfectionism, adaptive perfectionism is associated with a bevy of benefits, including higher self-regard,[1] higher levels of work engagement and psychological well-being,[2] and lower levels of perceived personal failure.[3] As opposed to engaging in negative coping styles like ruminating or avoiding conflict, adaptive perfectionists take problem-focused and solution-oriented approaches to stress.[4] Compared to their maladaptive counterparts, adaptive perfectionists demonstrate higher levels of motivation to achieve goals; they also worry less and are more optimistic when thinking about future performance.[5] This is perhaps because adaptive perfectionism has been shown to be a significant predictor of encountering "flow" states, moments of intense yet effortless engagement with a task or goal.[6]

Psychology professor and researcher Dr. Joachim Stoeber is a leading expert on perfectionism, as well as the author of the book *The Psychology of Perfectionism: Theory, Research, and Applications*. In a groundbreaking review of perfectionism research, Stoeber joined esteemed academic scholar and researcher Dr. Kathleen Otto to explore the ways in which adaptive perfectionists thrive. The review was notable because Stoeber and Otto didn't just compare adaptive perfectionists to maladaptive perfectionists, they also compared them to non-perfectionists. Among the three groups, adaptive perfectionists demonstrated the highest levels of self-esteem and cooperation, in addition to demonstrating *lower* levels of "procrastination, defensiveness, maladaptive coping styles, and interpersonal problems; and somatic complaints."[7]

Additional tripartite research (where adaptive, maladaptive, and non-perfectionist groups are compared to one another) indicates that of the three groups, adaptive perfectionists report the highest levels of meaning, subjective happiness, and life satisfaction.[8] In line with preceding studies, adaptive perfectionists are the least self-critical[9] and the most interested in working with others.[10] Because adaptive perfectionists demonstrate the lowest levels of both anxiety and depression among the three groups,[11] additional research was conducted to explore whether or not adaptive perfectionism can serve as a protective factor against anxiety and depression. Can adaptive perfectionism increase emotional safety and promote well-being? It turns out it can.[12]

Mainstream discourse on perfectionism doesn't include adaptive perfectionism. Instead, we decry and reduce the entire spectrum of perfectionism into its negative iteration. This means that the prevailing dialogue about perfectionism is not actually about perfectionism; it's about maladaptive perfectionism.

It's not uncommon for the wellness industry to truncate differentiated schemas into one generalized concept. Recall the low-fat craze of the 90s, where all fat was considered bad and unhealthy. There was no differentiation between the unsaturated fats found in avocados and the trans fats found in doughnuts. Fat was bad. Low-fat was good. Fat-free was best. As our understanding of perfectionism develops, we'll abandon polarized views of the construct.

For now, the monolithic place in the modern psyche where we know "perfectionism is bad" remains stable. We think that if we could just figure out how to get rid of our perfectionism, as all the self-help books instruct us to do, every single layer of our lives would be improved. Which is to say that if we just weren't perfectionists, if we could once and for all get it right and learn to be a different version of ourselves (specifically, a more "balanced" version), then we could finally take a breath, be happy, *actually enjoy our lives*. If only.

Beyond the blanket pathologizing of perfectionism being a gross misrepresentation of the broader construct, the eradication approach (*here's how to get rid of your perfectionism*) simply does not work.

Managing perfectionism by telling perfectionists to stop being perfectionists is like managing anger by telling people to "calm down." Never in the history of the world has this approach worked, yet we continue to barrel through on this dum-dum quest to get perfectionists to fall in love with average.

It is not going to happen.

Thinking of yourself as a perfectionist is an enduring identity marker. We don't talk about perfectionism episodically because we don't experience it episodically. For example, a person may say something like, "I went through a depression after college," but we don't "go through" perfectionism. Perfectionism is experienced in a visceral way, as a deep and integral part of selfhood, as opposed to something external that you encounter.

Perfectionists never stop noticing the gulf between reality and the ideal, and they never stop longing to actively bridge the gap. The noticing and the longing last a lifetime, hence the psychical constancy to perfectionism. People who relate to being perfectionists relate to that identity interminably. In addition to finding this to be true in my own work, the notion of "perfectionist" as an enduring identity state achieves consensus in the research world and among other clinicians, too.[13]

Trying to get rid of your perfectionism is like trying to get rid of the wind by whacking it with a broom. Perfectionism is too powerful for an eradication approach. When you try to get rid of your perfectionism, all you're doing is hemorrhaging energy at the opportunity cost of attending to your wellness.

Perfectionism is meant to be managed, not destroyed. (Perfectionism is also meant to be enjoyed, by the way, but we'll get to that later.) To manage anything successfully, you need to be able to recognize it in its inception as well as in its most advanced iterations, and everything in between. To begin, we need a better understanding of what perfectionism is.

Describing Perfectionism

Like love or grief, certain words are described more than they're defined because they don't fit inside a definition. It's easy to define what a light bulb is; it's not as easy to define what humor is. Psychological conceptualizations of any kind are designed to contain something inherently elusive, which is the extraordinary experience of being human. At best, we can hope to scaffold enough language around a concept for us to be able to move up, down, and around it, to peer into it from the windows, to see it from as many angles as possible.

With the capacity to be expressed in both constructive and destructive ways, perfectionism is a natural human impulse that we animate through our thoughts, behaviors, feelings, and interpersonal relationships. Persisting across time and cultures, the universal desire to actualize the ideals we imagine is as healthy as the impulse to love, to solve problems, to make art, to kiss, to tell stories, and so on.

People don't experience natural impulses in the same manner or measure. The impulse to tell stories is as natural as the breeze (*You'll never guess what happened to me on the way home from work*), but writers feel this impulse so powerfully that stripped of the tools and time they need to write, they will author entire anthologies in their minds. Forbid a true artist from making art, and they are guaranteed to make art in secret. Some people can go months or even years without having sex and be perfectly happy. Others, not so. The point is, not everyone is piqued by the natural impulse of perfectionism.

Ambition is not a universal trait. Some people are not interested in continually pushing themselves towards their highest potential or chasing an ideal. They may not ever even think about it. Writer and spiritual teacher Eckhart Tolle calls such people "frequency holders."[14] Those who contribute to society by maintaining a consistent level of engagement with the status quo. According to Tolle, the role of frequency holders is as vital as the role of those who create, advance, and work to revolutionize. By "just being," frequency holders offer collective stability[15] and install a solid ground from which to push off. Too much chaos would ensue if everyone tried to break all the limits at once.

Perfectionists have trouble relating to people who don't hold a strong impulse towards perfectionism, and vice versa. The more intense your impulse towards something is and the more natural it feels for you, the more you secretly or openly think, *Everyone has to feel this too, right?*

No, they don't.

Unlike perfectionists, some people can enjoy daydreaming about ideals without experiencing attendant pressure to work towards actualizing them. Feeling their potential press upon them from the inside out daily and acutely is not their experience, as it is for perfectionists. They don't encounter a chronic restlessness to achieve, excel, and advance. They're not haunted like you will be if you don't give yourself the opportunity to grow into your best self.

Some people like to work as little as possible, watch some TV, enjoy their hobbies, chill by themselves or with others, and do the same thing again tomorrow. Perfectionists wonder if those people might be depressed in some way: "If you just applied yourself more, you could turn this hobby into a real business. Don't you want to turn off the TV? If you woke up one hour earlier, you could clear your inbox, learn French in a year, have the garage cleaned out by spring. Are you okay? Do you need to talk?"

Similarly, non-perfectionists look to perfectionists with some degree of confusion and judgment-laced concern: "Why do you always have to be taking on another challenge? Can't you just sit still? Can't you just relax? Are you okay? Do you need to talk?"

Neither is better or worse; they're different.

Everyone has perfectionistic tendencies about something. When those tendencies (the desire to bridge the gulf between an ideal and reality) present more often than not and are accompanied by the impulse to actively strive towards bridging that gulf, you can consider yourself a perfectionist.

Like every identity structure, being a perfectionist operates on a continuum. To say that there are gaps in our conceptual understanding of the perfectionism continuum is a severe understatement. Appreciating what those gaps are and why they exist requires an understanding that the field of mental health is built on an illness model of care.

Illness + Wellness

In the world of health care, there are two main frameworks for addressing patient care. The first is an illness model (also called a *biomedical model, pathology-centered model,* or *treatment model*). Illness models are invested in efficiency and diagnostics; the goal is to figure out what's wrong as quickly as possible so it can be treated as quickly as possible.

Illness models are also based on atomism, which supports the idea that the source of what's wrong can be traced down to one thing. Wellness models, conversely, are based on holism (the opposite of atomism). Holistic care is the idea that each aspect of self (your social environment, work life, genetic predispositions, etc.) is interconnected within an indivisible whole. When you approach your health holistically, you're not just trying to find one wrong thing and fix it, you're working to strengthen each part of yourself so that you can become healthier overall.

While illness models are appropriate and the best course of action in certain situations, they have one major problem: they rely on the presentation of negative symptoms. Under this model, perfectionism can't hit the radar until it escalates into a dysfunctional state.

Operating under an illness model of care doesn't just carry powerful implications for the way we conceptualize perfectionism, it impacts the way we conceptualize every aspect of mental health. The slightest pang of sadness, a drizzle of frustration—we register any decline in positive emotion with an assumption of pathology. It's a cultural tic.

The tic is born from the pathology-centered illness model we operate under. Before we seek to understand, we seek to diagnose. Instead of saying, "Let's figure out what's happening here," we say, "Let's figure out what's wrong with you."

The elemental pathologizing embedded in the field of mental health is also why we're so confused when we hear the phrase "mental health." Does mental health encapsulate mental illness? Is mental health more about thriving and wellness, thereby rendering mental illness into its own separate category?

The supercategory of mental health includes both mental illness and wellness. While we're making great strides in proactively incorporating the wellness part into mental health, we're still overindexed on reactive approaches to illness. We wait for a tendency to express patterned dysfunction, then we try to suppress its symptoms.

Nowhere is our reactive instead of proactive model of care more apparent than in the stupefying fact that you currently need to be diagnosed with a mental health disorder to receive insurance reimbursement for mental health counseling. That's like needing to have the flu before you're allowed to wash your hands.

Perfectionism is a phenomenon, not a disorder. The larger culture is more focused on dysfunctional iterations of perfectionism because the mental health industry is built on an illness model; we're more focused on dysfunctional iterations of every psychological experience.

The Power of Perfectionism

When you consciously or unconsciously harness the power of perfectionism to help you and heal you, that's adaptive perfectionism. When you consciously or unconsciously harness the power of perfectionism to limit you and hurt you, that's maladaptive perfectionism.

As we discussed in the introduction, perfectionism is a power. Like any kind of power (love, wealth, beauty, intelligence), an inherent dichotomy of potential exists within it. Love can build relationships that are healthy and toxic. Wealth generates philanthropy and exploitation. Beauty inspires art and objectification. Intelligence eliminates communicable diseases through vaccines to save mass human life and builds atomic bombs to destroy mass human life. You need boundaries around any power, perfectionism included.

Maladaptive perfectionism will ruin your entire life, then have the nerve to charge you a destruction fee, with interest. There is no inner-field debate on this. The serious risk factors associated with maladaptive perfectionism are something that every informed therapist, researcher, and academic agrees on without equivocation. We'll talk about those risk factors a lot throughout this book so that you can learn to both identify red flags *and* respond appropriately to them (which, let's be honest, we can ascertain from past experiences that identifying red flags and backing away from red flags are two separate skill sets).

Where there are risk factors there are also protective factors: conditions to create and build upon to increase emotional safety and promote well-being. Mitigating the risk factors and emphasizing the protective factors from an informed, emotionally aware place is what managing any aspect of your mental health looks like.

Where eradication fails, integration succeeds. Taking an integrative approach to perfectionism requires you to think outside the box, then throw the box away. That kind of thinking starts now.

Think Outside the Box, Then Throw the Box Away

You've been taught that being a perfectionist is who you are before you learn to be healthy. Kindly get that "I'm a recovering perfectionist" nonsense out of your head. There's nothing about who you are that you need to recover from. That's number one.

Number two is that you need to start appreciating what you have. Stop taking your perfectionism for granted. Not everyone gets to experience that impulse you carry, pushing you to explore the bounds of possibility for yourself and the world around you. Perfectionists don't allow themselves to be constrained by what's "realistic"; that one mindset advantage alone is invaluable.

As a perfectionist, you have a lot of energy inside of you, more than you might know what to do with. But what if you figured out what to do with it?

As long as you're playing small, that energy rattles inside you and makes you ache. Stop cursing the ache and become curious about why it's there. If you're a perfectionist, you want more of something. What is it? Why do you want that? How do you imagine getting what you want will make you feel? Perfectionism invites a deep, unending exploration of who you are and what you most desire from this life.

After you figure out what it is that you want, the attendant pressure of your perfectionism will be there to motivate you towards your goal. Unlike an idealist, you won't be satisfied daydreaming; you'll have to do something about it. This actionable quality of perfectionism is annoying, frustrating, and often overwhelming at first. The more you learn to manage your perfectionism, however, the less you're overwhelmed by it.

You begin to appreciate the drive inside you. You see that your drive isn't there to hurt you, it's there to usher you towards your potential. You shift from avoiding your drive to honoring it, which requires you to stop misdirecting your energy. *Then you get to grow beyond your wildest dreams.* The school of perfectionism is a top-to-bottom gift.

Number three: you're perfect. Yes, perfect. Not "perfectly imperfect," not "good enough"—you are perfect.

It's something between sad and strange, how defensive we become about being called perfect:

How can you say that?!

You don't even know me.

I can't believe you would use that word.

No, no, no, no, no, I'm definitely not!

That's just not true.

We feel righteously entitled to our defensive posture, so much so that we immediately feel comfortable rejecting the categorization out loud and in the moment to anyone who dares label us that way. Meanwhile, we rarely defend ourselves out loud and in the moment (or even quietly, later) when someone needles us with a criticism or judgmental remark. We don't feel instantaneously entitled to reject negative categorizations about ourselves because the bad stuff is easier to believe.

The word *perfect* comes from the Latin *perficere, per* (complete) and *fi-cere* (do). Something considered perfect is that which is completely done; it exists in a state of completion, wholeness, perfection. When we describe something as perfect, what we're saying is that there's nothing we could add to it to make it better. Nothing more is needed because you can't add to something that's already whole.

Think of someone you love. Now think of the sound of that person's laughter. Is that sound not perfect? There's nothing you could change about that laughter to make it better; it's already complete, it's already whole. We use the word *perfect* to emphasize completeness. When you say someone is a "perfect stranger," you're not saying they're a flawless stranger, you're saying they're a complete stranger to you.

You're not flawless—none of us are—but you are whole, you are complete, and you are perfect.

We so effortlessly acknowledge perfection in children, nature, our best friends—but we deny perfection in ourselves as grown women because what would happen if we didn't need to add anything to ourselves? What would happen if we understood deeply that we're not broken, we're whole? That we've always been whole. That we don't have to fix anything to be ready for life. That we can just show up, now.

The answer is not "We would become powerful." We already are powerful. The answer is that we would be people who feel entitled to step into the internal power we already possess. What would the world look like if we felt as entitled to step into our power as we do to renounce our wholeness?

My favorite definition of *perfection* comes from Aristotle's *Metaphysics*,[16] a fourteen-book philosophical treatise on all matters pertaining to existential life and the essence of being. In this delightfully light read, Aristotle lays out three components that render something perfect:

1. *"That is perfect which is complete, which contains all the requisite parts."*

   You're perfect because you're already a complete and whole human being. You already "contain all the requisite parts." You never had to do anything to become perfect. When you were a baby, you were perfect before you opened your eyes. You didn't become more of a whole human being after you learned to spell or walk or get good grades or make people laugh. You don't earn your wholeness; you're born with it.

   Being whole never inoculated anyone from feeling broken. Sometimes you can only see tiny divisions of yourself. Sometimes you can't relate to your whole and true self at all. Limited perceptions don't dictate reality. The moon is always full and whole, even when it hangs like a slither in the sky, even when you can't find it in the sky.

2. *"That is perfect which is so good that nothing of the kind could be better."*

   You're perfect because the uniqueness of who you are is "so good that nothing of the kind could be better." No one could ever do a better job of being you than you. You're not "one in a million," you're not one in a billion, *you are the only one.* Take that in.

3. *"That is perfect which has attained its purpose."*

   You're perfect because your being alive in the world fulfills a purpose. You attain your purpose by existing, by being the one and only you. As Tolle puts it, "You are a presence in the world, and that is all you ever need to be."

   On the day you were born, you were worthy of all the love, joy, freedom, connection, and dignity in the world simply because you were in it. All of that is still true. Everything you achieve in this life is just the clapping after the song. You are the song.

In a world where the desires and ambitions of women are pathologized as a matter of course, the messages in this book may sound radical— they're not. The opposite of radical, these are basic starting points: you're already whole. There's nothing wrong with you. You're not a tumbling barrel of weaknesses. You possess rich strengths, and you can use those strengths to lead your life in any direction you choose. With the same ease that you so willingly accept the veracity of "experts" who are constantly telling you that you're fucked up in some way, entertain the idea that you're not.

What if there's not one thing—not even *half* a thing—that you need to add to yourself before you can live in the way you want to live? What if all you need is enough openness to see yourself from a different perspective? What if you don't need steady correction, you just need steady connection? These are not rhetorical questions.

The Perfection Paradox

Perfection is a paradox—you can never become perfect, and you already are perfect. A perfectionist in an adaptive mindset believes both those statements are true. A perfectionist in a maladaptive mindset believes both those statements are false.

If you listen to the most enlightened spiritual teachers in the world, it won't be long before you hear the perfection paradox come up. The greatest teachers will tell you some version of how you need to accept that perfect doesn't exist, and that the sooner you accept that, the sooner you'll be free. They'll tell you that nobody is perfect, *least of all them*, and they'll tell you that's a good thing because otherwise life would be terrible and boring. They'll tell you not to let perfect be the enemy of the good, to strive for progress not perfection, and that done is better than perfect. Then they'll look you straight in the eyes, smile a wide, beautiful, beaming smile, and announce to you with all the certainty in their soul, "You are perfect."

On all accounts, they are telling you the absolute truth.

An Inspired Life

All perfectionists chase that which is unattainable, "unrealistic," an ideal. Unlike a perfectionist in a maladaptive mindset, however, adaptive perfectionists understand that ideals are not meant to be achieved, they're only meant to inspire. That's how adaptive perfectionists get to spend their lives, inspired. Pulled towards something bigger than themselves, a grand task they can never finish, something worthy of a lifetime of striving.

To lead an inspired life yourself, you're going to familiarize yourself with the perfectionistic impulses inside you, give yourself permission to embrace the energy of your perfectionism, and learn to work *with it*, not against it. The work is not about fixing anything, getting rid of anything, or correcting anything; it's about connection.

You've been connecting to your weaknesses and faults for long enough. You can tell me if it's fair to say that you've gone beyond connecting, that you've centered your identity on those weaknesses. In either case, we're done with that. Now we'll be connecting to your strengths.

Once you're connected to your strengths, you'll have the perspective required to integrate your perfectionistic tendencies into your life in a way that feels healthy for you. Healthy means safe; healthy means empowered; healthy means reflective of your authentic self. Healthy does not mean happy all the time.

Eudaemonic + Hedonic Well-Being

Well-being can be divided into two basic branches. *Hedonic* approaches to well-being seek to increase happiness and avoid pain, whereas *eudaemonic* approaches to well-being seek to increase meaningfulness.[17] Happiness and meaningful experiences are by no means mutually exclusive, but one does not beget the other.

Perfectionists find hedonic approaches to wellness to be underwhelming and basic. That's part of the reason that people complain that perfectionists don't know how to have fun. It's not that perfectionists don't know how to have fun; it's that perfectionists have strong eudaemonic orientations. Inviting new challenges and building meaning around the ways in which you conquer those challenges *is* what's fun for perfectionists, not playing frisbee or whatever other people do.

Eudaemonic lifestyles have been described in the research world as "the striving for perfection that represents the realization of one's true potential."[18] Your strong eudaemonic orientation is an important feature of your perfectionism to keep in mind as we move forward. There's no need to feel like you're failing because you're not happy all the time. The absence of cheerfulness is not a disorder.

Your goal is not to be constantly happy or revel day and night in the dopamine-coated candy of immediate gratification. If that were your goal, you'd be hedonically oriented; you'd be a hedonist, not a perfectionist.

Perfectionists are bored by hedonism. Perfectionists love working. Perfectionists love a challenge. Perfectionists want to contribute, create, and grow.

Adapting from the Inside Out

Whether you've always had a naturally strong impulse towards perfectionism or whether a latent impulse emerged because of your experiences, it doesn't matter. Whether your perfectionism is a steady companion, a boon that rushes in under pressure, or a risky tendency that pops up in vulnerable moments, none of that matters either. What matters is that as an adult, you are the person in charge of your perfectionism, and you can learn how to steer it in an adaptive direction.

And what would you be adapting to, exactly? You're adapting to the most authentic version of yourself. Adaptive perfectionists don't acclimate to external environments or expectations; their adaptation is an internal process. You're going to adapt from the inside out.

Adaptive perfectionism involves a skill set that can be learned. Not only are you about to learn that skill set; you'll soon be enjoying the parade of benefits that comes along with it. For example, adaptive perfectionists get to enjoy being highly driven to succeed.

But I'm already driven to succeed.

Maybe you are and maybe you aren't. A lot of perfectionists *think* they're driven by success when what they're really driven by is the avoidance of failure—two very different animals.

When you're driven to achieve success, that's called *promotion-oriented motivation*. When you're driven to avoid failure, that's called *prevention-oriented motivation*.[19] In their article "Do You Play to Win—or to Not Lose?" esteemed psychologists Dr. Heidi Grant and Dr. E. Tory Higgins explain these two underlying motivations well: "The promotion-focused are engaged by inspirational role models, the prevention-focused by cautionary tales."[20]

As you learn the skills to adapt inwardly, to *your* version of success based on *your* values, your striving takes on more excitement, more meaning, and—most significantly—more joy. Why?

As research suggests, adaptive perfectionists play to win; they're more likely to enjoy the process because their efforts are fueled by optimism and reward seeking. Maladaptive perfectionists, on the other hand, play to not lose; they're more likely to experience stress and worry because their efforts are fueled by fear.[21]

When you understand that you are the person who oversees defining what's meaningful to you, you connect to the power of embracing success on your own terms. As you continue to succeed on your own terms, you build a confidence that's all your own, one that external accolades have no say in. For adaptive perfectionists, "winning" through traditional markers of success is nice (sometimes it's *really* nice), but that's all it is.

External wins and losses don't make or break you when you're connected to your inherent self-worth. Along those same lines, it turns out "failure" isn't that big of a deal to adaptive perfectionists either.

Adaptive perfectionists don't register setbacks as failures; instead, setbacks are experienced as opportunities for growth and learning. It's not that adaptive perfectionists are magically inoculated from feeling disappointment; it's that their appreciation for what they learned and the thrill of trying itself eclipses the disappointment.

You can see then how boldness is a natural side effect of adaptive perfectionism—how could it not be? People hold themselves back because they're afraid to fail, but when you learn to extract meaning from the process instead of the outcome, you can't fail. It goes back to eudaemonic living—finding the meaning *is* the success.

Incidentally, do you know how much more often you win when you're not intimidated by losing? As Thomas J. Watson said, "If you want to increase your success rate, double your failure rate."

Maladaptive perfectionists don't chase success, they run from failure. Maladaptive perfectionists are driven to avoid failure because maladaptive perfectionism is driven by shame avoidance.

As we'll discuss more in chapter 4, shame avoidance is one of the most exhausting and futile emotional exercises a person can engage in. You can't enjoy the process when you're in a maladaptive space—for the same reason that you wouldn't enjoy being in a car accident just because you weren't critically injured. When your entire goal is to win for the purpose of avoiding shame and then you win, it doesn't feel good—it just feels like you weren't critically injured.

This central shift from avoidance of failure to the pursuit of self-defined success is, in a word, freedom. In two words, it's adaptive perfectionism.

It sounds too good to be true—can you really enjoy all the perks of perfectionism without the self-flagellation that tags along? Can you really learn to use your perfectionism to get you far in life without allowing it to ruin your life? Can you really take pride and joy in what you're doing even if you're failing horribly at it, so much so that failing feels the same as winning? Yes, you can. Adaptive perfectionists do it every day.

Embracing Adaptive Perfectionism

Being healthy is not the decision to stop being unhealthy; it's the decision to rise to the occasion of your life. Committing to adaptive perfectionism isn't a single choice you make once and then you're done. Embracing adaptive perfectionism involves a series of choices made repeatedly over time, the first of which is choosing to focus on a growth mindset.

You're probably familiar with Stanford psychologist Dr. Carol Dweck's theory of "growth mindset" versus "fixed mindset." Dweck's idea is that people operate under one of two basic belief systems; they either believe they're capable of growth and development (they have a growth mindset) or they believe their capacities are static (they have a fixed mindset).

According to Dweck, your mindset impacts much of your decision-making in life, and your subsequent satisfaction with life. How you respond to personal failure as well as the success of others, your willingness to put in effort, the goals that you set for yourself—all these sorts of things stem from your mindset.

For example, if you operate with a fixed mindset and lean towards believing you can't learn something, you *maybe* give it one or two tries before throwing your hands up in the air and saying, "See, I told you I was no good at this." If you believe you're capable enough to figure it out, you persist where you would otherwise be too overwhelmed to continue.

It's the same logic behind why people enjoy completing thousand-piece puzzles. They work on these puzzles because they're certain the puzzles can be solved, and they believe they're capable of solving them. When you know success is just a matter of trial and error, you don't mind the trial and you don't mind the error. Not only do you not mind working on the puzzle; you also extract enjoyment from working on the puzzle.

Research indicates that adaptive perfectionism is positively correlated with adopting a growth mindset.[22] It doesn't have to be to the point of certainty, but cultivating openness about your capacity for growth is beneficial.

I've worked with so many perfectionists in maladaptive spaces who start therapy with a fixed mindset about what's possible for them. The general sentiment goes something like, "I know I'll never be happy-happy, but I'd like to be less unhappy."

People use the point that they've tried so many times to be healthy and nothing has worked as evidence that they're destined for permanent malaise. It's unfair to arrive at the conclusion of defeat without considering that the source of the dysfunction is the approach, not the person.

The current approach to managing perfectionism is a disaster on rails. As we touched on earlier, the whole strategy is based on forceful eradication. Hence why so many perfectionists are given the terrible advice to be mediocre on purpose. Get a lower grade on purpose, show up late on purpose, force yourself to present work you're not proud of on purpose.

Hoping it will break their perfectionism like a fever, perfectionists follow this advice. Not only does the approach not work; it also ends up making perfectionists feel worse because they assume they must be doing something wrong.

Your history of false starts is not evidence that your capacity to heal, grow, and thrive is static. Your history of false starts is irrelevant—I don't care about it, and neither should you. Allow your history of long and winding false starts to represent your abiding commitment to discover your authentic self.

Recognize that none of the solutions to managing your perfectionism have worked thus far because they're all solving for the wrong problem—they're trying to get you to stop being a perfectionist. You don't heal by changing who you are; you heal by learning how to be yourself in the world.

To challenge a fixed mindset, understand that when you misidentify the problem, you misidentify the solution. You've been relying on a faulty solution: trying to be less of yourself, trying to control who you are. The solution is to be more of yourself, in a healthy way.

Choosing a growth mindset requires you to take a moment to hold space for possibility. Holding space for possibility looks like taking a breath. A real breath. Get the air past your throat. Consider that a life in which you readily and often feel joy is possible for you. The number of times you laugh in a week, the quality of your relationships, your ability to sleep through the night, your professional fulfillment—it can all change for the better.

Even if it's just an intellectualized acknowledgment of objective possibility, it's important that you open yourself to the idea that change is possible for you. If you try and still can't create any openness, that's okay. Your reading this is open enough.

Boldness, authenticity, an endless drive you don't even have to try to cultivate, the confidence to fail, learn, and grow as you saturate your life with more and more meaning and improve yourself and the world around you—that's perfectionism. You can resist perfectionism or you can embrace it.

When you stop resisting perfectionism, you're practicing nonresistance. Engaging in nonresistance frees up energy. You are the person responsible for directing where your newly liberated energy goes next.

If you direct your energy in curative and intentional ways, you can build a life that you want instead of a life that feels hard all the time. In case no one's mentioned it before, when you build a life you want, it still feels hard a lot of the time. The difference is that the difficulty feels, to say the least, worth it.

3

Perfectionism as Disease, Balance as Cure, Women as Patients

A MODEL FOR PATHOLOGIZING WOMEN'S EXPRESSIONS OF POWER AND AMBITION

There has been little to describe the psychological lives and
ways of gifted women, talented women, creative women.

DR. CLARISSA PINKOLA ESTÉS

I passed by my next client, Rupa, working in the honeycombs—a cluster of small, individual pods within Google's New York City offices. I don't think she saw me. In my office ten minutes later, I mentioned that I saw her there, and she made a string of small-talk comments about being a "busy bee," which she then seemed immediately mortified to have done. As someone who cannot muster up small talk for all the riches and spoils in the world, there are few things I find more endearing than disastrous, caught-flames failed attempts at idle chatter. I smiled without responding to her small talk, then she started with the big talk.

Rupa was doing all the things. Every morning after her workout, somewhere between making coffee and getting on the subway, the haptic feedback on her fitness tracker celebrated her effort with a jaunty little fireworks circle: "movement goal complete." Honoring her New Year's resolution from the year before, she hired a financial advisor and was already making money decisions she felt good about. Very much into mindful eating, she simply wasn't distracted by Google's indoor food trucks, its waffle-making stations, the brick-oven pizza, none of it. She not only had friends, *she regularly spent time with them.*

Aspects of her relationship with alcohol made her uncomfortable, so after a difficult back-and-forth, she had finally cut drinking out. Her career in digital marketing did leave her with some creative longings, so after thoroughly researching the best protective gear and hiring the right HVAC contractor to ensure she had an adequate updraft ventilation system in place, she purchased an at-home kiln, transforming the extra bedroom in her apartment into a pottery studio. She was dating and traveling and going to the dentist every six months and buying books from independent booksellers and giving herself permission to do nothing.

There was so much she loved about this life she had worked so hard for; she stressed this to me, how hard it had been to get here, what a mountain it all was to climb. Rupa came to see me, she said, because sometimes she didn't sleep through the night.

"How often is sometimes?" I asked.

"I'm not sure, I don't keep track."

We began keeping track. Rupa woke up about four nights out of the week, usually around 2:00 a.m., for no apparent reason. She'd stare at her patchy dark ceiling, mostly resisting the urge to reach for her phone, sometimes reaching for it immediately.

She'd fall back asleep after an hour or so and ultimately got enough rest, but understandably it bothered her. She told me she honestly didn't feel that stressed. She didn't drink caffeine after noon and avoided too-sugary foods. Rupa was physically tired, but as she put it, "I just can't turn off my brain or something. I don't know."

When people say they don't know why they can't sleep, what they usually mean is they're not ready to explore the possible reasons out loud. Saying words out loud changes something.

Sometimes you say a thought out loud to give it weight because it matters. Sometimes you say a thought out loud to let it go because it's trivial. Until you allow the words to hit the air, it can be difficult to tell which is which. The stakes are higher when you say something out loud because the truth becomes clearer to you.

We also don't speak what we know out loud because while acknowledging the truth can be liberating, it's almost always painful first. When you can't sleep, at least some part of you knows why; otherwise, you'd still be sleeping. I had no idea why Rupa was waking up in the middle of the night, but I knew that on some level, she did.

The night before that busy-bee session (we hadn't been meeting for that long—a few weeks, four or five times) had been a particularly rough one for Rupa.

"It happened again," she said, sitting perfectly upright. "I'm so tired I just want to cry."

"What stops you from crying right now?" I asked in earnest.

Something about her energy shifted. It was as if on the inhale she was one person, and on the exhale, she became someone else. Her body seemed to deflate on the couch, and her voice fell with it. Rupa was a dynamic person with many authentic sides. It's not that she had been posturing; this was just another side—a less decorous one.

Rupa's expression reminded me of the look my college roommate would get when she ran out of cigarettes, a thought that I shared aloud. Rupa stared off into the nothingness of the corner. A good ten seconds went by. Rupa broke the silence: "Everything in my house smells like clay. I smell like clay, too." Now she looked as if she were about to cry.

It made no sense that we would both start laughing in that moment, but that's what we did. She started talking fast and handsy, explaining that she got the kiln because she thought she needed an official hobby, plus it made it easier for her to turn down requests for houseguests, but now her whole life smelled like clean spa mud.

Rupa was riding the extremely thin line between laughing at the ridiculousness of it all and having a full-on breakdown. She was taking the emotional risk we all take when we narrate our stream of consciousness without filtering it first, and what struck me was how visceral it was for her. Most of the work in therapy is done outside the therapist's office, but Rupa wasn't sharing an epiphany she'd experienced a few days ago—she was sharing it in real time. It was like one of those red ON AIR signs were lit. She went live.

I felt nervous on her behalf as she continued, doling out one confession after another: She liked the money-management stuff, but what was she saving for, anyway? Not drinking was a genuine improvement that she would continue, but now she couldn't decide who was more annoying, sober people or everyone else. She wasn't eating intuitively, she was just copying an idea—the way she *thought* intuitive eaters ate, which meant she ate a lot of almonds. She loved her friends but never wanted to see them. She also didn't like dating at all. "At all" as in she hated it. "At all" as in she wondered if she might be asexual. She vastly preferred to stay at home, watch TV, masturbate, ruthlessly judge others' dating profiles, give herself a drugstore facial, and go to bed alone. She resented something that she couldn't name, but she knew exactly what it smelled like. Pottery clay.

Rupa had made a rookie mistake, a mistake so common for women that it can unfortunately be considered a rite of passage into womanhood: trading the self-defined life for prescriptive balance. Rupa felt cheated out of the peaceful-yet-engaging, healthy, emotionally regulated lifestyle promised to her if she worked less, found a hobby, socialized more, ate well, and focused on "putting herself out there" romantically. It was a broken trade from the start; it always is.

Have you ever seen those cautionary-tale pictures about ordering furniture off eBay without paying attention to the dimensions? With a person displaying a realistic but miniature item in the palm of their hand? Adhering to prescriptive balance is like that, except instead of holding on to a tiny Eames chair, you're holding on to a tiny life, one you're too big for, one that can't possibly fit the magnitude of who you are.

If you're lucky, you won't be able to settle for someone else's version of success, nice and likable as it may be. Something will tap tap tap on the glass of your life, trying to get your attention. Maybe after work, during the quiet walk from your driveway to the front door—or in the morning, while you scramble the eggs. Perhaps most commonly, as was the case for Rupa, the tapping will arrive in the guaranteed stillness of the middle of the night. Something will press upon you from the inside out, eagerly demanding more from you. A better life, a bigger life. A life that fits. *Can you guess what that something is?*

Rupa was staring at her patchy, dark ceiling approximately four nights a week because she was coordinating her life to a grid: what she was told to do on the horizontal axis, who she was expected to be on the vertical. Layer atop this grid the ever-pressing dictum for women to be, as writer Karen Kilbane puts it, "pathologically grateful," and you get a silent, invisible, internalized sense of failure: *What's wrong with me? Anyone would be grateful for this. I can turn this around. I need to get it together.* This is the way so many ambitious women spend their twenties, thirties, and beyond— building the "balanced life" they were told everyone wants, then not wanting it themselves.

Rupa finished her "be balanced" to-do list, then she waited. Nothing. The opposite of satisfied, she felt a crawling, muffled, scratchy anxiety. It's always a sobering sight to behold—the quiet, anticlimactic, slow-drip shock of the "finally balanced woman." Sitting on my couch too exhausted to do anything other than tell the truth, asking me (which is to say, asking herself) some version of the brutally rhetorical question *Is this it?*

In stark contrast, I notice a bright, expansive quality whenever women describe the joys and benefits of getting older. Their description always goes something like this: "When you get to a certain age, you've learned to no longer care. You finally accept that you can't please everyone, so you try to please yourself. You trust yourself to know what you need. You do your best to get to the most conscientious place possible, and from that place, you say and do what you want. Let the chips fall where they may." Men never describe getting older in this way.

Balanced Ever After

I don't know one balanced woman. I know a lot of women who are two extra days in a week away from feeling balanced, or one professional housecleaning service away from feeling balanced, or one generous extension on the deadline away from feeling balanced, or three entire days of their children in someone else's loving and competent care away from feeling balanced. I know a lot of women who, like Rupa and like old versions of myself, structured a very balanced-looking life only to feel something between fidgety and haunted by the tap tap tapping. It's easy to get hooked on the feeling that you're really close to achieving balance, like a gambler at a blackjack table playing just one more time for the fifty-fourth time—but alas, the house always wins. Balance remains one step ahead, the ever-elusive prize of female modernity.

And yet, in my practice, women are constantly reporting their failure to achieve balance to me as if everyone but them has it figured out. My response is less "Don't worry, we all struggle to figure it out," and more "Don't worry, balance doesn't exist." It's a fairy tale for adult women wherein the prince has been replaced by balance: one day, if you just keep being nice and virtuous and doing all the things you're supposed to do, if you can just make the most out of being trapped and/or unconscious for a *teeny* bit longer, then balance will come and rescue you, everything will be okay, and you'll live happily ever after.

We buy into the admittedly alluring goal of balance because we believe two false promises. The first promise is that life is generally static. Sure, there are occasional bumps along the road, unforeseen circumstances and the like, but those are the exception, not the rule. The rule is that if your life isn't automated and flowing seamlessly from one day to the next, you're doing something wrong.

Since life is generally static and thereby easy to automate, you just need to find the right plug-in formula to make everything run smoothly, the way it's supposed to. This catalog-ordered, matchy-matchy approach to fulfilment pairs each problem with the Instant Pot version of its solution, and ta-da! Problem solved.

The second promise is that all your most basic and complex needs, longings, desires—all those lush, rolling, verdant, dewdrop-dotted hills of wanderlust inside you, all your curiosities big and small—could be met in the first place, *and* that they could be met simultaneously, *and still*, that they could all be met simultaneously while you're also reasonably meeting the innumerable social, professional, and familial obligations that result from being a basic contributing member of society.

Our contemporary view of balance is based on the notion that your life could ever fit on a to-do list in the first place, and that once you finish the to-do list and match your problems to their adjacent solutions, you can expect to feel a satisfying click, like a seat belt snapping into place. If you haven't experienced the clicking yet, it's because you're not balanced enough. You're not doing it right. Being "balanced" has become synonymous with being "healthy." If you're not a balanced woman, you're not a healthy woman.

As you may have noticed by now, those occasional bumps? Those unforeseen circumstances? They are the rule, not the exception. Life is not static at all. It's okay, natural, and healthy to encounter moments during which your life is eclipsed by something, internally or externally—perhaps both. This eclipsing, which one could consider the opposite of balance, occurs over and over again in our ever-fluid, never-static lives.

The eclipsing is not the problem; it's the point: to be alive and engage with life, not to sequester yourself behind portion-controlled aliveness and call it balance. Some seasons of life are for work. Some seasons are for sex. Some seasons are for three of the things. Some seasons are for nine of the things. Some seasons are for meandering through depressing emptiness doing negative two of the things.

What does balance look like when you're falling in love, renovating your home, or navigating through grief? How about during a divorce? The morning your car won't start? Your third month of job hunting with no leads? Most women have a #metoo moment—what did balance look like during yours?

Tell me what balance looks like the year after you've had your second baby, or while you prepare for your first round of series A funding, or when an elderly parent gets sick and needs a higher level of caregiving? How about while finding the right hormonal birth control? What is the appropriate level of balance while a family member is suffering through a bipolar episode and no one has heard from that person in three days? Tell me what balance looks like when the company you work for is bought by a conglomerate and your job stability is tentative for months, or during a particularly destructive hurricane season in your corner of the world? What's the right formula for balance during a global pandemic? How about after the pandemic is "over," but you're still processing all the ways it's changed you and everyone around you?

The pursuit of balance is curative within its original construct, which is based on the goal of balancing energy (the philosophical notion of "yin and yang," reverence for chakras, etc.). To enjoy optimal vitality, you pay attention to the internal energy system within you and calibrate it according to your needs. Balancing energies is markedly different than balancing tasks, the latter of which is what the colloquial meaning of balance has come to represent.

To say that a woman balances her life well is not to say that she's discovered her sweet spot of energetic equilibrium, it's to say that she's able to juggle several tasks and responsibilities at once. She can keep adding to her schedule without dropping the ball. We've hacksawed the definition of balance to mean being good at being busy, which has nothing to do with health. When I refer to balance henceforth, I'm referring to this stripped-down, cardboard-cutout version of balance.

A close friend of mine once shared a legal-industry saying with me, which was that making partner at a law firm is like a pie-eating contest where the prize is more pie. Balance is a lot like that. The more tasks you're able to successfully balance, the more bandwidth you create to, drumroll . . . balance more tasks.

In addition to balancing tasks, women are also expected to preemptively balance other people's emotional experience of them. In my favorite scene from Apple TV+'s *The Morning Show*, Reese Witherspoon plays local news anchor Bradley Jackson, who gets a big break on network TV. While begrudgingly shopping for the appropriate on-air wardrobe, Jackson describes what she dubs the "aspirational, inoffensive dream girl": "I've only been told about a thousand different ways I'm too liberal, too conservative, too in-between. You have too much chin. You're not smiling enough. You're too brunette. Do you want to go blonde? Where are your boobs? Quick, put your boobs out. Wait, put your boobs away. You're attracting men! You're scaring women. You know, try not to be so confrontational—men don't want to fuck you. Don't be so angry—women feel criticized."

I pushed rewind twice. It was so satisfying to watch because it was this truncated, accurate punch of an explanation articulating just a few of the diametric dictums women are constantly confronted with. Every day. In all the places. At all the hours.

"How do you balance work and motherhood?" It's a question every professional woman with kids is regularly asked. Professional men who are also parents are not asked the paternal version of this question because fathers are not expected to be primary caregivers. Men are expected to focus their primary energy on work, then be secondary caregivers or a tertiary presence in the lives of their children. Hence, women who work outside the home call themselves "working moms," but men who work outside the home don't call themselves "working dads." This is also why fathers don't experience the same level of guilt over competing demands in their work life and home life, because they don't share the same level of competing demands (excel professionally while also managing the children's care, school schedules, playdates, and doctor's appointments; the couple's social life; the housecleaning; etc.).[1]

Perhaps this is a good place to note that the goal is not to be treated like men. You know when you should absolutely know who someone is but you don't so you google it? Someone once told me I shared a birthday with Rudyard Kipling, and I was like, "Great!" Then I googled him and read some of his poetry. I came across a line in "If," a poem about being a man.

In the context of the poem, the line is optimistic and encouraging. Regardless, it jumped out at me as a stand-alone line, sealing itself in my mind as reminiscent of every man I've ever worked with: "And never breathe a word about your loss."

Among a litany of private sufferings we don't allow men to even *begin* to feel, let alone express, men suffer from being unchallenged in their unbridled response to perfectionism. "Being a man" calls for a blankness that doesn't fit the rich sensitivity, humor, creative power, abiding compassion, intelligence, and beauty of men. Anyone who's raising a little boy will tell you that this one is the sweetest boy who ever existed. All that kindness, affection, and curiosity that so readily bursts out of little boys' hearts is exactly what men are taught to smother if they want to be taken seriously in the world.

Men's sense of self-worth is precarious beyond all our mainstream imaginings. We pretend men are fine. Men are not fine. They're not sitting high atop their patriarchy thrones laughing down at everyone else. They're teetering on the corner inch of the fictitious gender binary, trying not to fall off a very real cliff.

I consider myself extremely lucky to have discovered Dr. Jackson

Katz's work early on in my career. His breakthrough book *The Macho Paradox: Why Some Men Hurt Women and How All Men Can Help* is a wonderful starting and continuing place for all the issues that are beyond the scope of this one. Internationally acclaimed writer and artist Alok Vaid-Menon's book *Beyond the Gender Binary* is also a wonderful starting and continuing place. For now, though, back to how there is no better or worse way to do something that is impossible, which is to find balance.

A Riddle

There are two women. Both are wives and mothers. Both wake up early, two hours before the rest of the members of their house. Woman One explains that she wakes up early because she loves having time to herself to bake fresh bread for her family in the morning, something about kneading the dough with her hands, the tactility of it. While the bread is baking, she cleans up. A clean house makes her feel centered. Because she's alone and doing it at her own pace, the cleaning feels more like a meditation than a chore. When she's done cleaning, she reads. She absolutely loves her mornings to herself.

Woman Two explains that she wakes up early to prepare for her workday at the office. Something about looking over her calendar and knowing that she's prepared for each meeting feels good, and identifying impending concerns helps her to identify impending solutions. She also loves the efficiency of responding to all her emails from the day before in one fell swoop. If she has time after her calendar inventory and emails, she reads. Her house is messy but not dirty-messy. The house generally stays this way unless people come over. Her kids eat cereal for breakfast so there's nothing to cook.

Which woman do you think is told to "be more balanced"?

It's a trick question—the answer is neither. If going before some sort of modern-woman council, these women would both be strongly encouraged to continue attending to themselves in whatever manner they saw fit. Both women would be met with a hardy "Good for you! Do what makes *you* feel like *you*! You have to put your oxygen mask on first, ya know. You can't help anyone else unless *you* take care of *you* first."

Then, just a quick follow-up question from this imaginary council. A minor formality really. Someone on the council asks, perhaps in a whispered hush, "Everyone's asleep, though, when you're doing all these things for yourself, right?"

That's the caveat. Do whatever you like—work out, read, join a club, stare out the window, invest in yourself and your career . . . do absolutely anything you want! *Just be ready when everyone wakes up.*

We hand women the boulder of balance, remind them that it's impossibly heavy and that's what makes them superheroes, and then parrot-preach self-care at them: "Balance and self-care, balance and self-care, balance and self-care." Yes, thank you. I heard you.

Women operate under the assumption that once you achieve balance, you'll be ready to unleash your power into the world. You don't need balance to do that. Balance is not a primer for being who you are. For most women, and damn sure for perfectionists of every type, living authentically looks on the surface like the opposite of balance. The most fulfilled women I know are terrible at being balanced, and I mean, truly, iconically awful at it.

Women feel an increasing sense of liberation as they age, not because they've finally achieved the balance they were searching for but because they've finally given up on it. Through painful trial and error women come to learn that, as my friend Miesha used to say, "You can't win for losin' around here."

With the energizing irreverence that comes with abandoning what no longer serves you, women crumple up their balance orders and toss them in the trash. Then they burn the trash. They're done. They quit.

Balance isn't real; it doesn't exist. It's just an idea. Balance is not possible in practical application due to issues such as time and reality. Balance is always around the corner, after the holidays, as soon as this very serious situation is handled. Balance never actually shows up, but we don't notice because we're too busy blaming ourselves for its delay. The "we" I'm referring to here is women.

Girl, You Are a *Hot Mess*!

There's a language catch for a woman who isn't demonstrating balance; we call her a "hot mess." Visibly failing to juggle the million things, she arrives late to the meeting, maybe her hair's a little messed up or her phone starts ringing five minutes after she sits down because she forgot to silence it. Whatever. The point is that she doesn't seem put together, and she doesn't seem balanced. She's allowing the competing demands on her time and energy to show, and we notice.

The "hot mess" language catch makes it easier to notice; it's easier to call something out when it has a name. When you think of a hot mess, you only think of a woman or an effeminate person. "Hot mess" is a descriptor reserved for femininity. Also notice that visibility is key here—if the "hot mess" person *looked* put together, if they do a great job of *pretending* to be balanced, they would not be considered a hot mess.

"Hot mess" is an external descriptor because the external is what counts; women's internal experience is secondary to the way they look. This mirrors the assumption that if women are thin, they're also healthy, regardless of what's happening behind the scenes. What's culturally incentivized is not being healthy for yourself, it's *seeming* healthy for others.

Obviously, the language we use reflects the culture we live in. Perhaps less obviously, the language we don't use can serve as an even clearer reflection of the culture we live in. For the same reason that the expression "guilty pleasure" doesn't translate well into French, there are no male equivalents for "bossy," "strong-minded," "hot mess," "mom guilt," or "resting bitch face." When applied to men, the implicit messages within those phrases don't align with our culture's value system. In other words, we don't say them because they don't make sense.

Pleasure is a natural, healthy, and encouraged part of French life; why would one feel guilty for allowing oneself access to pleasure? Men are supposed to be authoritative, so how can they be bossy? Men aren't supposed to be constantly smiling and pleasant, so when they display a neutral facial expression, why would you call it anything but normal? Men aren't expected to be perpetually balanced, so they can't be hot messes. "Dad guilt" is not a thing because men aren't getting the message that they should feel guilty for working. The "strong-minded" descriptor assumes a superfluous quality when applied to men.

We broadcast implicit gender-performance expectations by nestling them into everyday language (i.e., "working mom"). Language also serves a regulatory function by reinforcing said expectations through varying degrees of punishment and reward, including the "reward" of no punishment. For example, deviating from implicit gender-performance expectations of appearing to be a healthy, balanced woman brands you a "hot mess" (a punishment). Incorporating gratuitous exclamation points into your email etiquette means no one can call you a "bitch" (the "reward" of no punishment).

Yes, there are women who subvert gender-performance expectations to successfully gain industry respect and power, but these women do so at tremendous personal and professional cost—not at tremendous risk; the risk is bypassed into immediate cost. A memorable example:

In what ESPN dubbed "the most controversial US Open final in history," self-proclaimed perfectionist Serena Williams lost a point and a game after receiving three code violations. The last code violation, verbal abuse, was given after Williams called the chair umpire a "liar" and a "thief." Williams met this violation with protest, calling for the referee: "This has happened to me too many times. This is not fair. Do you know how many other men do things that are much worse?" Williams continued to assertively defend herself: "There's a lot of men out here who have said a lot of things, but . . . because I'm a woman, you're going to take this away from me. That is not right."

In the postgame media firestorm that followed, *Sports Illustrated* writer S. L. Price agreed with Williams's declaration that men have done much worse, citing Wimbledon and US Open champion Jimmy Connors's repeatedly calling a chair umpire "an abortion" and telling him to "get out of the chair you bum" during a US Open match, without any consequence. Connors went on to win that game.[2] In the words of iconic feminist writer Dr. Phyllis Chesler, "How bizarre, how familiar."

The Opposite of a Balanced Woman

Being considered a hot mess, whether by yourself or others, is a punishment for not appearing to be balanced, but it's not the opposite of being balanced. The opposite of the healthy, balanced woman is the perfectionist.

Perfectionism can be your downfall, but as previously noted, any power without boundaries attached to it can be your downfall—so why do we single out perfectionism?

A better question: *Why do we single out perfectionism as a negative marker in women?*

There's a reason you've never once heard a man refer to himself as a "recovering perfectionist"—because men aren't taught that they need to "recover" from their perfectionism. Men are taught to integrate their perfectionistic strivings, insistence on high standards, at times inefficiently meticulous, at other times interpersonally destructive drive to excel into the more holistic sense of who they are. Men are taught to pursue their ambition unapologetically. Not only do we expect male perfectionists to do this; we celebrate them for it. The on-screen persona of British chef turned media mogul Gordon Ramsay is an easy example.

Women, as we're rather aware of at this point, are conditioned to be chronically apologetic. After a 2010 study confirmed that women apologize more than men do, we began to notice the pattern of women cushioning requests and general statements with the word "sorry":

Sorry, can you pass the coffee? Sorry, I have a question. Sorry, it's my birthday today.

Becoming attuned to the tendency for women to overapologize didn't happen overnight. This tipping point in cultural awareness only happened because so many companies, media outlets, and individuals repeatedly pushed against this phenomenon. Directives to pay attention to your usage of the word "sorry" rolled around the zeitgeist like socks in the dryer. It rained op-eds and Ted Talks, and the word "sorry" was podcast fodder galore. Amy Schumer did a comedy sketch starring overly apologetic women; Pantene based an advertising campaign on the issue. Our awareness was flooded.

Now we're done apologizing, and we're *almost* done apologizing for no longer being apologetic. University of Zurich researcher David Matley studies, among other things, digital culture and the interplay between social media, the presentation of self, and relationship management. In examining the hashtag #sorrynotsorry, Matley found that it's used in a highly pragmatic way, "as a non-apology marker in a balancing act of (im-)politeness and self-presentation strategies . . . allowing [users of the hashtag] to take both oppositional and complicitous stances on evolving norms of appropriateness online."[3] We used #sorrynotsorry to defiantly announce that we didn't care what anyone had to say about our choices— while simultaneously trying to stay palatable by acknowledging that we knew the choices we were broadcasting were "against the rules." If you *had* to put money on it, who would you say used the hashtag #sorrynotsorry more, men or women?

Right now, women's expressions of ambition and power seeking are being suppressed by funneling those expressions into the concept of perfectionism, then pathologizing perfectionism ad nauseam; this is one of the most widely propagated implicit drivers of our culture's sexist agenda. Reinforcing the tempering of women's expression of power is billed as "finding balance," an instruction overwhelmingly directed towards women, not men.

For women, perfectionism is a sickness that requires a lifelong recovery period. The implicit message behind the word "perfectionist" is: *you're doing too much.* Balance is offered (proselytized) as the corollary cure. The implicit message behind "finding balance" is to take care of yourself by getting calm and slowing down while also taking care of everyone else by being all things to all people at once.

Celebrated Female Perfectionists

Being a female perfectionist isn't always pathologized. If a woman deploys her perfectionism in adherence to traditional standards of femininity, her perfectionism is recognized as excellence, and rewards are bestowed. If a woman deploys her perfectionism in historically male-dominated arenas or in adherence to traditional standards of masculinity, her perfectionism is pathologized, and punishments will ensue.

This is why, as I mentioned in the introduction, Martha Stewart can build an empire on her perfectionism and is perhaps the most celebrated female perfectionist of our time, but again, notice what her company Martha Stewart Living Omnimedia centers itself on: brunch recipes in a pinch, all things holiday entertaining, paint palettes that pop, weddings. These are archetypal homemaker interests. Martha Stewart can wear her perfectionism on her sleeve to roaring acclamation instead of being told to "be more balanced" (i.e., temper her powerful drive) because her interests stay within the realm of what is acceptable for women to be publicly ambitious about. Why does it feel so "off brand" to point out that the impressively industrious Martha Stewart was a stockbroker on Wall Street before starting *Martha Stewart Living*?

In 2011, Japanese organizing consultant Marie Kondo wrote *The Life-Changing Magic of Tidying Up.* My poor friends. For so long, I would not stop talking about this book. I loved it. From start to finish, *Tidying Up* is perfectionism on parade. Every shirt must be folded perfectly and vertically. Intention is central to even the smallest of decisions. Absolutely no loose change anywhere in the home. There is an ideal state, and you should try to achieve it, *and* that effort should be joyful—it might as well be called *The Perfectionist's Guide to Cleaning*.

Tidying Up has sold more than eleven million copies in forty countries around the world, spent over 150 weeks on the *New York Times* bestsellers list, and inspired the hit Netflix series *Tidying Up with Marie Kondo* because . . . we hate perfectionism? We think it's bad? We know it's so unhealthy?

Please.

We love perfectionism; we can't get enough of it. *Of course*, we don't love maladaptive expressions of perfectionism. Unless the dysfunction is packaged for Bravo, we don't love maladaptive expressions of anything. If it's delivered in the right context, our culture extols perfectionism. An exploration of what the "right context" is doesn't take long.

Do you think it's a coincidence that our culture embraces, celebrates, and syndicates female perfectionists when their perfectionism is expressed through improving and decorating the home, hosting social gatherings, and tidying up? The celebration serves as both reward and signal: this is how to behave.

"I'm Such a Perfectionist"

In the same way the word *bossy* served to regulate authoritative, traditionally masculine behaviors in girls and women, the word *perfectionist* has quietly risen to regulate ambition and power. As with all implicit messaging, we not only unconsciously hear it, we unconsciously internalize it. I'll give you an example.

One afternoon, in a shared workspace, I found myself sitting close to an area a photographer had staged to take photos of her clients. Throughout multiple shoots, the photographer continued to make statements such as these:

I'm such a perfectionist, I know, but can you put your hand a little closer to your hip?

I'm kind of a perfectionist, it's so annoying, I know! But can you turn your face a little more towards the window?

Okay, I'm going to be a little bit of a perfectionist about this and ask that you keep your chin at a ninety-degree angle from your chest.

The photographer may or may not be a perfectionist; I don't know her. What I do know is that she's a professional photographer whose job it is to cast the subject of her photography (in this case, other people) by directing them in both specific and general ways. She is repeatedly mitigating her directives with the vague qualifier of "perfectionist" to maintain palatability while also maintaining power over the shoot. Power that, in this dynamic, is pre-granted. She is the agreed-upon expert here, yet she still seems to feel the need to verbally qualify the enactment of her power. Every time she wants a better shot, she cushions her communication within the context of being a perfectionist.

Implicit communication requires subtlety. The marker of successful subtlety is an abundance of plausible deniability. It's easy to deny perfectionism's regulatory function by saying something like "Perfectionism can be really unhealthy—*that's* why women are encouraged to be less perfectionistic and balance themselves out." Like a pill in applesauce, the repression of women's drive to excel is swallowed without detection when mixed into the already-ambiguous, lumpy concept of perfectionism.

The push for increased balance is not a response to the state of women's health; it's a response to the state of women's power. Unfortunately, the implicit messaging works. Women scatter their energy on a wild goose chase to find balance while internalizing their perfectly healthy desire for more as a deficiency in gratitude.

None of this is to deny that perfectionism can be a destructive force in one's life. Perfectionism can be harmful or helpful to anyone, depending on how that person manages it. Until we acknowledge the dichotomous and gendered nature of perfectionism, we are agreeing to sit idly as misguided men fly themselves straight into the burning sun, and as women's wings are clipped off in the name of protection.

More

If you're not leading a balanced life right now, that doesn't mean there's something wrong with you. You don't have to "hit the gym" until you're too tired to be mad or make longer lists in your gratitude journal until you stop wanting things. You can be angry and full of love. You can be grateful and want more. You do not need to balance any of this out.

You are allowed to want more and get it. Wanting more is healthy. Your desires are real and important, and they do not have to make sense to anyone other than you.

Wanting more may feel subversive and "dirty" to women who are taught that their perfectionism (read: ambition) is bad and wrong, in the same way that being sexually aroused can feel subversive and "dirty" to women who are taught that their sexual desire is wrong. Wanting more is an affront to everything you've learned about how to be a grateful, healthy, and balanced woman. A woman who wants more is ungrateful, a man who wants more is a visionary. A woman who seeks power is "power hungry," a man who seeks power is an "alpha male." These narratives are boring and raggedy. Be done.

Do not allow your ambition to be pathologized. Refuse to apologize for or disguise your insatiable desire to excel. Reject entirely the notion that you need to be fixed. Reclaim your perfectionism now.

If only for the briefest moment, allow yourself to consider a radical thought in a misogynist world: *there's nothing wrong with you.*

4

Perfectionism
Up Close

A DEEPER UNDERSTANDING OF PERFECTIONISM
AND THE FLUIDITY OF MENTAL HEALTH

There's nothing fixed in matters of the mind and heart.

DR. HARRIET LERNER

Lena was tired that day. She had already committed to so much. When the email came through, she immediately knew she should say no. She wanted to say no. Perhaps more accurately, she wanted to want to say no.

But the idea of saying yes to the opportunity thrilled Lena, even in her tired state. Taking on slightly more than she could handle had become a philosophy for her. She read the email aloud in our session and without pause, began building the case for saying yes:

"What would ever actually get done if I only took on what I had the bandwidth for? I mean, honestly. Nothing. And how exciting would my life be if I made sure I had time to do everything? Not very." She replaced the plastic worms for the live therapist bait: "How much would I grow if I always made what I knew was the 'technically healthier' choice? I'm here to grow."

Now it was my turn to read an email aloud. I pulled up the one Lena had sent me last fall, when she first requested an appointment. She cut me off the second she recognized what I was reading, "Okay, I get it, I get it—you can stop." She quieted herself.

In the email, Lena described a "deep and necessary" desire to change her lifestyle. A part of her wanted to stop pushing herself, stop feeling compelled to rise to the occasion of being her best self. She wanted to figure out how to be her average self without feeling like a loser.

Operating just beyond her capacity had always energized Lena, except, of course, when it hurt her. Lena had written that email to me in a state of pain. The underbelly of ambition is a pain perfectionists know well— you realize you're overextended, but you can't see any alternatives other than to keep pushing.

Then again, Lena had a point. It does happen that you know something will be too much, but you say yes to it anyway, and you spend the rest of your life grateful for that version of you who said yes—to having another kid, to being the keynote speaker, to throwing the party and officially celebrating, to accepting the job offer. We don't know what we were thinking when we agreed to fix up the fixer-upper, or start the podcast, or rescue the dog that chewed everything in sight. It was too much, it is too much, but we wouldn't have it any other way.

Because balance doesn't exist, you're either operating under or over your energetic equilibrium. In other words, you're in the realm of being either underwhelmed or overwhelmed. Perfectionists reliably choose to operate over their equilibriums. For perfectionists, the risk of being underwhelmed is much scarier than the risk of being overwhelmed.

We reviewed all this, Lena and I. We discussed boundaries, burnout, and the infinite dividends of rest. We also explored the excitement she felt, whether or not she could step away from present commitments to successfully step into this one, and what it would cost her to say yes or no.

I wasn't trying to get her to arrive at a particular conclusion. I was trying to get her to weigh her options against the backdrop of her values, her limitations, her dreams, and what she'd learned about herself so far.

Lena held the tension for as long as she could, which was three days. Then she decided.

Perfectionism + Tension

We all feel tension at times. We notice the space between the ideal we envision and the reality plunked down in our laps. The noticing creates a tightening, which then seeks an outlet for release.

Feeling the tightening and seeking release is an everyday experience for perfectionists. Perfectionists live with a tension inside them that never goes away. Like a light that makes a sound when it's on, you get used to the hum.

Tension doesn't always feel good, but there's value in it. Tension energizes and stirs awareness. Tension catalyzes action. Tension makes everything more interesting. What we do with the tensions we experience is what makes life such a colorful, redemptive, tragic, joyful, and surprising experience. Tension is the wild card.

Perfectionism draws on a prototypical tension—wanting what you can't have. You want the ideal to be the reality. Ideally, Lena could figure out how to engineer life such that she could keep taking on opportunities without it costing her anything. How close could she get to the ideal without destroying herself? That's really what all her questions were asking.

Perfectionism Is Highly Individualized

The tension of perfectionism emerges from the constant clashing between the two most fundamental aspects of your identity—you're a full-of-flaws human with significant limitations and you're a perfect being with unlimited potential. Reconciling the backseat fighting between your limits and your potential is the underlying challenge of perfectionism. Still, as I mentioned in the introduction, describing perfectionism isn't as simple as saying, "Perfectionists want things to be perfect all the time."

The ideals that perfectionists seek are not generic; they reflect an individualized "perfect" vision of success themed around the highest priority for the perfectionist. It's one of the most misunderstood features of perfectionism—people think, "Well, I can't be a perfectionist because I'm never on time . . . I can't be a perfectionist because I don't mind a little mess." Perfectionism expands so far beyond the little ring box we've been trying to squeeze it into.

For example, a Parisian perfectionist may be fine coasting through the same job with no upward mobility for years because their drive to excel, achieve, and advance towards the ideal is expressed through interpersonal dynamics. Parisian perfectionists want ideal connection—*their* version of the ideal friendship, or ideal romantic partnership, or ideal connection to self, or ideal connections to colleagues, family, communities, perhaps all of the above. The individualized component of perfectionism is also why an intense perfectionist can hold exacting standards at work, then come home to a house that looks like it just got ransacked.

Perfectionism Is Compulsive

As we touched upon earlier, perfectionists are people who notice the difference between reality and an ideal more often than not and who feel compelled to actively bridge the gulf. While compulsivity is often used as a clinical marker for dysfunction, it's not automatically dysfunctional.

In adaptive perfectionism, healthy compulsive strivings are value driven, fulfilling, and executed in ways that aren't harmful to the perfectionists or others. In maladaptive perfectionism, unhealthy compulsive strivings are not fulfilling, and they're executed in a way that can harm the perfectionist and others.

Accepting that perfectionism is compulsive means accepting that, as a perfectionist, you will always be compelled to actively strive towards the ideal your perfectionist type represents. If Lena suppressed her compulsion to excel towards her specific ideal—if she set her speed to average and pushed cruise control, something inside of her would go dark in the same way that if an artist suppressed their compulsion to make art, something inside of *them* would go dark. No matter what the artist does, no matter how much they achieve in other areas of their life, they'll feel like a loser until they make some art. This can't be helped. It shouldn't be helped.

It can feel scary and limiting to accept the compulsive nature of perfectionism, to accept the compulsive nature of any strong natural impulse. We want to control the degree to which we are compelled to do anything. We want to feel free.

You don't achieve liberation through control; you achieve liberation through acceptance.

As much as she tried to find a way to let go of her impulse to strive—as hard as she tried to "relax" and embrace average without feeling like a loser, Lena couldn't. You won't be able to either.

This is always the most provocative part of explaining perfectionism— saying that unless you're striving to excel in some way, you're going to feel like a loser. People don't like to hear that. For one, it sounds like a judgment against average, which it's not.

Average is not a bad thing. Perfectionists are totally fine operating at an average and below-average level in a lot of areas, just not the areas they long to excel in.

Secondly, it sounds much more palatable and appropriate to say that healthy people are the ones who figure out how to be content with enough. That's true. You can't be a healthy perfectionist unless you learn how to cultivate and recognize an appreciation for enough. But you can appreciate enough and still want more. That's healthy, too.

Sometimes I use florid language to cushion provocations: if you don't honor the drive in you to actively explore the ideal, you're likely to experience an enduring sense of defeatism. (In other words, you're gonna feel like a loser.)

I don't mean "loser" in the socially comparative context, in relation to others, but in the sense of losing touch with one's full self. Perfectionists "confess" in therapy that when they try to stop excelling, they feel muted. They feel like they've lost something; they feel like losers. The trick is not to figure out how to stop wanting to excel so much—for true perfectionists, that always backfires. The trick is to figure out how to excel based on your values, not someone else's values.

We'll return to Lena and values in chapter 8. For now, let's talk about how to know if you're a true perfectionist.

Differentiating Perfectionism

The compulsive and active quality of perfectionism is what separates idealists and high strivers from perfectionists. Idealists can be happy talking about or daydreaming about ideals; perfectionists feel compelled to engage in the active pursuit of an ideal. High strivers can choose to stop striving and be at peace with that choice; perfectionists cannot.

A high striver, for example, who has enjoyed an industrious and rewarding career might decide, *You know what, I'm gonna call it. I'm done working*. High strivers could retire young, say at fifty-five, sit on the beach all day, and soak in the pleasure of doing nothing, indefinitely, for years. While the beach scenario is the dream for millions of people, it would be an exile of sandy horror for perfectionists. An absolute nonstarter.

Narcissists may also appear to be perfectionistic or hold themselves to a higher standard in pursuit of their goals. According to the fifth edition of the *Diagnostic and Statistical Manual of Mental Disorders* (*DSM*), however, narcissists are able to believe they have achieved perfection after completing their goals.[1] They may think, *I was the perfect boss, I created the perfect program*, or *I made perfect art*. Even when perfectionists achieve deep satisfaction upon the completion of a goal, they always notice areas that could technically be improved upon. Aside from the fact that narcissists demonstrate a consistent lack of empathy for others, another key difference between narcissists and perfectionists is that narcissists don't struggle with self-criticism in the same way that perfectionists do.

All perfectionists have vocal inner critics. Adaptive perfectionists learn how to respond to their inner critics with compassion, thereby disabling negative self-talk from having power over them—but the tape still plays. Narcissists don't have inner critics as much as they have inner superfans telling them they're geniuses, they're the best, and that the rules shouldn't apply to people as special as they are. Narcissism involves a sense of grandiosity that perfectionism doesn't.

Narcissists are highly sensitive to criticism from others, referred to as *narcissistic injury*, but their pain stems from confusion: *How can they not see how wonderful I am? Why don't they understand that I deserve special treatment?* To mend their narcissistic injuries, narcissists require a continuous and excessive amount of admiration and reassurance from others, referred to as *narcissistic supply*.

Conversely, a perfectionist in an adaptive mindset sources their primary sense of validation from themselves, while a perfectionist in a maladaptive mindset doesn't feel soothed by reassurance. For reasons we're about to delve into, excessive admiration and reassurance in fact makes the maladaptive perfectionist feel *more* insecure.

People also conflate obsessive-compulsive disorder (OCD) with perfectionism; the two are quite disparate. A person suffering from OCD may experience intrusive thoughts revolving around a certain obsessional theme—for example, contamination or harm. They may worry that, say, someone they love is going to get hurt, then see an image in their mind of that person getting hit by a bus over and over again. The obsessional thoughts of someone suffering from OCD can be intrusive to the point of feeling alien, as if your brain has been hijacked and you're being forced to repeatedly encounter a thought or image you don't want to be experiencing.

Overwhelmed by unwanted thoughts, a person suffering from OCD may then engage in a ritualistic, compulsive act to neutralize the threat and anxiety generated by their recurrent thoughts. There can be a degree of magical thinking that exists within OCD: *If I keep all the vases on the shelf perfectly symmetrical, it will protect the people around me from getting hurt.*[2]

In contrast to the general compulsive strivings perfectionists display towards ideal chasing, compulsivity in OCD manifests through specific acts, such as counting to a certain number, washing hands, or repeating an exact phrase. Compulsivity in OCD can also reflect rigid rules applied for no logical reason: *I can't walk into a room without first tapping on the doorframe three times.* Perfectionists may also engage in rigid behaviors, but the rigidity holds a connection to reality and logic: *I can't send an email until I read it three times over because it may have grammatical errors and I don't want to seem incompetent.*

To be clear, perfectionism is not considered a disorder. Unlike narcissistic personality disorder and OCD, there's no standardized criterion one can meet to be clinically recognized as a perfectionist. These differences reflect my conceptualization of the perfectionism/perfectionist construct.

The clinical disorder most adjacent to maladaptive perfectionism is obsessive-compulsive personality disorder (OCPD). The name sounds a lot like OCD, but it's a very different illness. OCPD can be marked by, among other diagnostic criteria, an excessive preoccupation with work at the expense of healthy interpersonal relationships, an obsession with control, and a preoccupation with orderliness and what the *DSM* refers to as, "rigid perfectionism."[3]

"Rigid perfectionism" is defined in the *DSM* as follows:

A rigid insistence on everything being flawless, perfect, and without errors or faults, including one's own and others' performance; sacrificing of timeliness to ensure correctness in every detail; believing that there is only one right way to do things; difficulty changing ideas and/or viewpoint; preoccupation with details, organization, and order.[4]

Note that the *DSM* is instituting the distinction of rigidity intentionally and with great consideration. The semantics allude to the body of research demonstrating that perfectionism can be both flexible and rigid, adaptive and maladaptive, healthy and unhealthy. The *DSM* is not in the habit of accommodating other such comparative distinctions; there's no "rigid narcissism" or "rigid bulimia" or "rigid agoraphobia" because narcissism, bulimia, and agoraphobia are understood to be uniformly maladaptive.

Also note that the clinical definition of *rigid perfectionism* does not currently include the emotional and interpersonal expressions of perfectionistic tendencies that we'll delve into later in this chapter; these, too, are features of perfectionism.

At first blush, it may be easy for any perfectionist to relate to OCPD. A deeper examination of the degree of rigidity involved in this disorder can be clarifying. As the *DSM* states, "Individuals with this disorder are [can be] rigidly deferential to authority and rules, and insist on quite literal compliance, with no rule bending for extenuating circumstances."[5] For example, if someone falls down on the grass and needs help, a person living with OCPD might not think it appropriate to walk onto the grass to offer assistance because of a Do Not Walk on Grass sign.

While you don't have to satisfy every diagnostic criterion to meet the diagnostic threshold of a disorder, other criteria for OCPD include hoarding tendencies and exhibiting a miserly relationship with money[6]—both of which revolve around an attempt to maintain extreme control over one's life.

More specifically, hoarding objects like broken appliances or thousands of old magazines is motivated by an illogical, extreme, and inflexible attempt to control for unexpected future events.[7] For example, a person with OCPD may think, *You never know what could happen, I might need an old toaster knob for something in the future, so I can't throw these seventeen broken toasters away.*

The extreme frugality that is sometimes present in OCPD is motivated by the same control-obsessed mechanisms. To deal with the fact that you can't control the future, you refuse to spend money in order to feel more prepared for and more in control of whatever comes your way. We're not talking about penny-pinching here. A person living with OCPD could be sitting on $2 million and still refuse to buy themselves lunch, opting instead to eat an array of free samples at the grocery store.

The *DSM* reinforces the difference between perfectionistic tendencies and extreme rigidity by emphasizing the following: "Obsessive-compulsive personality traits in moderation may be especially adaptive, particularly in situations that reward high performance. Only when these traits are inflexible, maladaptive, and persisting and cause significant functional impairment or subjective distress do they constitute obsessive-compulsive personality disorder."[8]

It's important to understand that just because the experience you're having isn't clinically recognized as an illness, that doesn't mean you're in the clear. Your work is to examine the degree to which your thoughts, feelings, behaviors, and interpersonal relationships are disrupting or enhancing your quality of life. Therapists, books, and personal-development stuff can offer you a supportive framework as you make those considerations, but ultimately you're the only one who knows what it's like to be you. As we move forward in our exploration of perfectionism, be honest with yourself about what's helping you and what's hurting you.

Perfectionism + Striving towards an Ideal

Perfectionists want to keep striving towards an impossible ideal throughout their entire lives; as we just discussed, they in fact need to. Adaptive perfectionists find it to be an honor and a privilege to have discovered an endeavor worthy of endless pursuit. When your bottomless striving is value driven and executed in a healthy way, it's a singular joy. The reward of doing work you know you can never finish is that you get to continue to do the work.

Compulsively striving towards an impossible ideal is the base of perfectionism. *Why* you strive and *how* you strive determines whether your perfectionism is healthy or not.

- **WHY ARE YOU STRIVING?** Is your motivation to bridge the gulf between an ideal and reality born from the desire to excel and grow (adaptive) or from the need to compensate for perceived inadequacies and avoid failure (maladaptive)?

- **HOW ARE YOU STRIVING?** Are you hurting yourself or others in the process (maladaptive)? Or are you striving in a way that feels good for you (adaptive)?

Identifying the motivation behind your striving (the "why" part) requires you to explore your sense of self-worth.

Perfectionists + Self Worth

Self-worth is about understanding that right now, with all the things you have yet to achieve, you are as worthy of all the love, joy, dignity, freedom, and connection as you would be had you already achieved them. You are worthy of all these things because you exist.

Your self-worth is prearranged; you have no hand in it. From the day you were born until the day you die, you remain worthy. You're worthy in every passing hour, through every mistake, in sun and in storm. Whether you accept or deny your worth is up to you.

Another way to understand what self-worth is is to understand what it's not. Self-worth is not self-esteem. As the ever-brilliant Dr. Brené Brown succinctly explains, "We *think* self-esteem"; self-esteem is not a feeling.[9]

Self-worth, on the other hand, is experienced more deeply. Self-worth is about what you feel and believe you deserve. The distinction is a source of confusion for those perfectionists who may have high self-esteem but who also find themselves feeling insecure.

For example, a hard-won promotion to your dream job is met with the following inner monologue: "I know I'm smart, I know I'm competent, and I know I'm performing well—so why do I feel so inadequate?" Yes, you know you're competent and smart, but do you *believe you're worthy* of having a job you love?

On the other side of the coin, perfectionists may find themselves in a hellish situation, yet unable to leave. For example, a person in a toxic relationship may understand that they're funny, attractive, smart, "a catch." They have great self-esteem, but they stay with someone who treats them like expired food in the fridge—kept only because the other person hasn't gotten around to throwing them away. They may say something like, "This is so unhealthy. I know I should leave, so why do I stay?" Yes, you know you're smart, attractive, and funny—but do you *believe you're worthy* of good, real love?

When people say, "You're enough," they're referring to your self-worth. They're saying, "Hey you, you don't need to do anything to deserve immediate access to love, freedom, dignity, joy, and connection. The 'admission fee' is paid for by your presence. You simply being here is enough."

Adaptive perfectionists are connected to their self-worth. When you know you're already whole and complete (i.e., perfect) as you are, you're operating from a mindset of abundance. You already have what you need, and you feel secure. For adaptive perfectionists, striving towards an ideal is a celebratory expression of that security.

Maladaptive perfectionists do not feel whole or secure. They feel broken, and they operate from a mindset of deficit. Their striving is driven by the need to compensate, to fix what's broken, and to try to offer substitutes for or try to hide what's missing.

A simplistic example of the different motivations propelling adaptive and maladaptive perfectionists can be found in those who strive to look their best. An adaptive perfectionist wants to look their best because they feel good inside. Animating and expressing that positive internal sentiment externally makes them feel more aligned with who they are, like they're celebrating themselves. A maladaptive perfectionist wants to look their best because they feel bad inside. They're desperate to look their best because maladaptive perfectionists feel so inadequate already that they feel like they better at least offer *something*.

Another way to think about it—adaptive perfectionists offer gifts; maladaptive perfectionists offer consolation prizes. A consolation prize is a gesture of apology. When you get a consolation prize, someone is trying to console you by saying, "You didn't win, and I'm sorry for that, but here's this less desirable thing so you don't have to walk away empty-handed." A perfectionist in a maladaptive mindset feels as if they already "lost" at being whole, good enough, or acceptable as they are. Maladaptive perfectionists strive to achieve goals (including interpersonal goals like people-pleasing) in the hope that others don't feel empty-handed in their presence.

It's impossible for you to ever show up empty-handed because you're always bringing you. When you're connected to your self-worth, you remember that; when you aren't connected to your worth, you forget it.

If you're in a maladaptive mindset, it's not necessarily that you feel worthless. You just don't feel fully worthy *right now*. You think that after you finish fixing yourself (i.e., making yourself superficially perfect and therefore worthy), *then* you'll finally deserve that which you most long for. You live in a state of waiting.

It's important to understand that detaching from your self-worth doesn't feel like *I'm a piece of trash, so let me desperately scramble to make up for that.* Typically, the disconnection is experienced more subtly. It's nuanced with a tinge of misguided optimism.

Being disconnected from your self-worth feels more like this: *Okay, I'm almost there, I'm close, so I'll be able to enjoy my life soon, as soon as I'm 'done,' as soon as I'm skinny, as soon as I make over X amount of dollars, as*

*soon as I get the job, as soon as I get pregnant, as soon as I'm accepted into
that school, or my children are accepted into that school, as soon as I make
partner, as soon as I'm in a relationship, as soon as I can buy the person I love
the present they want, <u>I can feel good about myself as soon as I've earned it.</u>*
When you're disconnected from your self-worth, you think your ability to
feel joy is won through goal attainment.

I wonder if I wrote this entire book just to write this next sentence: *You
don't earn your way to joy.* Joy is a birthright. So is love, freedom, dignity,
and connection. As the inimitable James Baldwin said, "Your crown has
been bought and paid for. All you have to do is wear it."

High self-esteem does not equal high self-worth. The other major misunderstanding we have about self-worth is that it's static. Self-worth is
fluid. Even the most self-assured among us aren't inoculated when it
comes to becoming untethered from their self-worth. The breakaway can
happen in an instant.

Target Parking Lot Moments

As civilized people do, my friend Selena texted me to ask if she could call.
I called her immediately. She was in a Target store parking lot, alone in
her car. As you and I both know, that could mean anything. I braced
myself.

SELENA: Hi.
ME: Hey, what's going on?

Then the inevitable "Excuse my momentary silence while I prepare to
have a breakdown" pregnant pause.

Through collapsed breaths and squeaky words, Selena explained that
today was Spirit Day at her kids' elementary school, but she didn't realize
that. Her two daughters went to school in regular clothes and everyone
else was dressed in green and white. The school sent a class picture to all

the parents, which she insisted on sending to me. "Don't send it, I don't need to see it," I said. "I just sent it," she said.

"Look, look at the kids on the left with the face paint." Her squeaks turned into stomps, "Who the fuck has time to put face paint on their kids in the morning?! I'll tell you who—the good moms. J's not even smiling. What am I going to say to them when they get home—'Sorry your mom sucks'?"

Selena knows she's an amazing parent, and at this stage in her personal development, she's almost always tethered to her self-worth. But that picture hit a nerve.

Three years out of a divorce, Selena had worked through so much shame and guilt in therapy about "ruining her kids' lives" because she didn't want to stay married. That was *after* she had worked through all the shame and guilt over the amount of time she spent at work (i.e., any amount of time). The lessons of her life curriculum had brought her to a point of feeling like, "Okay, that was all hard, but I did it! I understand all the lessons now. Now I can just enjoy the rest of my life."

For at least the last year, she'd felt assured and free, as if the work of connecting to her worth was behind her. Then the Spirit Day picture landed in her in-box and as quickly as she tapped that email open, she felt a cruel shove back to emotional square one.

You may in this moment feel very connected to your self-worth, like you're "done" learning the critical lessons. No matter how tremendously you've grown, you *will* encounter your own version of questioning your worth in a Target parking lot at some point in the future.

It's not that you're back at square one; it's that self-worth is fluid. The more you've established a connection to your self-worth, the more easily you can realign yourself when you lose your footing, but we all lose our footing.

Some days are a lot. Some days aren't a lot and we lose our footing anyway. Derailing from your center can happen in a blink—when everyone in the meeting laughs, and you're not sure if it's with you or at you;

when your credit card is declined at the grocery store; when you see something you weren't expecting to see on social media; when someone you're dating or building a new friendship with stops texting you back. Self-worth is fluid because all mental health is fluid.

Mental Health Is Fluid

I internally lose it whenever I hear a statement like, "One in five Americans suffers from a mental health condition." Statements like that are, for me, the statistical equivalent of seeing "Your great" in print. I always want to make a request into the void like, "May I please have a word with the other four Americans?"

Nobody is inoculated from "mental health conditions"; mental health conditions are human conditions. We all have the capacity to dip, dive, coast, float, and soar. We're all up and down at different times, in different ways, and for different reasons. This is all fine and as it should be; it's also exactly why we need one another.

If you're wondering whether you're an adaptive or a maladaptive perfectionist, spare yourself the trouble, you're both. Anyone who's a perfectionist is both.

We love to think in binary ways. We're depressed (damn it!), or we're not depressed (phew!). Mental health doesn't work like that. While it's both useful and convenient to rely on the diagnostic thresholds that categorical models of mental health are built upon, mental health is *way* more context dependent and trait based than we currently perceive it to be. When I use the terms "adaptive" and "maladaptive" to describe perfectionists, I'm referring to the mindset the person is in, not the person themselves.

The best way I can explain the fluidity of mental health in general and perfectionism in particular? At the risk of you closing this book, then burning it, I'm going to tell you something a professor told me my junior year of college, from which I have yet to fully recover: "There are no grades in this class."

The Raw Manifestations
of Perfectionism

Because we're so used to reductive conceptualizations of perfectionism, it's easy to overlook how dynamic the construct is. Since perfectionism is fluid and context dependent, it's helpful to strip perfectionism of personality overlays and examine the spokes that keep it turning.

The following are the raw manifestations of perfectionism I've encountered in my work:

Emotional perfectionism: I want to experience a perfect emotional state.

Cognitive perfectionism: I want to understand perfectly.

Behavioral perfectionism: I want to behave perfectly in my roles and perform perfectly in my tasks.

Object perfectionism: I want this external thing—art, the surface of my desk, my face, the movie I'm directing, the presentation deck, the "About" page on my website, my child's hair . . . to exist in a perfect state.

Process perfectionism: I want this process (an airline flight, sobriety, going to church, giving a presentation, a marriage) to begin, continue, and end perfectly.

Different facets of perfectionism emerge and retreat depending on the contexts we find ourselves in. For example, during the holidays, object perfectionism comes on strong for me, and I lean more towards being a classic perfectionist (which is not my regular mode of perfectionism). I plan the day by the hour. I wear plaid pencil skirts and actually blow-dry my hair. Last year, I spent thirty minutes at a Christmas-tree stand on the corner of Seventy-Second and Amsterdam in the pouring rain, looking for the perfect door wreath.

The first year I moved to New York, my sister and I hosted Christmas for our family in the fifth-floor walk-up apartment we shared. My sister asked which jobs she should do. My response? "What would be great is if you could let me do everything."

I had to have walked up and down those five flights of stairs a hundred times in the span of three days—groceries, decorations, laundromat runs. I could not stop preparing. There was a cute thrift store a few blocks away where I found a beautiful set of vintage holiday goblets. Green holly and red berries were etched along the bowl of the glass, which was lined with a festive gold rim. I became obsessed with serving traditional eggnog in those glasses.

Another trip up and down those stairs to get fresh vanilla seed straight from the pod. It was worth it. You could see the gorgeously tiny black specks of vanilla magnified through the thick goblet glass. Or at least I could see them; no one else cared.

I topped the frothy drinks with a generous dollop of freshly whipped cream, the faintest dusting of grated nutmeg, and a cinnamon stick as a vanity stirrer. When I served the drinks, one of my brothers said, "Thanks!" as he unceremoniously removed the cinnamon stick from the glass and slung it onto a napkin.

I stared blanky at him as a nostalgic mix of holiday songs played at the perfect background volume. "What?" he said. I patiently explained that he had to put the cinnamon stick back into his drink because it was part of the holiday. He obliged without speaking, then went to the kitchen to pour more rum into his eggnog.

Classic perfectionists easily become fixated on object perfection, but anyone can become fixated. Assuming the perfectionist is in an adaptive space (which I was not during that particular holiday), focusing on object perfectionism can be satisfying, emotionally regulating, meditative, and meaningful.

Adaptively expressed, object perfectionism helps enhance a feeling of wholeness and perfection that already exists within you. Maladaptively expressed, object perfectionism reflects your dependency on an external object to make you feel whole and perfect on the inside.

That first Christmas in New York, a part of me honestly thought that if I offered the perfect food and decor, if I created the perfect holiday playlist and curated the perfect activities, then that would make everyone feel connected, centered, and whole. Once everyone else was all set, then *I* could feel connected, centered, and whole. My job would be done, and I could finally relax and enjoy the moment. After all that work, I certainly would've earned the joy.

I wasn't connected to my self-worth in that moment, though, which didn't mean I felt totally worthless; it meant I was holding off on fully living my life—enjoying the present moment—until I earned it. I made my joy contingent upon my performance instead of my existence. In this case, my performance centered around my ability to successfully control other people by making them feel relaxed and happy. Embracing my power would've looked like giving myself permission to experience joy without conditions—and letting other people be who they are and feel what they feel.

Each type of perfectionist has their own way of expressing the dynamics inherent in maladaptive perfectionism, but regardless of context, the raw formula is the same: you get separated from your self-worth, and you think restoring your worth hinges on an external outcome. You start trying to compensate for something you don't need to compensate for. You start trying to earn something that already belongs to you.

Your maladaptive perfectionism swoops in thinking that it's saving the day, that it's going to fix the situation, that it's going to protect you from getting hurt. Maladaptive perfectionism will have you thinking a cinnamon stick is the missing key to unlocking peace. Maladaptive perfectionism only makes it worse.

For Parisian perfectionists, maladaptive perfectionism looks like people-pleasing at the expense of pleasing oneself. For procrastinator perfectionists, it looks like waiting too long and then never doing it. For messy perfectionists, it looks like sabotaging yourself by saying yes to everything while committing to nothing. For intense perfectionists, it looks like operating as if achievement will give you what only connection can. For classic perfectionists, it looks like refusing to acknowledge that no matter how much predictability, exterior beauty, and organization you create, some moments are uncertain in a way you can't control.

For everyone, maladaptive perfectionism looks like taking a moment of disconnection and responding to it in a way that renders you isolated. Instead of harnessing your authentic power, you double down on superficial control.

Superficial Control + Authentic Power

Like lust and love, power and control can look identical. They're not the same thing. Control is limited and transactionally owned. If you're a person in a position of control and you give someone else control, you have relinquished your control. Power, by contrast, is unlimited and can be shared. If you're a person in a position of power and you empower someone else (you give someone else power), you haven't lost any power.

Power is understanding the immutability of your worth. From that place, you're not desperate for an outcome to unfold in a particular way, because you know you're already worthy of whatever the outcome would grant you. You give yourself permission to feel joy, love, dignity, freedom, and connection now. You already won.

The confidence of having already won liberates your potential. When your self-worth isn't on the line, it becomes easier to take risks. You get more of what you want because you're more willing to risk trying.

When you're disconnected from your self-worth, you're fixated on control. You may be experienced as demanding or needy to be around because you're so attached to a specific outcome's unfolding. You *need* something to happen in a certain way to feel relief. Whether you realize it or not, you are desperate.

People can feel the attendant anxiety of a person who is desperate. If you want to be a leader in your field, in your family, in your community, in the world, you need to learn how to be powerful, not controlling. Nobody wants to work for or be around people who are controlling.

Control encourages restriction; power encourages freedom. Control is petty; power is generous. Control micromanages; power inspires. Control manipulates; power influences. Control is myopic—you have to plan everything one precise move at a time. Power is visionary—it affords you the great luxury of taking leaps of faith. Power is the upgrade.

Relying on a strategy of superficial control instead of accessing your power is tantamount to moving a car by pushing it from the bumper instead of getting inside and driving it.

Think about the leaders you gravitate towards. Is their authority based on control or power? You can be an authority figure without having power (the boss that no one listens to or respects), or you can be a leader without having official authority (the one employee who influences the decision-making of the entire team). Power isn't granted by titles. Anyone can be powerful.

Perfectionists + Mindfulness

Few words have been more radioactively commodified than "mindfulness" has. I saw a brand of mayonnaise called Mindful Mayo once. It's a strange world. Anyway, I much prefer the word *presence* to describe one's ability to consciously bring their whole self to the present moment. An abiding relationship exists between seeking perfection and seeking presence.

When something is experienced as "perfect," it's for no other reason than because the person experiencing it is present. Even when something is functionally perfect, if the person isn't present, they're destined to find fault with it.

Your memories of perfect moments are memories of moments in which you were most present.

Perfectionists are perfectionists because they love to court ideals. Goals are terminal; ideals are continual. After a perfectionist reaches a goal, they always create a new goal, a bigger goal, because their true interest lies in chasing the ideal that the goal represents.

By definition, ideals are not possible to achieve; achieving presence is the exception to the rule.

Perfectionism reflects our natural desire to experience total alignment with our inner and outer worlds. It's an attempt to merge the ideal (embracing what's possible) with reality (embracing what is). The only way to fully bridge this gulf is to become present. When you're present, you embrace both what is and what's possible simultaneously. You're achieving an ideal—the ideal state of awareness.

Being present means you are in touch with this moment. The fact that you're reading this sentence. The fact that you're taking breaths, shallow as they may be. The fact that instead of being dead, you are alive, here, now.

There's an odd irreverence that accompanies being present. You don't need anything to happen. You don't need anyone to like you. You're fully relieved of the small-mindedness of your thoughts, detached from the strain of trying to bend the future towards you and make everything happen now.

When you're present, your life now is not dictated by that of your past; it's dictated by possibility. You're encased in your own wholeness and at the same time, you are utterly free.

A misconception about being present is that presence equals happiness. We take deep breaths, fix our posture, then wait. We're waiting to feel something. Shiny, clean, ready—*happy*. The way people in car commercials look like they feel.

You can be present and feel tired. You can be present and feel heart-broken. You can be present and not feel ready. Presence guarantees freedom, not happiness.

Being present is not a state of mind; it's a state of being. Ergo, being present doesn't just change the way you think and perceive; it changes the way you move, the angle at which you choose to hold your head, the tone and speed of your voice. Whether you pull your breath in below your collarbone and deep down into your belly, or let it dangle from the ceiling of your throat like a chandelier made of air. Whether you notice or miss entirely the vibrancy of the colors surrounding you. Whether you interrupt others or listen. Whether you pick away at some part of your skin or let your hands be still. These are features of the quality of your presence.

Presence changes how judgmental, compassionate, and solution-oriented you are. Being present invites relief from living in a world where what's missing and wrong relentlessly eclipses what's good and already there.

Even in the moments when being present is hard because embracing reality is painful, presence retains an ameliorative quality. Being present is the only attainable ideal, which is why perfectionists are magnetically drawn to it.

So why aren't all perfectionists basking in inner peace and higher consciousness?

Because, at least initially, perfectionists try to reverse engineer the experience of being present. Perfectionists think, "If I can get this thing/myself/others to be perfect, then I will feel perfect."

You think that once you manufacture perfection externally, *then* you'll feel fully alive, satisfied, connected, in touch with possibility, spacious, whole, centered—all the things people feel when they're present. The inverse is true. The more you cultivate presence internally, the more you allow yourself to feel whole, alive, and connected, regardless of what's happening around you. The more present you are internally, the more you recognize perfection externally.

When I listen to people describe perfect moments, they're not describing the material; they're describing feeling whole and connected. When I listen to people describe moments that "should've been perfect" but weren't, they're describing exterior, superficial perfection amidst an internal sense of feeling fragmented.

We find superficial perfection to be stilted and dull because it's not imbued with presence; other people can copy it. You can perfectly paint by numbers without making a single mistake, but you'll never create a masterpiece that way. Something will be missing; it's your signature presence—that's what makes it "completely done," that's what makes it perfect.

It's not a coincidence that the people who rise and remain at the top of their fields are the ones who feel present doing what they're doing. Those are the people whom we feel do their job "perfectly." When Beyoncé steps onto a stage, she's not entertaining us with a performance; she's inspiring us with a showcase of her presence.

What Beyoncé has mastered is not a sequence of dance moves or the memorization of lyrics sung beautifully—a lot of people can dance, a lot of people have a beautiful voice. What Beyoncé has mastered is her ability to consistently access the power of her singular presence.

Because Beyoncé is a master of presence, she could walk on stage in a bedsheet, stand still, look you in the eye, and you would still be captivated. Do you know what you'd be captivated by? Her power. Do you know where her power comes from? Her presence. Do you know what her presence feels like? Perfection.

When people say that everything you need is already inside you, they're talking about the power of your singular presence. When someone's fully present with you, it's hypnotic. You think, "I've never met anyone quite like them." Because you haven't. Everyone has a signature presence.

We appreciate being around people who are present because they awaken us to our own presence. It's hard to recognize the power of presence in another and maintain amnesia about our own power.

Your presence is the epicenter of your power. Everything you need to be present, you already have.

For a perfectionist in an adaptive mindset, presence is the main priority. Whatever you're doing, thinking, or feeling, you seek to be present first. Some people describe this level of engagement with the present moment as being "in the zone." Psychologist Mihaly Csikszentmihalyi calls it being "in flow."

Being present can also be described more generally: freeing yourself, letting go, opening yourself up to possibilities, living without dictation from the past or instruction from the future, making room for spontaneity. What all these descriptions have in common is their emphasis on losing control.

When you're present, you don't have control, and you don't care. When you're connected to your power, you don't need control.

The opposite of presence is absence. When you're absent, you're disconnected from your power. Instead of feeling worthy, you're waiting to feel worthy. Instead of feeling spacious, you feel emotionally claustrophobic. Instead of taking up full residency inside yourself, you vacate the property. Instead of accepting what is (which doesn't mean you have to like it), you bleed energy rejecting and resisting the reality of the situation you are currently in. Your identity is replaced by your output—what you do and how well and fast you do it becomes who you are.

For a perfectionist in a maladaptive mindset, performance is the main priority. You must excel, even if you don't care about what you're doing, you don't want to be doing it, you take no joy in doing it, or it actively hurts you to do it. Control is maximized because when you feel powerless, being controlling feels like the responsible thing to do.

A Thousand Daggers

The greatest, most catastrophic heartache of seeking peace through external performance happens when you achieve your goal. Finally, you're number one. You're the best. You've earned what you consider to be tangible proof of your worth. Maybe it's the sleek office with the fancy title. Maybe you closed on the big perfect house. Maybe you can fit into the jeans. Maybe you received a heavy award with your name etched onto the base. The point is that you got everything you said you wanted. For perfectionists in a maladaptive mindset, that's when you're struck with a thousand daggers at once.

It's been one of the most baffling and noted aspects of perfectionism, reported on by countless therapists, researchers, and perfectionists themselves: the observation that when maladaptive perfectionists do achieve "perfect," when they hit their goal, even far exceed their goal, they still aren't satisfied.

Pioneering psychoanalyst Dr. Karen Horney described this dissatisfaction as an "inverse ratio" between success and inner security: "instead of feeling, 'I have done it' he merely feels that 'it happened.' Repeated achievements in his field do not make him more secure, but more anxious."[10] Modern-day perfectionism experts Dr. Paul L. Hewitt, Dr. Gordon L. Flett, and Dr. Samuel F. Mikail add that the persistence of perfectionism in lieu of chronic dissatisfaction is especially perplexing because it "directly contravenes decades of research and thought on reinforcement."[11]

Numerous studies highlight the point that achieving goals doesn't just fail to bring some perfectionists satisfaction; often, achieving their goals makes perfectionists feel worse.[12] Why in the world would anyone feel worse after getting exactly what they want, even after *exceeding* their goals?

Because the experience of winning forces you to realize that there are no substitutes for self-worth or presence. Not one.

Using Your Perfectionism to Help You

The notion that you never have to try to be perfect because you already are perfect is foreign to those of us who have been taught to experience ourselves as broken, inadequate, almost there. There is no almost there. There is only here, now.

I used to feel a knot in my stomach when November hit. The holiday season was so loaded for me; hence, my maladaptive perfectionism trying to swoop in and save the day. The knots are gone. I've learned to use the first signs of my burgeoning object perfectionism as a cue to get present and stay connected.

I access the wealth of power inside me instead of trying to win at scratch-off control. In practice, enacting power looks like reminding yourself that you're already whole and perfect. Enacting power looks like maintaining self-awareness by taking time to check in with yourself and ask how you're feeling, as you would a friend (in chapter 8, you'll learn why you should do this in the third person). Enacting power looks like freely giving yourself access to goodness instead of waiting to see how things turn out before deciding how much goodness you deserve. Enacting power looks like putting boundaries around the people and things that make it harder for you to believe in your worth and stay present.

I still do all the festive classic perfectionist tasks during the holiday season, but I do them from a place of joy and detachment from outcome. I love the holidays so much now, which I never thought I'd say.

Every aspect of your perfectionism is a meditation. Each is a ringing bell that chimes when you need certain reminders:

- The past is over, it may as well have been eight thousand years ago, and the future is not something you can control—choose presence.

- You're already whole and perfect; you don't need to become something you already are.

- You're worthy of peace now; you're worthy even as you sleep.

- Your potential is endless, it's calling you, and wouldn't it be exhilarating to answer the call?

After you internalize the reminders, your perfectionism goes, "Okay good, you got it—now let's go have some fun!" You're free to unleash the intensity of your striving in service of your highest potential and deepest desires. You become more of who you are, and you get more of what you want. When you learn to use your perfectionism to help you, you will love that you can't shut that impulse off. You will love being a perfectionist.

The takeaway here is that you have to consciously respond, instead of unconsciously react, to perfectionism in order for it to be healthy. You can't consciously respond to that which you are unaware of. Accordingly, we need to return to the raw manifestations of perfectionism.

The Raw Manifestations of Perfectionism Continued

In addition to object perfectionism, which we discussed previously, I've also observed behavioral, emotional, cognitive, and process-oriented iterations of perfectionism in my work.

Behavioral perfectionism in a literal sense is doing something perfectly (scoring 100 percent on a test), but it can also include mandating yourself to behaviors you believe demonstrate the perfect way to act in the roles that you play (daughter, boss, woman, confident person, parent, etc.).

Behavioral perfectionism is adaptive when it inspires improved performance without cost to your wellness and without attachment to outcome—for example, *I want to master this piano piece because it feels good to work hard at what I love. If I mess up on the day of the recital, then so be it, but I deserve to give myself the best chance to excel.*

When you engage in behavioral perfectionism at the expense of your wellness, it's maladaptive. For example, even though it makes you uncomfortable for a variety of reasons, you continue to say yes to your in-laws staying with you whenever they're in town because that's what you think the perfect daughter-in-law would do. Or you're lost in the meeting and you want to ask a question. Instead, you stay quiet because you want to be the perfect employee who always has their finger on the pulse.

Everyone at least occasionally encounters difficulty acting on behalf of their most authentic self. When the inability to act on behalf of your most authentic self develops into a patterned response, that indicates dysfunction. When we regularly feel obligated to act in ways that betray our needs, goals, and values, the obligation is usually to a standard of behavioral perfection we don't realize we're adhering to.

Cognitive perfectionism involves being able to understand X perfectly. There are some systems and formulas that can be fully understood from a cognitive perspective—for example, *Here's every detail about how a package gets shipped from our warehouse to our customer's door.* While there's utility in the analytical comprehension of a process, outside of strictly formulaic systems, the desire to perfectly understand or know something can keep you stuck and lost.

A procrastinator perfectionist, for example, might get stuck on the cognitive perfectionism loop that says, "I need to perfectly understand how every aspect of urban planning works before I apply for the job."

With regard to loss, consider the firm grip that the need to completely (i.e., perfectly) understand "why" can take—for example, trying to pin down the exact reason why a person left us or the need to know every point of logic behind why we didn't get hired. That's cognitive perfectionism.

We think perfectly understanding "why" can help us control our negative feelings about what occurred. Power is found in accepting and processing the undesirable feelings within you, not by erasing them.

Cognitive perfectionism is adaptive when it's driven by curiosity and learning without attachment to outcome. For example, a neurologist who dedicates their life to researching why we dream. At the end of decades upon decades of research, the neurologist may say, "I don't really know why we dream." They didn't get an answer or closure, but they thoroughly enjoyed decades of meaningful work. The neurologist could retire, but it wouldn't matter. In one way or another, they will never let go of trying to answer the question.

Process perfectionism involves wanting a process to begin, continue, and end perfectly. The "perfect" ending in a long-term process can be for the process to not end at all. Accordingly, if a process ends (e.g., a marriage that results in divorce) or absorbs meaningful disruption (e.g., a relapse from recovery), the entirety of the process is considered a failure.

Process perfectionism can also include self-imposed standards and preconceived notions about the amount of time, energy expenditure, and help a process requires. A perfectionist might, for example, pass the bar exam but still experience the victory as a failure because in their mind, they shouldn't have had to study as intensely as they did to pass.

Zooming out, consider process perfectionism as it relates to identity formation. If you perceive your childhood to have been dysfunctional and you're stuck inside the notion of process-oriented perfectionism, you feel you're sentenced to a life in which you're perpetually "behind." The process of becoming who you are didn't start out perfectly, so how could it ever be any good?

An opposing but similar manifestation of process perfectionism arises in the perfectionist who feels they were given a "perfect childhood." The process started out perfectly, so the pressure is on; the rest of their life must unfold perfectly because in their eyes, they have no excuse for it not to.

Procrastinator perfectionists have to put in the work to not be overwhelmed by their desire for the process to begin perfectly. Messy perfectionists get stuck when the process doesn't continue along perfectly. Intense perfectionists are fixated on the process ending perfectly (achieving the goal). Because their goals are more interpersonal in nature, Parisian perfectionists don't care about which stage of the process they're in as long as they feel connected to others. Classic perfectionists also don't care about which stage of the process they're in as long as they can exert organization and generate some stability.

Like all modes of perfectionism, process perfectionism is adaptive when you use it to serve you as opposed to allowing it to dictate your quality of life. Aubrey was a client of mine who saw the world through the lens of process perfectionism. Waiting for the bus, picking up her dry cleaning, watching TV—they all left her with an acute awareness of the ways in which the process could be streamlined for an optimal experience.

For years, Aubrey fought against the frustration of her lens while trying to be like everyone else. Others didn't seem to notice or care that their experience could be improved. Her world burst open as we discussed ways in which she could deploy her perfectionism towards that which she most valued.

Aubrey was a waitress and, like any perfectionist, she valued a job well done. She didn't feel she could do her job well without having a wait time to offer customers who were asking where their food was and helping manage the expectations of those who hadn't yet asked.

Aubrey searched for solutions and in doing so learned about electronic kitchen-display systems, something she noted she "oddly enjoyed." She wanted the restaurant to invest in one.

Aubrey was excited to present her idea to management, who shut it down twenty seconds into her pitch because of cost issues. Undeterred, Aubrey then suggested that the specials be served as a "flight"—a row of single-bite servings to every table as customers settled in. The specials were being made anyway, the portions were nominal, and the unexpected offering delighted customers while also giving them something to focus on during an unpredictable wait. The solution was a hit.

Next, why was the eyesore coatrack right next to the host stand? Aubrey was practicing her speech to management on me: "Should a bunch of other people's coats be the first thing our customers see when they enter this establishment?" The "establishment" in question was a glorified college bar, but Aubrey didn't care.

She made more improvements in three months than the restaurant had seen in the past five years. Profits (and tips) shot up. More importantly, it felt rewarding and joyful for Aubrey to feel and see her own agency in action.

What used to exist as a daily frustration for Aubrey is now her pocket ace. Aubrey's goal is to open a warm, casual, community-supported restaurant (the restaurant version of a CSA). From start to finish, Aubrey wants to offer an unforgettable dining experience. It's not a question of whether Aubrey will do this, but when.

Possessing a gift without the chance to hone the skills around it and without being able to enjoy it for yourself or share it with others—that's painful. Possessing a gift that you interpret as a burden—that's even more painful.

Certain sectors are well suited for a person who can naturally see or anticipate the micro-processes inside a larger process—industrial design, directing, the entire hospitality industry. Still, you don't have to deploy process perfectionism in a formal or professional capacity for it to benefit you. If you find yourself mired in process perfectionism, use your awareness of wanting the process to be perfect as a cue to get present and get perspective.

Emotional perfectionism is the desire to be in a perfect emotional state. A perfect emotional state here does not mean happy or at peace; it means you want to perfectly control what you feel, when you feel it, and the degree to which you feel it.

For example, a perfect emotional state for a mother might include a tolerance for being slightly annoyed with her child when her child is being loud. What she feels is annoyed, when she feels it is during moments when her child is being loud, the degree to which she feels it is slight. However, should she find herself exceeding what she views as the "perfect" experience of annoyance, she becomes vulnerable to self-censure.

Let's say the mother becomes annoyed when the child is not being loud, or the child is loud for a moment and the mother is intensely annoyed, perhaps to the point of rage. Any experience that deviates from the perfect emotional state is experienced as a failure for a perfectionist in a maladaptive space.

It's not uncommon to take a portion-controlled response to embracing undesirable feelings: *Okay, I'm going to let myself be sad about this for five minutes, and then I'm moving on.* For someone stuck in a maladaptive iteration of emotional perfectionism, encountering their internal world through rationed emotionality is a mainstay strategy. Research supports this notion; maladaptive perfectionism is correlated with using emotional suppression to cope with stress.[13]

For perfectionists struggling with emotional perfectionism, everything is timed and measured. They attempt to control their feelings like a volume knob, and not just the "bad" ones.

The perfect emotional response can also involve attempts to force yourself to feel appreciative when what you feel is resentful, attempts to force yourself to feel excited when what you feel is bored, attempts to make yourself feel thrilled with your body when you don't feel thrilled with your body, and so forth. When you fail to properly control your feelings, you become punitive with yourself.

When adaptive perfectionists notice their emotional response is different from the ideal response they're holding in their minds, they get curious (not punitive) about why that's happening; they wonder what they might need. Instead of running from their feelings, adaptive perfectionists work to regulate their emotional experience in healthy ways. (We'll talk about how to do all of this in the second half of the book.)

Emotional perfectionism is also adaptive when you create an ideal emotional state marked with flexibility and intentionality and then use your ideal to help motivate you towards positive change. For example, you're miserable at work, so you consciously conjure up an ideal emotional state for how you want work to feel:

When someone asks me what I do, I want to feel excited to discuss it. I don't need to feel thrilled to jump out of bed and go to work every single day, but I do want to feel an overall sense of pride in my work. I want the hard days to not feel like a direct threat to my mental health. I want the feeling of forcing myself to do my job to be gone. I don't need to feel at ease all the time, but I want to feel comfortable enough to laugh a few times a week at work.

Then, remembering that ideals are not meant to be achieved, only meant to inspire, you use this ideal to guide you in your search for a new job.

The chase for emotional perfection is one of, if not *the*, most over-looked components of perfectionism. Emotional perfectionism flies under the radar because it's not as simple as wanting to feel happy all the time; it's such an individualized, private experience.

Nowhere is emotional perfectionism more evident than in the perfectionist's vision of what it means to be healed. As "proof" that you've healed, you want to feel a specific way to a specific degree in a specific circumstance. That's what happened with Marissa.

Marissa worked with a man whom she described as the love of her life. They dated for a few weeks but ultimately decided not to see each other because of professional complications. The two remained "friends." A few weeks after their last tryst, he began dating another woman they both worked with, whom he married within six months.

After her former paramour announced to the office that his new wife was pregnant, Marissa expressed to me her deep desire to feel "purely happy for him." Instead, she felt devastated. Her solution? Control the hell out of the situation. Her perfectionism (which typically operated à la Parisian) went into overdrive in every direction.

To begin, she insisted on throwing the couple an office baby shower. She needed to be the perfect friend (behavioral perfectionism), she needed to feel perfectly happy for them (emotional perfectionism), and she needed the shower itself to be perfect (object perfectionism). If she could achieve all the control she was seeking, including having one final closure conversation with him about exactly why they didn't work out (cognitive perfectionism), then she would achieve her outcome of being totally over him and ending their connection in a perfect way (process perfectionism). It was a setup of epic proportions.

We started with the emotional perfectionism.

> ME: What do you think would be a reasonable emotional response when you see them together at the shower, smiling, his hand on her baby bump?
> MARISSA: I'd like it to feel nice in a forgettable way. Like the way it feels to notice a ladybug.

I said nothing.

> MARISSA: It could happen! You don't know what's going to happen!
> ME: In this case, I think I do. I think you do, too.

Marissa's goal, like the goal so many of us fall prey to, was not to process what happened but to learn how to control her feelings about what happened. Preconceived notions about what it means to be "officially healed" loiter around in our minds and hearts. These imaginings of what we think our healing is supposed to look like are always wrong. You have no idea what form your healing will take.

One way to define healing is becoming open to possibility. When you focus on emotional control, you close yourself off to possibility. Power lies in understanding that whatever you feel, you have agency over every moment in your life. The exception to this rule is trauma.

Perfectionism + Trauma

Trauma unfolds when you are unable to access your power or when you have no power to begin with (as is the case with childhood trauma). Trauma changes you in such a way that you cannot reacclimate to the person you were before experiencing the trauma. The way you heal from trauma is not by returning to the person you used to be but by evolving into the person whom you decide you want to be now. Maladaptive perfectionism can manifest as a reaction to trauma, as it did with Naomi.

Naomi was raped in her hotel room while on a ski trip with friends. Like many rape survivors, Naomi's memory of the experience was sensory, not chronological. She vividly remembered the cool, dry scent of fresh snow coming in through the open balcony door. Naomi told herself what it would look like to heal, which was to encounter the smell of snow in the air without the memory of being raped as her first thought.

More than anything she had ever wanted in her life, Naomi sought to reclaim the simple pleasure of taking in the cold, blank, invigorating scent of snow. Determined to achieve this self-imposed "treatment goal," every winter for the last three years, she regularly forced herself to lie down on her back directly in the snow, close her eyes, and take in the air.

It wasn't working.

She hated the snow even more now. She hated movies with snow. She hated the winter. She hated the weather app on her phone. She hated space heaters. She hated heavy coats. She hated the summer because it left her. She hated the sky because that's where the snow came from. She hated new things every day. "I'm here," she told me, "because this has to be the year. I need the smell of snow to bring me joy again."

It was September in New York.

As I listened to Naomi describe her method of lying on the snowy ground in greater detail, I put my two hands together as if in prayer position, touching my pointer fingers to my lips. This seemed to bother, or at least confuse, Naomi. Upon finishing the description of her self-prescribed desensitization technique, she followed the two-second silence with, "Aren't you not supposed to do that?"

"Do what?" I asked.

"I thought therapists weren't supposed to get emotional."

In addition to the steel anguish I felt from Naomi, I recognized her projection of emotional perfectionism onto me. If I were going to "fix" her, I'd need to be able to put my feelings away to focus on generating results. She wanted me to engage with her from a purely intellectualized space because she wanted to learn to engage with her trauma from a purely intellectualized space.

As is the case for many victims of trauma, being present with her pain felt too unsafe for her. Naomi couldn't predict or control her emotional response, which she experienced as a personal failing. Witnessing the slightest emotional reaction from me made her feel unsafe and uncertain about my ability to help her, as if I were failing her, too.

The collision of trauma and unmanaged perfectionism results in what Horney called "the supremacy of the mind."[14] Integration (i.e., real healing) is not seen as an option. As Horney describes, "No longer mind and feelings but mind versus feeling, mind versus body, mind versus self . . . His brain then is the only part of him that feels alive."

Perfectionists intellectually understand that they cannot change the past, but that doesn't stop them from trying to change the fact that the past had an impact on them. To accept the latter is to encounter too great a sense of losing control, of defeat, of failure.

The "logical" solution becomes to split the experience between the event and the degree to which the event impacted you. You accept the event and reject the impact. You say some version of "Yes, that happened but I'm fine." The splitting is a math of sorts, a long division for trauma.

Power lies in accepting that while you can't control what you feel or the fact that the past impacted you, what happens next is entirely up to you. Power is understanding that your life can become a conscious choice to pursue whatever you want; it doesn't have to be an unconscious reaction to run from what already happened.

Continuing to bring awareness to the formulas and allowances you're holding for your various "perfect emotional states" can be helpful in dismantling the notion that any prescriptive emotional response is ever required of you.

Developmental Antecedents
to Perfectionism

How much do parenting styles have to do with the development of perfectionism in either direction? In a call for more research in this area, Dr. Cláudia Carmo and her colleagues point out, "Several studies support the idea that perfectionism develops more easily in families with extremely critical parents and that an authoritarian parenting style may lead children to adopt a perfectionist orientation during the course of their lives. However, it is still not clear whether parenting styles are directly linked to the development of adaptive or maladaptive perfectionism facets. . . . Although progress has been made regarding the empirical support for the role of parents in the development of adolescents and children's adaptive and maladaptive perfectionism, research is still relatively scarce and inconclusive."[15]

My perspective on developmental antecedents to perfectionism, while informed by the research that is available, is derived mostly from my clinical work. I offer my clinical experience only as a single point of reference.*

As we discussed in chapter 2, perfectionism is a natural impulse; some people are born with a high propensity for it. Based on my conversations with perfectionists, perfectionism in kids can manifest through curiosities and interests that can be obsessional, sometimes including compulsive, self-directed behaviors. As a child, for example, Marie Kondo was obsessed with interior design and organization. She declined recess and instead opted to stay in her classroom to organize bookshelves. At home, she snuck into her siblings' rooms to secretly purge clutter.[16]

Beyond the standard "watching their favorite Disney movie for the hundredth time" type of childhood obsession, naturally perfectionistic kids may direct intense focus in a specific activity that may appear

---

* See author's note for elaboration.

random to others because it's not necessarily "kid friendly"—setting up aquariums, collecting matching luggage sets, listening to opera classics. It's not random; it's a reflection of something inside these children that's springing to life—the development of their individual ideal.

When we don't understand something, we lean towards either fear or curiosity; most people lean towards fear. Kondo's recess-skipping, compulsive, clutter-purging behaviors likely alarmed her teachers and caregivers at the time. However, when examined within the context of her lifelong passion (particularly when that passion has been so successfully monetized), the once alarming behavioral pattern becomes a charming anecdote.

If you forget that children are not mini-adults, it's easy to misinterpret some of their behaviors as perfectionistic. For example, if a four-year-old child throws themselves on the floor in a crying fit because they couldn't find the perfect-colored crayon to complete their unicorn picture, they're not necessarily being perfectionistic.

Kids are learning to emotionally regulate; they're not supposed to have the same capacity as an adult does for gaining perspective and managing negative feelings. Being overwhelmed by emotions such as frustration or disappointment and then engaging in disproportionate reactions to said emotions can be developmentally appropriate—not just for toddlers and tantrums but in different iterations for children of all ages.

There are times when children engage in rigid perfectionistic tendencies in a patterned way that is clearly unhealthy because it causes meaningful disruption to the child's functioning, in addition to causing distress. This is when you recruit an arsenal of added support via school counselors, community connections, family therapists, and the like. Current research is exploring rigid perfectionism's relationship with a myriad of mental health illnesses.

Generally speaking, rigid perfectionism is considered to be a transdiagnostic trait, which means it's present in some form across multiple mental illness diagnoses. Transdiagnostic mechanisms are risk factors and maintenance factors for disorders, meaning they make it more likely for a disorder to show up, and they make it more likely for a disorder to continue.

All that said, and though of course it happens, I've never talked with a parent who is concerned about unhealthy perfectionistic tendencies in their child without that parent acknowledging their own unhealthy relationship with perfectionism. In my opinion, modeling (demonstrating a behavior firsthand) is the most effective way to teach a child. Whether you're modeling healthy or unhealthy behaviors doesn't matter; the child learns one just as easily as the other. James Baldwin's words are once again apt: "Children have never been good at listening to their elders, but they never fail to imitate them."

Developmental Antecedents to Maladaptive Perfectionism

If you grew up knowing that you were loved, it's nearly impossible to relate to having to wonder if you were loved, or to flat-out knowing that you were unwanted and unloved. The screen-saver thought that is ever-present for so many—"Does anyone really love me?"—is simply not present for children who experience the unparalleled emotional safety of unconditional love.

Similarly, if you grow up in an environment of abuse, neglect, or conditional love, it's nearly impossible to relate to the idea that someone could love you no matter what you do or fail to do in this life. When someone who is loved conditionally is told, "I love you," what they hear is, "I love you for now, so don't mess up." Conditional love isn't love, it's a contract. We all know contracts include fine print and that contracts can be voided.

Developmental theories of maladaptive perfectionism all echo the same sentiment: when basic needs for love and belonging go unmet in a child, all the energy that would normally go into building a healthy sense of autonomy (exploring self-interests and building healthy relationships with others) gets redirected into trying to belong and earn love.[17] This appeal for connection can take the form of trying to be superficially perfect: *I'm doing everything perfectly, so will you love me now?*

Perfectionism as a response to abuse and neglect is not only about wanting to be loved but about surviving. Your caregivers aren't just there to be your cheerleaders and give you hugs; they also give you food, shelter, and clothing—you're totally dependent on them. When that primal attachment isn't secure, being anything less than whatever their perfect version of you is can feel imminently dangerous. Walking-into-traffic dangerous.

I started my career in social work; doing home visits to check on kids who may be living in abusive environments was part of my job. I'll never forget the chilling advice my boss gave me before I went into the field for the first time. She said, "Look for the kids who are behaving perfectly; those are the ones who are terrified."

Internalizing someone else's perfect version of you doesn't always look like getting good grades or appearing perfect; it can include being the child who is silent and unseen, the one who has no needs, the one who provides steady distraction through jokes or troublemaking.

Children who don't feel loved will do anything to earn that love. *You need a distraction? I'll become a project. You need to not be sad? I'll be happy enough for the whole family. You need me to be less of a burden? I won't even make a sound when I chew.*

Everything a child who does not feel loved does is done to answer this question:

Am I worth loving yet?

The child asks some version of that question indefinitely, but not forever. When the answer to the question continues to be perceived as "No," the message is internalized:

Oh, I'm not like other people who get to be happy and loved. I'm not worthy of love, safety, or goodness.

An invisible switch is flipped. In the child's unconscious mind, freedom to be who they are is no longer an option. It's too unsafe and too destabilizing. With freedom off the table, two choices remain. The first choice is performance. They choose to play the part of someone who is worthy and hope to God no one finds out they're pretending. The second choice is destruction. They choose to destroy themselves with the mentality of "If no one else cares about me, why should I?"

For those who choose performance, the pressure to perform perfectly is everything. It's sort of like how, when people are lying, they often add so many details to their false stories because the lie doesn't sound true in their own heads. Maladaptive perfectionism operates in the same way. The perfectionist feels they're telling a lie—they're only pretending to be worthy, so they better get their story straight. They better perform perfectly because any holes in their story will reveal their deception.

While these patterns of relating to oneself and others can stem from the family of origin, they can also stem from feeling rejected or unloved by the larger culture, school environments, religious institutions, and so forth.

Unconscious patterns of performance and destruction continue until they're disrupted by conscious intervention. Once consciousness comes into play, anything is possible.

Belonging

We talk about love and safety as if they're nice things to grow up with. A big backyard is a nice thing to grow up with. Love and safety are needs. We don't just need to grow up with love and safety, we need to cultivate love, safety, and belonging as adults, too.

Anyone who grows up in isolation or who lives in isolation as an adult is going to encounter patterned distress—depression, excess anxiety, maladaptive perfectionism, addiction, you name it. Human beings are not meant to be isolated; we're meant to connect.

Connection is the source of all growth and healing. Connection is a need. In the absence of healthy connections, we become dysfunctional.

Chronic dysfunction increases your vulnerability to mental illness, including suicidality. The next section discusses perfectionism and suicide. If you decide it's better for you to skip this section for now, you can turn to the next chapter.* If you're not sure, take your time and save the rest of this chapter for later. It's not going anywhere.

Perfectionism + Suicide

For three years, Simone was my 9:00 a.m. Monday session. I knew from the general practitioner who referred her that she was "not feeling like herself" following a breakup and that she was taking antidepressants prescribed to her by a psychiatrist she had met with once, five years ago.

In the first month of our work, I encouraged Simone to meet with a trusted psychiatrist colleague of mine so that she could reevaluate her medication regimen. The new medication helped her faster than she was expecting it to. (I don't think she was expecting it to help at all.) I remember how afraid she was that her sense of relief was merely a placebo effect that would soon wear off. She didn't want to have to "go back," as she put it.

I asked Simone the lifesaving question directly, which is the only way to ask it: "Have you ever thought about ending your life?" Her answer wasn't a hard no, which translates into a yes.†

---

* If you're experiencing suicidal ideation and you don't trust yourself to make safe choices for the next twenty-four hours, connect to support. Let someone in your trusted circle know what's happening and that you don't feel comfortable being alone, or call 988 to reach free mental health crisis support 24/7. English speakers can also text 988 for mental health crisis support. The Substance Abuse and Mental Health Services Administration (SAMHSA) is currently working on enabling Spanish speaking text services for the 988 lifeline, but for now, Spanish speakers should call 988 instead of texting. Also know that you can always walk into a hospital or call 911 to have an ambulance come get you.

† To be clear, even when someone answers the lifesaving question with an adamant no, that doesn't necessarily mean either that they're telling you the truth or that they're not at risk. Please visit suicidepreventionlifeline.org for more information on how to have these admittedly challenging conversations.

Simone and I began to talk about suicide a lot, and that was a good thing. It doesn't scare me to have conversations about suicidal ideation. Not talking about it is what's terrifying. Our collective avoidance of discussions around suicide is both understandable and eerily, gravely negligent. We're in the midst of a fully-fledged public health crisis. We're not approaching the red zone; we're in the red zone.

In the last twenty years, the number of people who have died by suicide in the United States has increased by a staggering 35 percent, according to the Centers for Disease Control and Prevention (CDC). A report released in 2019 by the National Institute of Mental Health (NIMH) identified suicide as the second leading cause of death for individuals aged ten to thirty-four, and, according to the same NIMH report, 1.4 million adults attempted to end their lives in 2019. The pandemic exacerbated the suicide crisis exponentially.[18]

According to the CDC, for example, in the one-month time span between February and March in 2021, ER visits for suspected suicide attempts rose by over *50 percent* among girls aged twelve to seventeen.[19] The CDC also states that twelve million Americans report seriously thinking about ending their lives each year.[20] What's the percentage of people who are seriously considering suicide without reporting it? Nobody can say, though we can assume the figure is higher than twelve million.

Sequestering conversations about suicide to the therapist's office and during the week after a famous person dies by suicide is not an effective way to engage in a deeper, collective understanding of this complex issue. It's statistically evident that some people reading this book have thought about ending their lives. Perhaps you're worried about someone you love who might be suicidal? It's important that we talk about suicide proactively, regularly, and substantively.

We don't talk about suicide because we don't know how. We have no idea what to say because we don't understand it. We don't understand it because we don't talk about it. Discussing suicide proactively yields immediate benefits, like understanding that there's no need to wait until the situation feels like a crisis to talk or text and get support. Also, crisis hotlines (which include text lines) aren't just for people who are thinking about suicide; they offer support for any mental health crisis, including substance use issues. Crisis hotlines are also for people who are worried about someone they care about and who want to gain a better understanding of how to deal with suicidality.*

As the classic therapy aphorism goes, "It's never about what it's about." When I talk with people who are intersecting with the suicide spectrum, it's not that they want to die; it's that they want to experience relief from the pain they're in. I use the phrase "suicide spectrum" because (similar to the way categorical models of mental disorders are an oversimplification of a person's contextual, ever-changing psychological experience) a person is not simply "suicidal or not suicidal." For example, some people are parasuicidal, which is defined by the American Psychological Association as exhibiting "a range of behaviors involving deliberate self-harm that may or may not be intended to result in death."[21]

Psychologist Dr. Adele Ryan McDowell is one of many therapists who advocate for detailed descriptions of additional points on the spectrum of suicide (as opposed to the basic three: ideation, ideation with a plan, and attempt). McDowell encourages the inclusion of the following markers:[22]

- **IDEATION:** thinking about ending one's life

- **ATTEMPT:** an attempted suicide resulting in survival[†23]

---

* You can call the Suicide & Crisis Lifeline anytime, 24/7, not just at the height of a crisis, and not just for issues surrounding suicide. As per SAMHSA's website, 988 is a lifeline that "accepts calls, texts, and chats from anyone who needs support for a suicidal, mental health, and/or substance use crisis." If you're a teacher, counselor, coach, etc., this hotline can connect you to best practices and resources for working with suicidal students, athletes, clients, etc.

† While some use the term "suicide gesture," I've learned that that language is unintentionally pejorative. As psychologist Dr. Nicole Heilbron, co-chief of the Division of Child and Family Mental Health and Developmental Neuroscience at Duke University, states, "Labeling of an individual's behaviors as 'gestures' . . . may communicate a dismissive

- **PASSIVELY SUICIDAL:** thinking about suicide without actively taking steps to end one's life. (Passive suicidality may be expressed indirectly, as an indifference towards death—for example, someone who is passively suicidal might say something like, "I wouldn't care if I got hit by a bus."

- **ACTIVELY THINKING:** developing a plan and working on the details

- **THINKING AND DOING:** McDowell says there are two types of thinking and doing—planned and impulsive. The impulsive type is "a flash of a thought and a rush of feeling that makes sense at the time. Frequently, this occurs with teens and young adults."

- **CHRONICALLY SUICIDAL:** chronically thinking about suicide, threatening to carry it out, or making multiple attempts

- **SLOW SUICIDE:** McDowell describes this as being "evidenced by a lifetime of self-harm that chronically erodes a person's health, well-being, mental stability, emotional resilience, and vital energy."

A major misunderstanding about suicide is that it unfolds in a linear progression. We think the way suicide "works" is that first you think about it for a while, then your thoughts evolve into making a plan, and then you carry out the plan—all while leaving red flags and signals for loved ones to catch along the way. As Dr. Paul Nestadt, a psychiatrist at the Johns Hopkins University School of Medicine, explained to Kim Tingley for *The New York Times*, "Suicide is also surprisingly impulsive. A majority who decide to do it act within an hour, and nearly a quarter act within five minutes." Tingley aptly points out, "Getting rid of guns or making access to them harder would prevent more suicide deaths, as would more affordable and widely available mental health care."[24]

If you don't understand how impulsive the act of suicide can be, it's

---

stance that may lead to a false sense of security regarding the individual's safety and needs for monitoring."

difficult to appreciate how strongly the presence of a firearm in your home can impact whether you or anyone in your household will die by suicide. Over half the completed suicides in the United States are by firearms. As the CDC reports, in 2018, twice as many people died from gun suicides as from gun homicides.[25]

David Hemenway, professor of health policy at Harvard University's T. H. Chan School of Public Health, explains the disconnection succinctly: "Differences in overall suicide rates across cities, states and regions in the United States are best explained not by differences in mental health, suicide ideation, or even suicide attempts, but by availability of firearms. Many suicides are impulsive, and the urge to die fades away. Firearms are a swift and lethal method of suicide with a high case-fatality rate."[26]

In your office, in your family, in your relationship, the last thing you may *want* to discuss is whether the people around you are suffering in a way that makes killing themselves feel like a solution, but we must have these conversations.

Do you know if those closest to you (including your children) have ever thought about suicide? Consider asking. The sense that you "plant" the idea of suicide by bringing it up is another misconception. Research suggests that acknowledging and talking about suicide reduces suicidal ideation and can lead to an increased willingness to connect to support.[27] As therapist Dr. Stacey Freedenthal writes for the wonderful website Speaking of Suicide (www.speakingofsuicide.com), "Where you worry you may be planting a seed, a large tree has already grown."[28]

Even after the significant relief her medication management offered, Simone experienced suicidal ideation every day for at least five months. It was one of the first things she thought about in the morning. Though her quality of life was improving, the thought of having to return to a state of pain that left her feeling so ragged, heavy, and notched up overwhelmed her. Simone's suicidal ideation served as a self-soothing technique: *If it ever gets that bad again, I can escape.*

Feeling better wasn't what decreased Simone's suicidal ideation. What decreased it was understanding that should her intense state of pain return, she was not helpless against it.

Simone found power in choosing to surround herself with protective factors (things that build resiliency). Things like going to therapy, taking lots of walks (which also helped her sleep), eating well, taking her medication consistently, and building her social connections. She started volunteering at the synagogue on her block, even though she's not Jewish. She signed up for NYU's "free and public" newsletter, even though she had graduated from college fifteen years prior and hadn't gone to NYU. It didn't matter; the offerings were for the whole community, as often are the offerings of most large institutions.

Simone slowly filled her life up with people and things that felt, as she put it, "nice and good." I cannot overstate how simple and yet impactful some of these "nice and good" additions were. For example, she had never heard of or tried chia seeds before. One day she bought a bag and started spreading them into the cream cheese on her morning bagel, and for some reason that made her realize that she has so much agency when it comes to her health. She started carrying chia seeds in her purse and putting them in and on everything. Pizza, iced coffee, eggs. Stir fry for lunch? Not without chia seeds on it. Ice cream for dessert? Not without chia seeds on it. It wasn't the chia seeds themselves that made the difference for Simone, it was the identity entrance they offered her. She began to see herself in new ways, as someone who could make healthier choices, as someone who could experience life in a different way.

Simone also found power in creating specific alternate paths to take should the desire or impulse to kill herself arise. She had the suicide hotline saved in her phone. We connected to a friend of hers who gave Simone a key to her apartment so that Simone could come over any time she didn't trust herself to be alone. Simone stored the address of the closest hospital under "saved places" in her Uber account. She had an overnight hospital bag packed in her closet and ready to grab, like pregnant women do.

Two years into our work together, Simone sent a greeting card to my office address. It had an orchid on the front and was blank inside. This is how she filled the space:

Who knows what life will bring. Whatever happens, I choose to stay.

See you next week,
Simone

It was the opposite of a suicide note.

For so long, it felt impossible for Simone to move and live with the weight of her pain. She's not alone, perhaps especially so among her fellow perfectionists.

Researchers have long explored whether perfectionism increases one's vulnerability to suicide. Though these studies are hard to interpret without a consistent definition of what perfectionism is, the short answer is yes. Perfectionism is positively correlated with suicidality.

Research suggests that "the most pernicious form of perfectionism [involves] perceived external pressure to be perfect."[29] It's what two of the foremost experts on perfectionism, researchers Dr. Gordon L. Flett and Dr. Paul L. Hewitt, whom I mentioned earlier, identified decades ago as "socially prescribed perfectionism."[30]

So much curative gold is tucked away in the obscure world of academia; the conceptualization of socially prescribed perfectionism (SPP) is one such treasure. SPP explores how your perception of the norms and expectations around you impact your mental health. Not only does Flett and Hewitt's context-driven framework enable powerful insights into the mechanics of perfectionism; if applied more broadly, it would offer deeper insight into the sociocultural influences behind a myriad of other mental health issues.*

---

* See Author's Note for more on this.

SPP is basically when you think others expect you to be perfect; it's more strongly correlated with maladaptive qualities in general (such as excess anxiety and procrastination) and specifically, with suicidality.[31]

External pressures to be perfect seem to be more problematic in relation to suicidality perhaps because of the roles of humiliation and shame. When you're imposing perfectionistic standards upon yourself independent of others' expectations, you're less prone to humiliation because you don't necessarily feel that others expect you to be perfect; your perfectionism is experienced privately. However, when you're imposing perfectionistic standards on yourself because you think others expect perfection from you, you may be more vulnerable to humiliation and shame because you feel there's an "audience" watching you.

If you or someone around you experiences increased visibility (e.g., a teen who makes class president, a local athlete who is written up in a national paper, an employee whose work garners significant industry buzz), suicidality risks associated with perceived external pressures to be perfect are something to keep in mind—an association not just for perfectionists to remember but also for social media companies, managers, coaches, teachers, employers, parents, and the like to remain sensitive to.

Also of note is the emphasis on *perceived* external pressure by the perfectionist. As a boss, parent, partner, leader, or coach, you may not at all feel that you're pressuring the people around you to be perfect. You may in fact be shocked to learn that anyone in your orbit feels such an immense amount of pressure from you. Your flexibility, openness, acceptance of mistakes (encouragement of mistakes?), and unconditional positive regard for the people in your world are points worth clarifying out loud and often.

Understanding dichotomous thinking (also referred to as *black-and-white thinking* or *all-or-nothing thinking*) helps clarify the development and progression of suicidality.

Perfectionists + Dichotomous Thinking

A telltale sign that a perfectionist is in a maladaptive space, dichotomous thinking occurs when the range of possibility is eclipsed by the extremes of a spectrum. There's no gray area in dichotomous thinking—for example, you've either succeeded or failed, you're beautiful or ugly, you're revered or the laughingstock.

You know how Simone first described her apathy towards dying? In a calm and logical manner, she explained, "Once I ordered Chinese food, and there was a staple, like a silver staple from a stapler, *in* the rice. So I checked for other staples in the rice. But even though I checked, I wasn't sure I'd checked well enough. For a few bites, I kept chewing the food slowly in case there was another staple. That was really ruining the whole meal, so I threw it away without finishing it. And that's what my life is like. There's a staple in the rice, and even if I take it out, it's already ruined everything, so what's the point."

When you're dealing with black-and-white thinking, there's half an inch of space across each thought, but underneath that half an inch is a thousand-foot drop. Quite suddenly, you're in the lowest coordinates on earth.

"So what did you end up eating?" I asked her.

SIMONE: What do you mean?
ME: For dinner that night, what did you eat instead?
SIMONE: Nothing. I told you, the meal was ruined.

And that's the real dichotomous thinking right there. It's not so much *The meal is either ruined or not ruined*; it's the blink and you'll miss it sequel thought: *Since the meal is ruined, there's no possible way I could eat anything else.* This is why dichotomous thinking is dangerous, because the speed and false logic behind an otherwise mild experience of displeasure can so easily spiral into existential turmoil over the entire point of your literal life.

We got in a huge fight, so the relationship is completely failing, so I'm completely failing, so my entire life is a failure, so what's the point.

I'm completely humiliated in this moment, so my self-confidence is totally destroyed, so I'll never feel good again, so what's the point.

I didn't get the job I wanted, and even if I get another job, it'll never be that one specific job I wanted, so I'll never be happy, so what's the point.

My car won't start, so things are always hard for me, so things will always be hard for me, so what's the point.

Dichotomous thinking presents both in micro form (you either did well in the meeting or you messed everything up) and in macro form (you either have a successful career or you're flailing). Left unchecked, dichotomous thinking consumes the psyche like water being absorbed from the corner of a paper towel. You did it perfectly or you should be ashamed of yourself; you're super productive or you're a bumbling slob; everyone loves you or you're a burden to the world; you're number one or you completely wasted your time.

Disrupting dichotomous thinking is easier once you become aware that it exists.

Once you're aware that you're engaging in dichotomous thinking, don't try to force yourself to stop thinking in black-and-white terms. If you can find some gray area, that's great. If you can't, reach out and connect to someone. Connection will hold you over when nothing else can.

In a previous office, I had an illustration of a gray background with the suffix "-ISH" in giant print, right in the middle. I love hearing people say, "ish"—*I'm happy-ish. My day was good-ish. I'm depressed-ish.* "Ish" is a single-syllable anthem you sing when you exit the land of black-and-white thinking and enter the land of the gray. In the words of my favorite professor from grad school, the brilliant Dr. Anika Warren, "You have to learn how to live in the gray."

Adaptive perfectionists learn to build the habit of "ish" thinking. They learn to choose presence over absence, power over control, and connection over isolation (the second half of this book is designed to offer specific strategies and tools involved in that learning). Adaptive perfectionists also learn how to stop making the number one mistake perfectionists make, which is to respond to missteps with self-punishment.

Everyone is punitive with themselves at times, but perfectionists take punishment to a whole other level. Perfectionists are the Olympians of punishment. Perfectionists have perfected punishment. Perfectionists go to law school.

5

You've Been Solving for the Wrong Problem

IT'S NOT THAT YOU APPROACH YOUR LIFE
WITH PERFECTIONISM; IT'S THAT YOU
RESPOND TO MISSTEPS WITH
SELF-PUNISHMENT

I met an old pastor's wife who told me that when she was young and had her first child, she didn't believe in striking children, although spanking kids with a switch pulled from a tree was standard punishment at the time. But one day, when her son was four or five, he did something that she felt warranted a spanking—the first in his life. She told him that he would have to go outside himself and find a switch for her to hit him with. The boy was gone a long time. And when he came back in, he was crying. He said to her, "Mama, I couldn't find a switch, but here's a rock that you can throw at me." All of a sudden the mother understood how the situation felt from the child's point of view: that if my mother wants to hurt me, then it makes no difference what she does it with; she might as well do it with a stone. And the mother took the boy into her lap and they both cried. Then she laid the rock on a shelf in the kitchen to remind herself forever: never violence. And that is something I think everyone should keep in mind.

ASTRID LINDGREN, IN HER 1978 GERMAN BOOKSELLERS'
PEACE PRIZE ACCEPTANCE SPEECH

Wednesday, 7:07 p.m.

Carla called. I picked up.

ME: Hey, everything okay?

7:00 p.m. on Wednesdays was Carla's session time, and she was never late.

CARLA: I'm okay. I'm outside.
ME: Is the buzzer broken? I'll come get you.

At the time, I was practicing out of a ground-floor office in an old brownstone on the Upper East Side. The buzzer stuck sometimes.

CARLA: No, I'll be in in a minute, I don't know.

With my pointer finger, I pulled the curtain at my window and saw her standing by the stoop. She was looking down. Her foot was fidgeting with the short iron fence around the sidewalk tree, and she was smoking. "I'm coming out," I said, and I hung up the phone. Without the pane of glass between us, I could see that Carla had been crying.

ME: I didn't know you smoked.
CARLA: I don't. Is it bothering you? I'm sorry. I know it's disgusting.

I sat down on the stoop; it looked like it was about to rain. A few people walked by, and we were silent as they passed.

I looked up. "I've never been able to decide if dramatic skies help or hurt in moments like this."

CARLA: Moments like what?

ME: I don't know, Carla, you tell me. What's going on?

Still smoking, Carla started pacing the sidewalk in long, wide steps, almost as if she were learning a dance. She told me she had had an argument with her mom that morning, during which she hung up on her mom. Carla felt bad and called her mom back to apologize, which seemed to go fine; her mom was understanding. Getting to this part in the story had taken ten minutes. I interrupted Carla, "Do you want to go inside?"

She put her second cigarette out, and we went in. As Carla walked me through her day, I was waiting for her to tell me something that you might only tell your therapist. That didn't happen.

She described a sequence of events in which she felt she had ruined the moment and then unconsciously decided to make the day harder on herself. For example, after she hung up with her mom, she went into a busy coffee shop and got coffee, despite already feeling "tweaky" and overcaffeinated, and even though she knew doing so would make her late to work (which stressed her out). She normally listened to music during her commute because it put her in a good headspace, but today she decided it would be better to "reflect" on the abruptness by which she had hung up on her mom. Carla repeated the incident over in her mind, alongside a negative commentary about how she was an ungrateful daughter and needed to work harder at being patient. Her commute was miserable, which helped her to feel that she was holding herself accountable.

As the day progressed, Carla continued to lash her brain with negative self-talk; she also canceled lunch with a friend in town for the day from Philly. I knew she'd been looking forward to that lunch. I asked her why she had canceled. Carla said something along the lines of how it's not okay to indulge in the frivolous when you're behind. That word stuck with me, "behind."

ME: What are you behind?

CARLA: I don't know.

ME: What's in front of you?

CARLA: My best self, I want to be my best self.

ME: You mean, you want to be perfect?

CARLA: No, not perfect; I know nobody's perfect. But I'm better than this, I just want to be my best. This isn't me.

ME: What's the difference to you?

CARLA: The difference between what?

ME: What's the difference between your best and perfect?

Silence.

A self-punishment is consciously or unconsciously returning to something that you know will hurt you, or denying yourself something that you know will help you. Punishments are designed to create more pain. When you're punitive with yourself, the grand plan is to hurt yourself in order to teach yourself a lesson. You punish yourself "for your own good." You're hurting yourself as a strategy for learning, growth, and healing.

Punishment doesn't work. When you punish someone, that person doesn't learn how to change; they learn how to avoid the source of the punishment. If you are the source of your own punishment (through critical self-talk, for example), then you learn to avoid yourself by numbing out. Numbing out looks like overeating, overspending, overworking, getting caught up in drama, substance misuse, mindlessly watching TV or scrolling social media, and so forth.

You don't heal yourself by hurting yourself. To sustain any kind of personal growth, we need to internalize the lessons of our past mistakes, understand what the healthier alternatives are, and believe that we are capable of change in the first place. Making positive changes in your life does not require any punishment whatsoever.

Even when punishments function to alter unwanted behavior to desired behavior, they're still ineffectual because punishments create more problems. If you own a restaurant and you don't want anyone coming in late to work, for example, target the unwanted behavior with punishment by firing the next three people who come in late. The following day, anyone who still works for you will be on time. Your punishment was effective, congratulations. You now have a staff that's arriving on time *and* telling absolutely everyone they know not to come to your restaurant *and* preparing to jump ship at the first chance to work somewhere else *and* operating at a bare minimum instead of bringing premium-quality work forward (and don't forget the two who are spitting in the food).

When you punish your employees, you *might* achieve the ostensible benefit of altering whatever specific behavior your punishment targets, but you achieve that shallow gain at the massive opportunity cost of bigger-ticket items like employee loyalty, retention, and self-initiative. You kill spontaneity and collaboration because punishments are demoralizing. Your company is where creativity and innovation come to die.

You're not addressing the problem when you use punishment; you're avoiding the problem and creating a new one.

Punishments are negative ways to approach problems. Punishments increase problems. Solutions are positive ways to approach problems. Solutions decrease problems. The opposite of a solution is not a problem; the opposite of a solution is a punishment.

The ineffectual nature of punishment is critical for perfectionists to understand because if there's one thing all the experts agree on, it's that perfectionists can punish the hell out of themselves.[1] When you're in a maladaptive space, punishment will be the go-to, default, cruise-control setting of your mind unless you consciously choose to disrupt it.

Understanding Punishment

Punishment is different from discipline, personal accountability, natural consequence, and rehabilitation.

The differences between punishment and discipline:

- Punishment seeks to increase pain. Discipline seeks to increase structure.

- Punishment is reactive. Discipline is both proactive and reactive.

- Punishment is solely focused on discouraging negative behavior. Discipline is focused on discouraging negative behavior through the promotion of positive behavior.

As psychotherapist and mental health advocate Amy Morin points out, punishment doesn't involve positive approaches to change, whereas discipline does. Positive approaches to change include interventions such as teaching positive coping strategies; praising people when they do well; and when they do something wrong, taking the time to teach them how to better handle a similar situation in the future.[2] Morin points out that punishment is about trying to control someone through pain. Discipline is about trying to teach someone to empower themselves through structure.

The differences between punishment and personal accountability:

Personal accountability is both proactive and reactive; it encourages always taking responsibility for oneself. When accountability is proactive, it engenders trust. What you trust is that the accountable person will take responsibility for their role in a situation independent of any external demand to do so. When accountability is reactive (i.e., when you take accountability for harm that has been caused), it offers healing. The reason healing is available through personal accountability is because personal accountability includes actively addressing those who were hurt.[3]

Holding yourself accountable is active; punishment is passive. Taking accountability involves openly recognizing how your behavior impacted everyone involved, acknowledging that you could've made a different choice, apologizing to those who were harmed, doing what you can to fix the problem, making a pledge to improve, and creating a plan to uphold that improvement.[4]

Personal accountability requires you to own up to your missteps, yes, but personal accountability is less about taking the blame for a mistake and more about taking responsibility for the solution.

Punishment, on the other hand, doesn't require an ounce of reflection, acknowledgment, responsibility, condolence, or a pledge and plan to improve. Punishment is lazy.

The difference between punishment and natural consequence:

Punishment relies on fear to motivate desired results. Natural consequence relies on understanding the impact of your choices to motivate desired results. The former engenders a mentality of "I'm scared to do the wrong thing." The latter engenders a mentality of "I actively want to do the right thing."

Punishment encourages the avoidance of the source of the punishment. Natural consequence encourages the avoidance of the negative choice in the first place, as well as the active pursuit of more positive choices.[5]

The difference between punishment and rehabilitation:

Rehabilitation and punishment are both reactive, but rehabilitation seeks to stabilize and empower, whereas punishment seeks to demoralize and disempower. Rehabilitation involves building positive growth on top of a newly stable and healthy foundation. Punishment doesn't care about generating positive growth, nor is it interested in altering the foundation through remedial work. Punishment just lays pain on top of whatever's there.

Punishment is a form of coercive control. Being in a relationship with someone by whom you are being coercively controlled (including your relationship with yourself) is not healthy. The reason we don't recognize the dysfunctional nature of punishment is because we live in a culture that broadcasts and actively promotes punishment as an appropriate and effective means of responding to unwanted behavior (even though it's neither).

Punishment is a through line in our culture, despite our knowledge that it's ineffective. We allow tens of thousands of kids to be hit every year in school with a paddle,[6] despite overwhelming evidence demonstrating that hitting children leads to increased aggression, antisocial behavior, and increased mental health problems. We respond to the extraordinarily high recidivism rates evident in the prison-industrial complex (which *scream* punishment doesn't work) with three-strike laws—more punishment—instead of increasing community resources in crime-ridden communities. We place human beings in solitary confinement and kill them through a variety of federally sanctioned methods, including by firing squad, lethal injection, electrocution, gas chamber, nitrogen hypoxia, and hanging. These punishments are not relics from a less enlightened time. On Christmas eve in 2020, the US Department of Justice quietly extended its execution protocols.[7]

In this retributive rather than restorative culture where punishment is the first line of defense, it makes sense that you've internalized punishment as *your* first line of defense against the qualities you don't like seeing in yourself. What does not make sense is for you to continue using punishment as an agent for positive change.

Look at punishment up close and what you'll see is desperation. When we feel desperate and out of touch with power, we grasp onto punishment to feel in control. Feeling in control is not a substitute for empowerment.

What Self-Punishments Look Like

Dismantling our motivation to punish ourselves requires us to recognize what self-punishment looks like. We tend to think of punishments in a visible, tangible way—going to jail, having privileges revoked, and so forth. But self-punishments are often neither visible, tangible, nor conscious.

There are more ways to punish yourself than there are coffee cups on a Monday morning, though each perfectionist tends to stick to their "go-to" self-punishment themes:

PROCRASTINATOR PERFECTIONISTS: Rumination

Negatively comparing herself to others as well as idealized versions of herself, she minimizes any success she's achieved thus far and focuses her energy on unproductive, circuitous thoughts about how she's not doing enough.

Imagine it: *She's riding the subway with a vacant stare, softly rattling in her seat. Lost in thoughts of regret and resentment over all the things she hasn't done, she misses her stop.*

CLASSIC PERFECTIONISTS: Dissociation

Going through the motions of her to-do list, she focuses on empty busyness as opposed to meaningful engagement.

Imagine it: *She dusts the headboard while she's having sex.*

PARISIAN PERFECTIONISTS: Endless people-pleasing

She insists on proving herself—"singing for her supper"—even when no one's asking her to. She prioritizes other people's pleasure and comfort over her own. Enacting a version of herself she believes everyone will most easily connect with, she denies herself the opportunity to authentically connect with anyone.

Imagine it: *In a sparkly little getup she stayed up all night making, she's enthusiastically tap dancing for hours, dripping sweat in front of an empty plate.*

INTENSE PERFECTIONISTS: Interpersonal turmoil

When she most needs love and support, she pushes everyone away with out-of-line behavior and social withdrawal.

Imagine it: *She walks directly over to the people in her life who most love her, and instead of saying, "Can we talk?" she pulls the pin out of a grenade and walks away.*

MESSY PERFECTIONISTS: Arrested development

She doesn't allow her ideas (or herself) to flourish, develop, and mature. Eventually she's forced to watch as her dreams die out.

Imagine it: *She's lovingly watering a thousand rows of seedling plants in the pitch-black dark.*

More general punishments look like:

- Critical and negative self-talk. For example, allowing the following narrative to play in your head: *How could I be so stupid?! I always fuck everything up. I might as well just stop trying. I'm so bad at this.*

- Self-sabotaging the good in your life. For example, you get an interview for your dream job but the night before, you stay out drinking. You wake up hungover and perform poorly at the interview. You don't get the job.

- Restricting yourself from an entire dimension of your life until you're able to perform in a certain way. For example, *I'll start traveling once I lose the weight.*

- Denying yourself the space and time to experience simple pleasures. For example, not allowing yourself to take a break from work to go for a walk, or to sit down to a conversation with a friend without an agenda.

- Giving yourself access to pleasure, but then lacerating yourself for it the entire time. For example, you sit down to relax and watch a show with the following running commentary in your mind, *You shouldn't be watching this, you have so many other things to do. Stop slacking off.*

What's the point of sitting down to relax if all you do is interrupt your-self with admonition the whole time? The point is to punish yourself. Again, engaging in your life punitively is often unconscious; it registers consciously as feeling "stuck."

Clients use that word, "stuck," to describe themselves as often as ther-apists say "boundaries." Occasionally, we're stuck because we're genu-inely confused about what's happening and what to do about it, but that kind of confusion is rare. Nine times out of ten, we know *exactly* what to do to improve our lives, and yet we struggle to do it. The reason we're struggling is that we're engaged in a cycle of self-punishment.

When you continue to use self-punishment as a strategy for positive change, you position yourself in a type of psychical purgatory—doomed to repeat the same mistakes over and over while hating yourself for it every time. You know you're stuck, you want to generate different out-comes, you are in fact *desperate* to generate different outcomes, yet you repeatedly make the same negative choices. The downward loop of self-punishment is a painful spiral. Let me give you an example of what I mean.

Ava

I used to run group therapy at a rehab center in Brooklyn. My Thursday night group was about the early stage of alcohol recovery, and it met until 9:00 p.m. At 8:58 p.m., we were ending the way I always did. We went around the circle and repeated a short statement that someone had said during the session that was meaningful to hear. When we got to Ava, she abandoned the exercise and instead, with some degree of stoicism, shared that she'd been drinking before group, she'd been drunk the entire time, and she was planning to go out and drink more afterwards.

This is what's known in the therapy world as an LMB—a last-minute bomb. Sometimes at the very end of a session, precisely *because* it's the very end of a session, a client will relay a critical, an urgent, or an otherwise dramatic piece of information to you. In other words, they drop a bomb. LMBs are positive because they demonstrate a readiness on the client's part; the client is ready enough to say something they're nervous to say out loud but not ready enough to say it when we actually have time to discuss it. Is there anything more relatable?

As is true for every experienced therapist, I could fill another entire book with the LMBs that have been detonated from my couch. To respect the boundaries of the session and despite the temptation, I don't engage them. I usually respond with something like: "Have you ever heard the phrase *last-minute bomb*? A last-minute bomb is . . . and you just dropped one. I imagine it was a hard thing for you to say, and I'm glad you said it. What you're telling me is important, and it deserves a bigger chunk of session time than we currently have left. I'm looking forward to talking about this next week. Right now, we need to end."

Typically, clients are relieved to get to leave immediately *and* know that I'll be the one bringing up the hard-to-bring-up issue the following week. Their work is done, and they're out! I didn't say any of that to Ava, though, because I was concerned about her safety. I excused the group and asked Ava to stay; as everyone else stood up to leave, she and I remained seated. The last person out shut the door behind them.

"It's gotta hurt to be back here," I said. Ava's stoicism broke; she scrunched her eyes shut and started nodding, holding her breath, and crying all at the same time.

A few moments later, I asked Ava what she would do if she hadn't drank before group. She answered me immediately, sounding desperate: "I'd take a bath. I've been cold all day. I just want to go home and take a hot bath."

Everyone who likes taking baths has a bath ritual. I asked her what hers was. She said she didn't have one. "Do you have one of those bath tray things that rests across the tub?" I asked.

She did not. She told me she lights a candle on a corner edge of the tub. She said that ever since she was little, she's always liked putting her ears underneath the surface and listening to the echoey sound of the water below. She said she doesn't read, play music, or bring her phone into the tub; she just sinks her ears in and out of the water. Sometimes she can hear the neighbors she shares the bathroom wall with moving around on the other side of it, speaking in muffles, clanking dishes. "I don't mind it; the noise is kind of relaxing," Ava said. She had stopped crying.

"I wonder if you'd hear them tonight, if you went home and took a bath."

There was a long silence between us. I asked her to imagine what she would be doing that night if she were five years sober. She made a sarcastic grunt and smirked, as if that could ever be her. Ava's answer was the same, "I'd take a bath. I just want a hot bath."

Here, Ava is stuck in a cycle of self-punishment. She knows what to do (go home and take a hot bath to begin restoring herself), but she plans on punishing herself instead (by drinking more and denying herself restoration).

"Why did I do that?" Ava began to lament. "I don't know what I'm doing. Why did I do that?"

I stood up to get the tissue box and scootched my chair beside her as I sat back down. Crouching over in her seat, Ava buried her face in the collar of her hoodie. She started sobbing. Side by side in a circle of otherwise empty chairs, I leaned forward beside her and let her cry.

Broaden-and-Build Theory

I wanted to say so much to Ava in that moment, but it wasn't the time for words. At the right time, a lighter time, I'd tell Ava about how Dr. Barbara L. Fredrickson is the Jennifer Aniston of the psychological research world. Everyone loves Fredrickson because year after year, her work just makes you feel good. A pioneer in positive psychology and one of the most highly cited scholars in the field, Fredrickson is best known for her "broaden-and-build" theory.[8]

The broaden-and-build theory asserts that if you can get yourself into a positive headspace, your "thought-action repertoire" broadens. When you're in a positive state, your thoughts about the possible actions you can take expand; you realize you can do a lot of different things, and you make choices that promote future positive states.

For example, if you feel happy, you're more likely to plan, say, a Sunday morning hike with friends next week. Because you enjoyed the hike, you're more likely to go home and enjoy your evening. Energized by your good mood, you decide to cook while listening to music. You make something healthy-ish for dinner, then go to bed on the early side—decisions that make you feel restored the next morning.

Nice and restored, you show up to work in a positive headspace. Some issues arise, of course, but it's easier for you to approach them from a solutions-oriented perspective because you're not weighed down with negativity. Because work isn't overwhelming you, you're able to have a good time where you would otherwise be forcing yourself to push through. Energized by rising to the challenge of the day's work, you spontaneously text the person you're dating to meet up later, a meeting you then enjoy. Your positivity is building upon itself and getting stronger.

As Fredrickson points out, positive emotions aren't just "end states" that *signal* optimal functioning; positive emotions *produce* optimal functioning. In Fredrickson's words, "Positive emotions promote discovery of novel and creative actions, ideas and social bonds, which in turn build that individual's personal resources; ranging from physical and intellectual resources, to social and psychological resources. Importantly, these resources function as reserves that can be drawn on later to improve the odds of successful coping and survival."[9]

Contrast moments when you're in a positive emotional state with those when you're in a negative emotional state, which narrows your thought-action repertoire. When your thought-action repertoire is narrowed, it's harder to see around the problem.

For example, if you feel bad because you got a negative performance review, you probably won't feel inspired to take on the night. You're more likely to think, *Well, nothing left to do but go home, order some food, and call it a day.* You watch TV for three hours after eating a junky dinner that makes you feel bloated and gross, and now it's 1:00 a.m. And you hate that it's 1:00 a.m. because you meant to go to bed early. Your negativity is compounding.

You get anxious about feeling worse and then you can't sleep. In the morning you feel worn down because of your sleepless night. At that point, you're not thinking, *How do I seize this day!?* You're thinking, *How do I get through this day!?*

When your thought-action repertoire is narrowed, your perspective is stunted; you can only see ten or twenty minutes in front of you. How do you broaden your thought-action repertoire? With self-compassion.

Practicing self-compassion expands your thought-action repertoire because it pulls you out of fear-based negativity and towards increased feelings of safety, reassurance, and positivity.

Research demonstrates self-compassion's positive association with a greater sense of self-worth, increased personal initiative,[10] increased resilience to stress, more realistic self-appraisals of strengths and weaknesses, lower levels of depression and anxiety, reduced rates of burnout, increased motivation to make amends for past mistakes, and the list goes on.[11] Self-compassion broadens your thought-action repertoire; punishment narrows it.

Let's return to Ava. While the research helps punctuate our understanding of the powerful correlations between self-compassion, constructive decision-making, and improved quality of life, we don't need empirical studies to tell us what Ava should do next. It's obvious to us that instead of drinking more, Ava should go home and restore herself.

More than ever, she needs her own emotional generosity. She needs to be compassionate with herself.

Not only is this obvious to you and me now, it was glaringly obvious to Ava at the time, too. There was no part of Ava's brain that thought staying out and drinking was the smarter option, so why didn't she just go home and take a bath? If self-compassion is so good for us and punishment is so bad for us, why do we keep punishing ourselves?

Three Main Reasons We Choose Self-Punishment Instead of Self-Compassion

1. WE MAKE OUR WORTH DEPENDENT ON OUR PERFORMANCE

Every perfectionist can relate to Ava's sense that because she drank three drinks before group, she ruined everything. Ava had avoided drinking every single day for the last four months, but her negative performance on this one day counted exponentially more to her than her positive performance over the previous 120-plus days.

In addition to not drinking, over those four months, Ava had begun to meaningfully reconnect with her family, she'd joined the Prospect Park Track Club and was meeting new people, she'd improved her eating habits, she'd replaced some negative coping skills with some positive coping skills, she'd forged a strong relationship with me—she'd done so many things right. For Ava, those four months instantly became meaningless the second she made one mistake.

Even in her intoxicated state, Ava still made it to group, was able to be immediately honest about her behaviors, and asked for help in the form of a last-minute bomb. Still, none of those instantaneous repair attempts mattered at all to her. All that registered for Ava was that she had consumed alcohol, so now she was a complete failure.

Recall from the last chapter that perfectionists in an adaptive space base their self-worth on existence, whereas perfectionists in a maladaptive space base their self-worth on performance. Ava was in a maladaptive space. As long as Ava performed well (i.e., stayed sober), that meant she was good, worthy, and undeserving of punishment. But Ava was not sober, which automatically made her bad, unworthy, and deserving of punishment.

Another way to say that you're worthy is that you believe you deserve something positive. Another way to say that you're unworthy is that you believe you *don't* deserve something positive. What Ava decided she didn't deserve was any compassion, comfort, or safety. That's why taking a hot bath, simple as it may be, felt genuinely impossible for her that night.

The conditions we place on our self-worth and the self-punishments we enlist when we don't meet those conditions are unconscious. We move through our daily routines without realizing that we have put our worth at stake. Ava didn't consciously think, "I'm making my worth conditional at the moment, so I'm going to punish myself by returning to behaviors that I know are hurtful to me and denying myself what I know would be helpful to me." Nobody actually talks to themselves like that in their head.

The thought that registered consciously for Ava was a one-dimensional, "I feel like shit, and I deserve it." With a narrowed thought-action repertoire, her second thought was, "Might as well stay out and keep drinking."

2. WE NEVER LEARNED THAT SELF-COMPASSION IS KING

We're all in pain, and most of us simply do not know what to do about that. Our main strategy is to play whack-a-mole with our pain because we think pain is automatically unhealthy. We've adopted this sanitized, "healthy people can bypass pain" view of emotional well-being (otherwise known as *toxic positivity*) because we prioritize analytical intelligence over emotional intelligence. We don't emphasize emotional literacy in school, so it shouldn't be all that shocking to us when we come careening into adulthood only to find that we're emotionally illiterate.

What's the difference between self-esteem and self-worth, or account-ability and punishment, or compassion and pity, or dignity and respect? What's a boundary? What's one healthy way to respond to guilt? We don't naturally know the answers to those questions any more than we naturally know the difference between an obtuse and an acute angle.

Still, somehow it *is* kind of shocking for us to realize that our basic emotional vocabulary skills are blurry, at best. The most jaw-to-the-floor shocking thing we come to discover is that feeling our feelings (otherwise known as *emotional regulation*) is something we actually have to learn how to do.

As an emotional-regulation strategy, self-compassion is king. Unfortunately, we never learned that. If we're being honest, we don't even know what self-compassion is (we'll delve into it in the next chapter). Because we don't know that much about it, we underestimate self-compassion.

We think of self-compassion as a sweet thing we can do for ourselves while we're putting lotion on our legs, not as a primary source of power. We think of self-compassion as optional, when there's nothing optional about it. You can't heal or grow without self-compassion. In the absence of self-compassion, the best you can hope for is stagnation.

Some of us think of self-compassion as an indulgence—emotionally petting ourselves while we avoid personal accountability. We don't realize that self-compassion is what ushers us into personal accountability.

3. WE MISTAKE SELF-PUNISHMENT FOR PERSONAL ACCOUNTABILITY

We've already addressed the basic differences between punishment and personal accountability, but let's dive a little deeper. It's also important to distinguish between personal accountability and other types of account-abilities. While external accountability can be imposed on you (someone can hold you legally accountable or financially accountable, for example), no one can "make you" take personal accountability except you. Personal accountability is a personal choice.

It sounds simple to point out, but you can't take personal accountability if you don't know what doing that looks like. We don't know how to take personal accountability, but we feel bad and want to do *something*. Enter the cultural and thereby individual default: self-punishment.

You think that if you punish yourself, you're proving to yourself that you mean business, you're disciplined, you're serious this time, you're ready to do the hard work.

First of all, it's not difficult to create pain and make yourself feel like shit, so you're not proving anything. Do you know how easily I could derail my entire life? I could do it in nine minutes flat with my eyes shut and no Wi-Fi.

Second, while pain can motivate the drive towards taking accountability, pain is not a requisite for accountability. You do not need to be a suffering and miserable person to be someone who can be trusted to do the right thing in the first place and to course correct when mistakes are recognized. In fact, being punitive with yourself only makes it harder for you to take accountability.

As Dr. Harriet Lerner explains, to hold oneself accountable, "a person needs to have a big platform of self-worth to stand on. From this higher vantage point, they can look out at their mistakes and see them as part of a larger, complex, ever-changing picture of who they are as a human being."

To take personal accountability during a misstep, you need to be able to acknowledge that while you made a mistake (or several mistakes), you're still a capable, strong, and good person who has the power to learn, grow, and thrive.

To punish yourself in the name of discipline, to deny yourself compassion in the name of accountability—these efforts are misguided.

Can I promise you something?

I promise you this: *we are all in enough pain already*. We don't need to invent more pain for ourselves through self-punishment. It's exactly what I wanted to say to Ava while she was sobbing into her hoodie: "Can't you see that you're already in enough pain? You don't need more pain; you need more compassion."

The Accomplices to Self-Punishment: Numbing + Blame

Since we're emotionally illiterate and don't know how to respond to pain in healthy, conscious ways, we unconsciously respond to our pain through the unhealthy habits of numbing and blaming.

Numbing looks like engaging in an activity that helps you ignore the feelings you don't want to feel. Unlike taking a break for the purpose of restoration, numbing behaviors are distractions designed to repress your emotions. You'll recall the examples at the beginning of this chapter: overeating, overspending, overworking, getting caught up in drama, substance misuse, mindlessly watching TV or scrolling social media, and the like.

We all need regular breaks and a little escapism. So how do you know if you're restoring or numbing? Restorative activities help you regulate your emotions and gain perspective—taking a walk to "clear your head," for example. Restoration regulates; numbing represses. After you restore, you feel reset. You feel recharged. Restoration feels good.

Numbing doesn't make us feel good; it makes us feel nothing. When the numbing wears off, we still have our pain to answer to. While numbing is an attempt to bury our pain, blame represents our effort to throw our pain out with the trash.

As Dr. Brené Brown's research demonstrates, "blame is an attempt to discharge your pain."[12] We think, *If something is your fault and not my fault, I don't have to deal with it, you have to deal with it.* Blame doesn't work like that.

Blaming someone else does nothing to absolve you of your pain. Blame is especially ineffectual for perfectionists because, as people who strive to be accountable (even when we don't understand what that means), guess who perfectionists blame first?

When you're in an adaptive space, you focus on personal accountability without fixating on blame. When you're in a maladaptive space, or you don't know what taking personal accountability means, blaming yourself seems like the right thing to do.

Messy perfectionists blame themselves for failing to follow through and blame the world for being too bureaucratic. Intense perfectionists blame themselves for not getting others to perform at a high enough standard and blame others for being mediocre. Parisian perfectionists blame themselves for caring too much and blame others for being "too unconscious." Classic perfectionists blame themselves for not being organized enough to manage a dysfunctional or uncertain situation and blame others for not being thoughtful enough to adhere to a plan. Procrastinator perfectionists blame themselves for not being perfectly ready and blame others for being so presumptuous as to dare to begin without being fully prepared, qualified, or perfect.

Numbing and blaming delay progress because they delay self-compassion. Negative self-talk also delays self-compassion.

The Most Common Self-Punishment: Negative Self-Talk

Self-talk is the way you talk to yourself about yourself. Negative self-talk is when you speak negatively about yourself to yourself: *I'm such an idiot, I can't believe I did that, no wonder no one wants to spend time with me,* and so forth.

Negative self-talk is a self-punishment and an extremely insidious one at that. If you make a habit of berating yourself, you'll experience chronic guilt that morphs into shame.

Unless you disrupt your self-punishment with some self-compassion, you'll eventually adopt a false, shameful identity as someone who is incapable, damaged, lazy, annoying, a mess—whatever mean adjectives you're using to describe yourself. Like all punishments do, negative self-talk causes you to be in more pain than you already are.

As your pain grows, at some point your primary goal shifts from growth to pain avoidance. Instead of being motivated to practice habits that support your goals, you become motivated to practice habits that support numbing your pain.

For example, let's say you give a poor presentation at work. If you practice self-compassion after that presentation, you recognize a need for improvement while also being kind to yourself. You acknowledge the presentation went poorly, but you don't allow your poor presentation to be a commentary on who you are as a human being.

Here's an example of a self-compassionate response: *Yeah, that didn't go well at all. I didn't realize how nervous I'd feel. It's okay that I felt nervous; I felt nervous because it was important to me. It's not like I'm the only person in the world to ever stumble through a presentation. This happens. I'm still cringing thinking about it, but that's not all I feel. I'm proud of myself for trying something I've never done before, and now I'm curious about what makes someone a good presenter.*

Feeling good gives you energy; feeling bad drains your energy. Because being compassionate with yourself helps you to feel good, you have the energy to think about who could help you improve your presentation skills. You ask someone who you think is a good presenter what their secret is, and they tell you about a bunch of YouTube videos they watched on the topic. Before your next presentation, you've watched those videos.

You also remember that there must be a TED Talk on presenting because there's a TED Talk on every topic on earth, so you watch one on body language, and that's helpful, too. The morning of your next presentation, following your newfound tips, you make sure you're not overly caffeinated, and you do some deep-breathing exercises. It feels kind of weird, but you light a candle in your office beforehand because one of the videos suggested it may help you relax. Whether the candle thing actually works or not, it feels great. You give presenting another shot.

It goes . . . okay. You still need some improvement, and you're honest with yourself about that. You've also improved meaningfully since your last presentation, and you're honest with yourself about that.

Conversely, if you engage in self-punishment via negative self-talk after a poor presentation, you acknowledge a need for improvement while also inducing shame: *That presentation was a mess. You're bringing the whole team down. You always knew you didn't belong at this company, and now everyone else knows it.*

In a state of shame, you believe that who you are is bad. Guilt says, *I'm sorry about what I did.* Shame says, *I'm sorry about who I am.*

It's hard to pivot from shame to skills building. It's easy to pivot from shame to numbing.

Because you're making yourself feel worse, not better, you have less energy. You don't have the energy to watch a TED Talk; that sounds so annoying to you. You look at a candle and you roll your eyes. You think, *Fuck lighting a candle; candles are stupid,* then you proceed with more negative self-talk that you may or may not even be aware of.

Eventually the negative self-talk overwhelms you, so you reach for numbing agents. You eat three bowls of cereal, even though you're not hungry; you drink another glass of wine, even though you can't taste it anymore.

In accidental moments of quiet, you replay other painful mistakes you've made, bigger mistakes. Because you haven't disrupted your self-punishment with self-compassion, your mind can only stay on one channel—the "every painful mistake I've ever made" channel.

At this point, you've convinced yourself that you're a terrible, bumbling, hopeless mess. You continue to make negative choices because terrible people don't deserve to feel good. Terrible people deserve punishment, right?

The cereal and wine aren't cutting it, so you start overworking, too. Unable to adequately prepare for your next presentation because you've ensured your schedule is grossly overburdened, you steamroll through it as quickly as possible, hate it, and experience the pain of having all your insecurities confirmed. But it doesn't matter because you can't feel the pain.

Your frenzied work life leaves you so exhausted that you no longer feel anxious about presenting. You in fact no longer feel anything except "tired all the time." Are you tired all the time, or are you numb?

The more pain you're in, the more compassion you need. Period.

In the same way that someone who believes that they deserve good things won't put up with bad treatment, someone who does *not* believe that they deserve good things won't put up with good treatment.

Until you can meet yourself with some compassion, you'll reject the good in your life. No matter how small the good is, you'll honestly believe you don't deserve it.

Can you see why taking a hot bath felt so impossible for Ava? She was too ashamed of herself to take a bath. Taking a bath didn't fit inside her story of how she's bad and doesn't deserve to feel good. Taking a bath fit inside the story of someone who was five years sober, not someone who came to group therapy intoxicated. In the absence of self-compassion, choosing the healthier option feels wrong.

Recovering

One of the greatest gifts my clients ever gave me (which is saying *a lot*) unfolded in that rehab. I saw so clearly that the people in recovery who were able to truly learn their lessons and recover were not the ones who came up with the smartest punishments. "Smart punishment" is an oxymoron. The people in recovery who actually recover are the ones who respond to their mistakes with self-compassion.

We're all in need of healing. We all have something to recover from.

Recovery of any kind runs in direct proportion to how much we are willing to abandon self-punishment.

In examining the difference between adaptive and maladaptive perfectionists, research has demonstrated that it's not perfectionistic strivings that are harmful to our mental health, it's the self-criticism we lacerate ourselves with that endangers our well-being.[13]

Pay attention to those who describe themselves as "recovering perfectionists." Notice that they aren't people who have lowered their high standards, learned to want less, or stopped chasing the ideal. They're people who have committed to self-compassion as a default emotional response to pain. That throbbing thorn in your brain isn't perfectionism; it's self-punishment.

Loopholes

"Okay so what about serial killers?" Keisha asked me with her arms crossed. Looking at me expectantly, she was trying to paint me into a corner about how not everyone deserves compassion, especially not her.

ME: Are you really comparing yourself to a serial killer right now?
KEISHA: I'm just saying, what if you go out and kidnap a nice family that's having a picnic and then you bring them into a secret room that you lined with industrial plastic and you cut up their bodies with a chainsaw while you listen to your favorite song. The day after that, when you wake up the next morning, *then* do you still deserve self-compassion?

I explained to Keisha that violent sociopaths don't need self-compassion because they feel no remorse, guilt, or attendant self-loathing in the first place. The morning after they commit some heinous act, they're not struggling to extend kindness to themselves; they're wondering whether to have scrambled eggs or Frosted Mini-Wheats for breakfast.

If you're determined to find a loophole for why you don't deserve your own empathy, you will find one. The reason you pick will feel like an excellent, irrefutable justification of why you're unworthy of compassion, patience, warmth, connection, basically anything good. Ava, for example, had what felt to her to be a bulletproof reason for why she didn't deserve goodness.

If you insist on punishing yourself, that is your choice. Others may or may not object to your decision; either way, their objections won't change your mind. No one has the power to change your mind except you.

Similarly, if you decide to love yourself as a matter of course, others may be quick to object, to subtly or overtly explain your unworthiness to you, or to assign stipulations to the degree to which you are allowed to be joyful and free. None of these objections can change your mind unless you allow them to. Understanding that permission to grant yourself compassion is a choice you can enact in any moment, that you are the person who can lead your mind in any direction you so choose—*that* is what it means to have power. You summon power by becoming aware of what you're choosing, why you're choosing it, and what you could be choosing instead.

The most common loophole people use as an excuse to withhold self-compassion is repetition.

When You Know Better But Don't Do Better

The exquisite and sage and everything wonderful Dr. Maya Angelou practically bottled self-compassion with her famous phrase "When you know better, you do better." An immediate invitation to kindness and understanding, Angelou's phrase acknowledges that you made a mistake, but it's okay, because you didn't know better. Now you know better.

You learned something important, so the mistake doesn't even count as a mistake; it's transformed into a valuable lesson. Don't even worry about it; just do better next time, and you'll be good. *When you know better, you do better.*

I love the phrase, and at the same time, I always want to add a footnote to it.

The reality is that a lot of the negative choices we make are repetitive. Particularly when we're stuck in a pattern of addiction (to a person, food, alcohol, work, etc.), *we already know better.* The other reality is, we already *know* we know better.

When you say to someone, "You know better than this," you're not imparting new information to that person. That statement is simply a shame trap unless it's followed by a question of genuine curiosity—for example, "You know better than this, what's going on?" or "You know better than this, what do you need that you're not getting?"

Left unchecked, the "You know better than this" self-talk metastasizes into "What were you thinking?! How could you be so stupid? What are you even doing with your life!?" From that shame-laden place, the very last thing you're going to do is reach for something that might help you and heal you because you're going to feel like you don't deserve it. In the moment that you need it most, you swiftly brush all compassion away, every bit of it, like sweeping muffin crumbs off a table.

If you don't respond to your repetitive mistakes with self-compassion, everything else becomes a punishment. Not only does withholding compassion hurt you; it hurts everyone around you.

When you withhold compassion from yourself, you withhold your gifts and unique presence from others. Trying to show up as your full self while simultaneously punishing yourself is like trying to give a massage to someone who's jogging. No version of it works. You can't be as patient, creative, strong, loving, or reliable when you're punishing yourself—you can't be you.

Denying yourself compassion reflects a misguided attempt to take responsibility and demonstrate that you're sorry. Skip the shame; the best apology is changed behavior.

Growth looks like two steps forward and five steps back sometimes. Healing isn't linear or iterative. Healing is a process, not an event, and in the process of healing and learning, repetition is important. Different iterations of the same lesson theme show up repeatedly, and each time they do, you understand the lesson a little more completely. That's how learning is supposed to work.

The fact that the learning process involves a lot of repetition is frustrating. We hate repetition. We automatically assume repetition means we're failing. Repetition can also mean we're learning. If repetition weren't necessary for our learning, that would mean we were robots.

A Paradigm Shift

Human beings are good at making rules, better at breaking them, and best at punishment. For perfectionists, mastery of self-punishment is almost always assured, a developmental milestone of sorts, the psychological version of learning how to feed oneself with a spoon.

Mastery of self-love, on the other hand? It seems we need years of therapy and yoga classes and carefully branded beauty products just to stand a chance with that one. What if we didn't, though? It is our choice, after all.

What if perfectionists everywhere decided to excel at loving themselves instead of punishing themselves? What if we just flipped the whole damn paradigm on its head?

That paradigm shift would look like you centering your identity on your possibilities instead of your limitations. It would look like you remembering that not only do we all make mistakes, we all repeat mistakes, sometimes for years. Most critically, that paradigm shift would begin and end with you extending some compassion to yourself. The next chapter will teach you how to do just that.

6

You'll Enjoy the Solution about as Much as You Enjoy Getting an A–

LET GO, FAIL FORWARD, AND BE COMPASSIONATE WITH YOURSELF NO MATTER WHAT

Maybe your life will work. Most likely it won't
at first, but that will give you poetry.

YRSA DALEY-WARD

5:30 p.m., Tuesday.

Immediately upon eye contact, Maya seemed different. She strolled in from the waiting room. As she walked over to the couch, she passed by a large piece of artwork I have hanging on my office wall. I watched from my chair as she ran her fingertips along the bottom of its bumpy gold frame.

ME: How are you?

MAYA: I feel . . . good.

ME: Tell me more.

MAYA: Well, I was late picking up Noa [her daughter] before I got here, but that happens. I wasn't *that* late; she's fine. We had a nice walk home actually.

Maya shared some funny things her daughter had said, and how connective the walk felt, even though it was only a few blocks.

ME: The last time you were late getting Noa was a big ordeal in your internal world. You were really hard on yourself about it.

MAYA: Yeah, I was.

ME: But that didn't happen today.

MAYA: Nope.

We were silent for a good moment. Something was off. Was she high? Manic? Tipsy? Did she somehow achieve enlightenment on the 4 train on her way to my office?

ME: I can't get an emotional temperature on you today.

MAYA: You know, I just, I'm *good*.

As she looked at me to find the right words to express herself, Maya started smoothing over the couch with her hand, almost like she was petting an imaginary cat. She glanced down at her hand and shot up to attention, which startled the hell out of me.

MAYA: This couch is green. Wait. *Is this velvet?!*

ME: Maya. I need you to fill me in on what's happening right now.

MAYA: I've been sitting on a green velvet couch for the past year, and I'm just noticing it now.

The realization produced a moment that Maya experienced as both sullen and hopeful. She'd been working on replacing self-punishment with self-compassion for months without noticing any changes. I noticed changes in her a while back and I shared my observations, but she didn't believe me: "You have to say that; you're my therapist."

Now the changes were starting to appear firsthand. The more she adapted inwardly, the more Maya's life reached out to her. Her life was shifting from black and white to color—in this case, to forest green.

Punishing yourself takes an extraordinary toll on your energy. Once you stop punishing yourself, you may be surprised at how much free space is cleared up in your mind, heart, and soul. When your energy comes back, the successive openness can be disorienting. You start to notice things you never noticed before; you start to see others in a different light.

With self-punishment out of the way, you also discover a new problem, a bigger problem (welcome to the world of personal growth). Your problem was never that you're a perfectionist, and your problem is no longer that you punish yourself. Your problem is that you're not being your full self.

I don't know exactly what you need to do to be your full self. Only you know that. What I can tell you is that to be who you are, you'll have to stop being who you're not. You'll need to let go of what no longer serves you, fail forward as you discover what's meaningful to you, and be compassionate with yourself no matter what. Enacting this trifecta calls for a focus on healing, not changing. In every way, the former is the harder curriculum.

Making technical changes in your life is just rebranding dysfunction. You're no longer dating Nicole the emotionally unavailable bartender, but now you're dating Arianna the emotionally unavailable analyst. Good job curtailing your tendency to numb out with food, but also not good job because now you're numbing out with overspending. Technical changes are trash trades. Change is not something you have to force; change is a natural by-product of healing.

You can change without healing, but you can't heal without changing.

When it comes to strategies for change, nothing surpasses the strategy of healing because healing automates change.

Perfectionists do not enjoy focusing on healing because healing is not a prescriptive endeavor. We much prefer that one big thing be very wrong with us (a cluster of many medium- or small-sized impairments is also fine) so that we can systematically annihilate all of our inadequacies at once and move forward with a perfect reset.

Healing is not about eradicating the parts of ourselves we most loathe, nor is healing won through achievement sprees. Healing is realizing that you are already whole (perfect) right now, as you are. In this moment, you are worthy of as much love, joy, freedom, dignity, and connection as any human being could ever deserve. If you could fully accept the immutability of your worth, that would be all the healing you'd ever need. This is very upsetting news for perfectionists. Perfectionists love a project.

Perfectionists want instructions and timelines. We want the handy acronym, the six simple principles, the thirty-day plan. Streamlined routes to change engender the temporarily buoying sense that addressing your problems is a simple matter of self-discipline. All you need to do is follow exacting advice about how to best live your life from someone who's not you and who doesn't know you. Follow the specific advice perfectly, and when you mess up (because plans like that are impossible) make sure to blame yourself and not the approach. Always blame yourself— that way you can stay in control, because if everything is your fault, you can fix it all when you finally get your shit together and become perfect.

Infomercial healing is so tempting, if only it worked.

What does work is to engage the invisible tedium of moving away from who you're not and moving towards who you are. It's not a glamorous process, you won't get any credit for it, there are no instructions, and there's no finish line because it never ends. Have fun.

Letting Go

Unless you consciously decide that you want to heal, you'll always choose familiarity and convenience over surprise and effort because that's what human beings are wired to do. Familiarity and convenience offer us control, which in turn offers us predictability. If we can predict our environment, we increase our chances for survival.

Surviving doesn't demand that you heal or thrive; surviving only requires that you don't die. If your goal is merely to survive, it's important that you close yourself off to any risk. If your goal is to extend your survival skills to "thrival" skills, it's important that you learn how to take risks.

Risks are not automatically dangerous; they're automatically uncertain. To take a risk, you have to let go of predictability. Relinquishing predictability is an ambitious task for two reasons. First, it makes you feel like you're losing control (because you are, and this is a good thing). Second, it takes continuous effort to let go of what's familiar and try something new. At least initially, you have to process so much more information than you otherwise would: *Do I like this? Is this what I want? Is this who I am? Is this working for me? Am I happier yet? Should I be crying right now? What is this doing to my relationships? How is this affecting my work? Is this worth my discomfort? Are there snacks here? What is happening?*

In the background of this psychological calculus is the evolutionary reflex to return to what's familiar. When you engage in a dynamic that's familiar, the incentive is that you don't have to process any new information. It's like getting out of an Uber without having to deal with paying; the experience is appealing because it's streamlined.

Your brain likes streamlined; hence, you gravitate towards what's familiar *even when what's familiar is hurting you and you know it.* The "devil you know" is more appealing to your brain than uncertainty.

The seductive ease that accompanies the familiar is constantly humming in the background of your healing. You don't want to go back to your old ways, but familiarity feels like home when you're in new and foreign territory. Familiarity *can* be home, but not when what's familiar is also the thing that hurts you.

You don't need to abandon everything you're comforted by in order to heal. You *do* need to differentiate between "good familiar" and "bad familiar," though, because both are deeply comforting, so you'll be drawn to both.

The more stressed you are, the harder it is to tell the difference between good familiar and bad familiar; all you register is comfort. When your stress response is activated, anything that's familiar feels like, *There it is, that's exactly what I need right now, thank God.*

It's especially easy for perfectionists to justify indulging in the immediate gratification of unhealthy familiarity because doing so doesn't look like slacking off; it looks like working harder.

Parisian perfectionists work harder to do more for other people at the cost of meeting their own needs. Intense perfectionists apply brute force to their work, clocking more hours with less rest alongside a disregard for the law of diminishing returns and the risk of complete burnout. Procrastinator perfectionists plan to make a plan about learning how to best make a plan. Messy perfectionists play Jenga with their goals, continuing to shift the top priority in a way that's built to collapse. Classic perfectionists jam structure into every open space they see, including the places designed to be breathing holes.

Letting go of the immediate gratification attached to bad familiarity is only the beginning. You also have to let go of the outcome of your striving.

Fear-Based Striving

We spend our lives confronted by two rotating fears:

I'll never get what I want.

I'll lose what I have.

What these fears have in common is that they're based on a future outcome. There are too many factors at play, factors you cannot possibly foresee, for you to ever be able to successfully manipulate every outcome in your favor. In other words, you cannot control the future. If you can't let go of your attachment to the outcome, you will spend your life trading one fear for the other.

Operating from a chronic state of fear is useless. Fear-based lifestyles are a perpetual scramble, a dizzying loop, a ring of fire. To exit the loop, you have to enter the present moment. You enter the present moment by letting go of the future outcome and focusing on what you're doing right now—otherwise known as *engaging in the process.*

Letting go of whether you win or lose to focus on "the process" initially feels like a distasteful apathy for most perfectionists. We don't understand the alternatives—so we're supposed to no longer care about achieving goals? That leaves us to do what, exactly? Replace our deodorant with essential oils and become one with nature? We think, *No thank you, I'll take the ring of fire, please.*

Letting go of the outcome doesn't mean you stop caring about goal attainment; of course you care. Goal setting isn't problematic. The problem arises when you hook your joy onto a future outcome: *I'll be happy when I get this* or *I'll be happy if I can keep this.*

You will never experience the future; you're always and only in the present moment. If you're waiting on the future to feel joy, you will never feel joy.

One big reason we resist letting go of the outcome is that we don't want to fail. We don't want to fail because we don't want to be failures, but there's a difference between saying *I failed* and *I'm a failure.* The former describes an event; the latter describes an identity. You can't control the outcome of your striving, but you do have the power to choose how you ascribe meaning to failure.

Fail Forward

When you allow setbacks, rejection, delay, or whatever you're perceiving as failure to serve as a commentary on who you are, it's hard to move forward because you stop believing in yourself. You lock yourself out of a growth mindset. When you're in a maladaptive space, failure has the final say on what's possible for you.

When you *don't* allow rejection, delay, or failure to serve as a commentary on who you are, it's easy to move forward because you still believe in yourself. You step over the failure like a napping dog and you keep going. When you're in an adaptive space, you don't give failure any power. Not only does failure not have the final say; it doesn't have any say.

To fail forward means that you allow yourself to grow from your failure, and out of that newfound state of expansion, you try again. You engage in the process for the sake of enjoying and learning from the experience, not for the glory of a future win.

But how?

How do you make the choice to switch your focus from the outcome to the process?

To focus on the process, you have to start honoring the process. Honoring the process can be divided into two parts: acknowledgment and celebration.

Honoring the Process through Acknowledgment

There are so many ways people try to teach us that the journey is the destination. We don't care. Perfectionists want to win. We focus on achieving the outcome because we think achieving the outcome will make us happy. Do you want the bad news first or the worst news first?

The bad news is that achieving a specific outcome (an award, a promotion, a relationship, etc.) is not going to make you happy. Building meaning is what makes us happy, not desultory acquisition. The worst news is that blazing through the process makes you feel worse because you put so much pressure on attaining the goal as your singular source of happiness, but hitting the goal can never make up for the fact that you were disengaged and not feeling any joy or connection the whole time you were in pursuit of it.

When you focus on the process, you focus on the victories that are happening now. You focus on what's ready to be enjoyed now. Acknowledgment gives you power because it widens your perspective, engenders positivity, and helps you broaden and build. For example, if we were to acknowledge the process you're currently in, the acknowledgment would look something like this:

Caring about becoming your authentic self and taking action to become your authentic self are two different things. Reading this book is evidence that you've arrived at the intersection of caring and active engagement, which is a milestone. Millions of people are stuck trying to get to the place where you are now. This is a big deal. All major progress begins and sustains itself through what you're doing right now, which is taking one step forward.

You worked hard to get here. You took on the gritty task of being honest about what wasn't working for you. You extinguished your tolerance for so much nonsense you used to happily wait in line for. There were so many trials that you had to overcome for you to arrive at the you who is here now reading this book. Lessons that you've mastered so well *you've forgotten they were ever a struggle*. Acknowledging the process requires you to give credit to yourself for the work you've done to get to where you are now.

Think of who you were five years ago and how much you've grown since then. If you could go back in time and transplant your brain and all that you've learned into the five-years-ago version of you, it would blow your five-years-ago mind. What used to be your ceiling is now your floor. You float across waters that you used to flail and thrash in.

Can you take in how far you've come? How much valuable experience you've gained? Can you appreciate how much discomfort and introspection you've worked through?

Do you understand the amount of strength and courage that is required to persist through all that you dealt with to arrive at the place where you are right now? Is it possible that you're already on the other side of the wall you've been trying to figure out how to jump?

Is there more work to do? Yes. No matter what ambitious people have done, they'll always perceive more work ahead of them than behind them—that's what makes them ambitious.

You cannot be a perfectionist without being ambitious. That sense you privately carry, that you still have so much work to do, that you'll never be done, that you've been working on self-improvement for so long and yet it feels as if you haven't even dented your vision—that represents your ambition, not your defeat.

In a world where we're taught to stay small and constantly second-guess ourselves, it's remarkable that you're seeking ways to thrive instead of ways to destroy yourself. This very second, you're actively choosing to focus on possibility; hence why you're reading this book instead of pursuing the ten million other things you could be doing. Your state of consciousness is a victory in and of itself that no one else could give you and no one else could take away. Step out of reflexive self-loathing and dare to be impressed with yourself as you are, right in this moment.

Celebrating completes the circle of honoring the process.

Honoring the Process
through Celebration

It's easy to think of celebrating as an expendable or indulgent act, but in the absence of celebration, something important is lost. The micro-rituals involved in celebrating (receiving an invitation, getting dressed up, clinking glasses, taking pictures) serve as steady anchors to connect us to the joy and momentum of our lives. Without anchors, we drift.

In the absence of celebration, a sense of buoyancy that carries us through the seasons starts to wane. Our ability to process change individually and collectively is disrupted. The pandemic delivered this lesson to our doorstep. When our ability to safely gather was gone, we instinctively fought for celebration because deep down, we understand how important it is. I'll always remember those yard signs: "Honk for our high school senior! Class of 2020."

Beyond helping us emotionally process the evolution of our lives, celebrating also boosts gratitude because we're acknowledging joy for what's happening. Everyone knows that increasing your gratitude makes you happier, but celebrating also increases our happiness because it gives us an opportunity to acknowledge all the people who have helped us and continue to help us along the way. The reinforcement of support and connection is a meaningful and often overlooked component of celebration.

Graduations, anniversaries, housewarming parties, weddings—they're all designed to help us announce how much a milestone (the very beginning or the very end of the process) means to us. But what about the middle points of a process? The middle is usually where we need the most connection, recognition, support, and encouragement.

There's no card at the store for the personal goals that you're investing so much of yourself into. When you lead a self-defined life, *you* have to be the one to put a stake in the ground and say: "This is important. This is a big deal!"

The middle of the process is invisible, soundless. If you don't add noise and visibility through celebration, the process goes by unnoticed. Not just unnoticed by others but also by you. No one, for example, is ever going to stop by your desk at work and say: "Hey! Great job on reducing your credit card debt by 12 percent over the last year! We should get drinks and celebrate your granular but steady commitment to financial freedom."

You have to initiate the celebration of the middle of the process yourself. This is how adaptive perfectionists live—inviting joy, connection, support, and gratitude into their lives *during* the process, not just after the win.

In the middle of writing this book, when it only existed as an unfinished Word document, I brought my daughter, Abigail, to a party-supply store. Post-vaccines, the world was opening again. Being *anywhere* was a thrill, let alone being in a party-supply store. I told her that we were going to have a big party with "me, you, and daddy."

To describe the maximum amount of anything, Abigail says, "All the numbers and letters." She's three, and what she knows for sure is that there are *a lot* of numbers and letters. She asked if the party was going to be "all-the-numbers-and-letters fun." "Oh, definitely yes," I told her. She started jumping and hugging my leg. The party prep was on.

I said we'd need special signs, confetti, balloons—all the most fun stuff. A few minutes later, while we were trying on plastic top hats, Abigail asked, "Mommy, is it my birthday?"

"No, honey, it's not your birthday," I said. "Is it you's or daddy's birthday?" she asked. I got down on eye level with her, smiled big through my mask, and said: "You know why we're having a party? Because Mommy's trying really hard at something! We're having a trying party!" She lit up with pure three-year-old glee, then she chose pink streamers.

Trying hard at something is a wonderful reason to celebrate, not that you need a reason. One afternoon, I was in session with a classic perfectionist client of mine who shared that she does a similar exercise as one I happen to do—we both keep lists of our favorite things to notice. Being a classic perfectionist, she of course labeled her list perfectly, the "Like List."

On my Like List, somewhere between swaying trees and people having full-on conversations with their dogs, as if their dogs are human beings, it reads, "Balloons that say, 'just because.'" In those moments of true confusion when you don't know whether you're starting something or ending something or winning or losing or what the word "process" even means, actively invite joy into your life anyway. Err on the side of just because.

A celebration is intentionally flooding the moment with gratitude and recognition to awaken you to the joy in your life. When it comes to inviting joy, anything goes. A celebration doesn't require a party, it doesn't require any money, it doesn't even require another person.

You can enjoy a peaceful and private moment of celebration by cooking a nourishing meal for yourself. You can take a celebratory walk with a friend. You can throw a loud-ass backyard barbeque, swim in the ocean, wear red lipstick, go to a real-life movie theater, or use the fancy thing you were saving. As the saying goes, "Don't save anything for a special occasion; being alive is the special occasion."

Leading a self-defined life means that you get to decide what success looks like for you, and you get to decide how and when to celebrate that success.

Some people don't like celebrating during the process because they don't want to jinx it. They don't want to mess up their chance of achieving the outcome by enjoying the moment "too early."

It may be the thing we forget the most: nothing is promised in this life. If we only celebrated what we could be certain of, that which we were sure we could never lose, we would never have cause for celebration. There is no such thing as officially having anything.

We often choose not to celebrate "too early" as a way of hedging our anticipatory grief. You're trying to control the amount of joy you feel now so you can control the amount of loss you absorb later.

Not once have I worked with someone who said: "Well, X important thing that I deeply wanted fell through, but luckily I didn't get too excited about it, so I'm inoculated from pain now. I'm not sure what to talk about today." The pain comes anyway.

You can't control grief by subtracting joy from your life. You can't control grief, period.

Approaching joy from a position of power looks like recognizing that joy does not need to be notarized by some external marker before you're allowed to officially feel it. The positive moments that are happening in your life now are real. Whether they stay or go does not make them less real now. Also, the positive moments don't have to be achievement-themed; they can be as simple as being present to the first sip of a hot drink in the morning. Anything that's on your "Like List" counts.

Get it out of your head that the only way to grow is through suffering. You can grow just as profoundly through joy. "Doing the work" is not solely about learning how to recognize and speak our sadness, our anger, and our angst. Doing the work is just as much (if not more so) about learning how to recognize, speak, and celebrate our joy. So often, the latter is in fact the more challenging work. This is especially true for perfectionists.

Celebration is important, you are important, and what you're doing is important. The projects and relationships you're working on are important not because they'll lead to a desirable outcome but because you have deemed them worthy of your precious time and energy. This is what it means to lead a self-defined life—it's understanding that whatever you choose to value is what's valuable and whatever you decide to care about is what's worth caring about.

Consider what your life would look like if the victory was experienced in the process, externally validated achievement was just a sentimental token, and failure did not exist as a schema in your mind.

Unforeseen Setbacks

A process can involve months, years, sometimes *decades* of progressive steps taken towards achieving a vision. Amidst any given process, something is always breaking and in need of repair.

If you think the fact that something is always breaking and in need of repair is about you—I say this from a place of love—then you need to get over yourself. The world is not revolving around you. Without exception, everyone experiences unforeseen setbacks big and small.

Embodying your power as you let go, fail forward, and encounter the unforeseen requires you to hone your instincts and clarify your intentions.

Accessing Your Instincts

When it comes to leading a self-defined life, your instincts are your greatest guide. We often conflate feelings and instincts, but they're not the same thing and should not be given the same weight when it comes to decision-making. Instincts and feelings both get a vote, but instincts get veto power.

Feelings are ephemeral and easily swayed by the most basic external circumstances—a rainy day, being hungry or hot, getting a free sample. Instincts are incorruptible. Instincts don't change based upon your surroundings, mood, or energy level.

Let's say, for example, that you know you need to leave your toxic job; it's an unmanageably stressful and dysfunctional environment.* Then your work hosts an Employee Appreciation Day. There's a delicious lunch at a new restaurant followed by a fun outing. Your feelings might start to say: *Hey, this job isn't so bad. Maybe I could stick it out for a little longer, this is kind of nice.* Your instincts, however, will not waiver.

Instincts never lie to you. Pay attention to the messages that don't change; those are your instincts.

We glamorize instincts when we assume they only arrive in bold "yes or no" packaging. Sometimes your instincts tell you to wait and see, to

---

* A job, a person, or a situation doesn't have to be toxic or abusive for you to know you need to leave. You can simply know it's not for you.

take it slow, to move one inch forward so you can peek around the corner. When your instincts are telling you to give yourself more time before you make a decision, it can feel like you're taking a passive role in your life. Patience is not passivity.

Knowing that you need to do something and knowing what exactly it is that you need to do are two different things; the knowledge of both strikes us simultaneously only in the luckiest of circumstances. An instinct telling you that you're not ready to decide is just as valid and vital as an instinct broadcasting a bold yes or no.

You can't force clarity by writing out the pros and cons list for the twentieth time. Gray moments of ambiguity are invitations to trust yourself. If you regularly check in with yourself, when the right thing to do becomes clear, you'll recognize it. As the poet W. H. Auden wrote, "Truth, like love and sleep, resents approaches that are too intense."

Other times your instincts tell you what you need to move away from, but they don't seem to be interested in giving you any follow-up messages whatsoever about what to move towards. It's frustrating when you don't have clear direction forward, but even in those moments, your instincts are still useful. You can know something and not be able to name it.

For example, you may not remember the name of the Italian restaurant you went to last month, but you'd know it if you heard it. When a friend asks, "Was it Celeste?" you say, "No, it was something else . . ." "Maybe Il Brigante?" your friend suggests. "No . . . not that one either," you say. Tip-of-the-tongue knowing is still useful because it allows you to immediately recognize what the wrong answer is.

When you don't know what the right answer is, use your instincts to identify the wrong answers and move away from them. Move away from that person who always leaves you with an uncomfortable feeling. Move away from spending your time in ways that aren't meaningful for you. Move away from spending your energy in ways that aren't reciprocated.

Focusing on what you need to move away from can make you feel like you're in a negative space; don't mistake honesty for negativity. The more you distance yourself from the wrong paths, the more likely it is you'll stumble onto the right ones.

It's okay if you find what's right for you through stumbling; that's how a lot of people find what's right for them. If you think everyone else is coming into their own by flying gracefully through the sacred night in steady line with the moon, you are mistaken. When it comes to finding the life that's right for us, everyone has two left feet until they don't.

Some people find themselves by already knowing who they are, then moving towards that. Other people find themselves by knowing who they're not, then moving away from that. Many of us work our whole lives at a combination of the two.

Listening to your instincts when they speak to you quietly about small things is as critical as listening to your instincts when they scream at you loudly about big things. Your instincts don't operate on a hierarchy. The more you honor your instincts, the deeper you heal.

Only you can honor your instincts because only you can hear them. Having access to your instincts makes you the most qualified expert on your true self. No one else knows what you know; *it has to be you.*

Letting go of control and stepping into your power looks like trading the question "What should I do?" for "What are my instincts telling me about this?"

Clarify Your Intentions

Intentions style your life. While a goal represents a clear demarcation of quantifiable achievement, an intention is more sophisticated. Intentions are expressed not through what you do but through how you do it, not if you do it but why you do it. Your intention is the energy and purpose behind your striving; your goal is what you're striving for.

Intentions can be attached to goals or not, and vice versa. For example, becoming a paid actor is a goal. Inviting others to stretch their capacity for empathy is an intention. You can be a paid actor without an intention, in which case you'll take on pretty much any role you get paid for; you could do a steady stream of toothpaste commercials your entire career. You can become a paid actor with the intention of inviting others to stretch their capacity for empathy, in which case you'll focus on roles in which you work to embody the character such that the audience feels what the character is feeling.

You can also honor your intention without hitting your goal—or even having a goal—by using your everyday life to bring your intention forward. For example, you might not ever "hit it big" as an actor, but you've found joy anyway because you discovered a way to honor the intention driving you to pursue acting in the first place.

Another way to say you're honoring your intention is that you're consistently animating your values. If kindness is a value, you're not just kind when people are watching, you're kind all the time. You're not kind because you get credit, and you don't need external validation to tell you whether you're being kind or not; you already know.

If there were an exclusive kindness award given to one person a year, and one year that person was you, well, that would just be so lovely and yet unimportant to you at the same time. When you operate from an intentional space, the primary source of reward lies in honoring the intention, not in getting credit for it.

When you set an intention, you're giving yourself a way to feel success, satisfaction, and enjoyment during the process, not just in the afterglow of goal attainment.

A key difference between adaptive and maladaptive perfectionists (what some theorists believe is *the* key difference) is that adaptive perfectionists find a way to enjoy the process of striving towards a goal, whereas maladaptive perfectionists don't. Perhaps that's because adaptive perfectionists set intentions and goals, whereas maladaptive perfectionists only set goals.

When you only set a goal, you win on one day, the day you achieve the goal. When you set an intention, you start winning from day one because you keep getting the opportunity to honor the intention.

People who don't set intentions will do some cutthroat shit to achieve their goals, then call their behavior "ambition." This doesn't happen because they're terrible people, it happens because they're desperate for validation. Chasing your ambition and running from your desperation are not the same thing.

If an adaptive perfectionist cannot achieve the goal without honoring the intention, they don't want the goal; it's not worth it to them. Abandoning a goal can look and feel like defeat. Look again.

We will quit listening to our instincts and quit imbuing our lives with intention long before we quit trying to achieve a goal that we discover is ultimately hurting us to reach. And for what? So others won't perceive us to be failures or quitters?

There is no other way to rise towards your potential than on your own terms. Letting go of a goal that isn't aligned with your values isn't quitting-quitting, it's power-quitting. It's like when your best friend finally breaks it off with her appalling, disaster-show ex who slept with her roommate and stole all her furniture. She's not losing; she's winning. Doves fly out of the group chat upon hearing the news—behold the glorious day. Yes, she has left something that she could not make work. No, she is not failing.

Power-quitting is important. If you've never power-quit anything, that's something to explore.

For adaptive perfectionists, success is not defined by whether you win or lose, stay or leave, push forward or quit. Success is experienced as an internal state. When determining their level of success, maladaptive perfectionists ask, "Am I meeting my goals?" Adaptive perfectionists ask, "Am I living up to my intentions?"

The more specific you can be about the intention behind your actions, the more likely you are to live up to the meaning driving your intention. Note the difference between the following general and specific intentions:

A) "I come home at 6:00 p.m. to spend time with my family."

B) "I come home at 6:00 p.m. to make fun memories with my kids."

We don't receive meaning automatically; meaning comes when we understand what's important to us. You can build your idea of success around what's important to you, or you can build your idea of success around what's important to other people who are not living inside your mind, your heart, and your life. The power to honor that which brings you meaning is yours.

Be Compassionate with Yourself No Matter What

Everyone needs compassion. You can't control whether others meet you with compassion or not, but you have the power to meet yourself with compassion. Exercising self-compassion is one of our greatest powers; it will change your life. When you learn to be compassionate with yourself no matter what, you carry safety with you wherever you go.

Perfectionists find an emphasis on self-compassion to be superfluous, "Uh-huh, be nicer to myself; got it." We're ready for the *real* solution. Unconsciously operating under the false belief that we learn more through punishment and suffering than we do through compassion and joy, we don't understand that self-compassion *is* the primary solution.

Self-compassion is not telling yourself, "It's okay, it's alright," when things are not okay and things are not alright. I call that type of generic reassurance *emotional petting*. Emotional petting doesn't feel good because we know it's not the truth. Self-compassion is honest. Self-compassion brings real relief.

Dr. Kristen Neff is to self-compassion what Dr. Brené Brown is to vulnerability. A pioneer in her field, Neff wrote the book on self-compassion (several books, in fact) and was the first to examine self-compassion from an empirical standpoint. Neff begins her definition of self-compassion in this way, "Self-compassion entails being warm and understanding towards ourselves when we suffer, fail, or feel inadequate, rather than ignoring our pain or flagellating ourselves with self-criticism."[1] According to Neff, there are three critical components to self-compassion: self-kindness, common humanity, and mindfulness.

Self-Kindness

To practice self-kindness, Neff says, instead of judging yourself, criticizing yourself, or feeling pity for yourself, you first need to recognize that you're hurting. Instead of focusing on your mistake as the primary issue, acknowledge your pain as the primary issue. As Neff explains, "We cannot ignore our pain and feel compassion for it at the same time."[2]

One of the most basic tasks for therapists involves offering simple permission statements:

You are allowed to be angry about that.

You are allowed to still miss them.

You are allowed to no longer care.

Self-compassion begins with giving yourself permission to encounter what you feel. Once you acknowledge that you're in pain, you need to respond to your pain with kindness instead of criticism.

Yes, your choices may have contributed to the pain you're in—perhaps you're certain that whatever you're struggling with is entirely your fault. It doesn't matter whose fault it is. Blame is a distraction in this work.

As you'll recall from the last chapter, you're blaming because you're contending with something that's difficult to feel, and you're trying to get rid of your pain. Paradoxically, giving yourself permission to feel your pain is what alleviates your pain.

Compassion means "to suffer with"; the word is formed from a combination of the Latin root *com* (with) and *pati* (suffer). When we feel compassion for someone's struggle, it's because we relate to them in some way. We've allowed ourselves to connect with the pain they're going through, and we see them as a whole person who in many ways is just like us. We're motivated to help precisely because of this connection—we are suffering *with* them—helping them helps us.

Feeling bad for people without working to understand or connect to them is pity, not compassion. Compassion is active; pity is passive. You pity someone whenever you see their negative situation and think, "That could never be me." Pity is the polite side of judgment. Nobody wants to be pitied or treated like a "charity case" because no one wants to be judged as less than.

Self-compassion and self-pity operate in the same way as the compassion and pity we hold for others does. Self-compassion makes you feel understood and strengthened; self-pity makes you feel powerless and pathetic.

Self-compassion requires kindness. Kindness means you act with generosity and without an agenda. Kindness is not *I've decided to be good to you, so you better be in an improved mood by tonight.* Kindness is simply *I've decided to be good to you.*

Kindness is a powerful choice because it disarms your defense mechanisms and helps you broaden and build a path forward. Think about the last time someone was kind to you—not just polite, but kind. Think about how that kindness melted something in you. You deserve to feel that way now.

Emotionally mature people recognize that the way they treat themselves is a choice, and they take responsibility for that choice. If you don't choose to treat yourself with kindness, what are you choosing instead?

Common Humanity

Neff's second component of self-compassion is *common humanity*, defined as "recognizing that suffering and personal inadequacy is part of the shared human experience—something that we all go through rather than being something that happens to 'me' alone."[3] As the writer Anne Lamott puts it: "Everyone is screwed up, broken, clingy, and scared, even the people who seem to have it more or less together. They are much more like you than you would believe."[4]

It's easy to presume that some people simply don't have "baggage," or if they do, their baggage is matching, cute, and carry-on size. Everyone struggles in meaningful ways. Still, when *we're* the ones who are clingy, scared, and making new mistakes with every blink, it can feel isolating. Our pain doesn't feel common in those moments; it feels uncommon.

Social media exacerbates our misperception to a dangerous degree—everyone is happy, hot, pregnant, professionally fulfilled, traveling the world, and surrounded by tons of friends. You don't see anyone's acne, or their sister living with the terrifying onset of undiagnosed bipolar disorder, or the affairs people are having to escape their lonely marriages. Domestic violence is undetectable on Instagram, as is a history of sexual abuse, experiencing suicidal thoughts, infertility, ambivalence about parenthood, being in debt, living with a chronic illness, being ghosted, caregiver burnout, an addiction of any kind, the unwieldiness involved in dating after a divorce, hating your job—*most of what we go through is invisible.*

Embracing our common humanity is understanding that we all encounter pain, we all get lost, we all have drama in our families—we all have so much happening behind the scenes. The more you see your problems as uncommon, unrelatable, and unnatural, the closer you move towards self-pity, not self-compassion.

Mindfulness

Neff's third component of self-compassion is mindfulness—feeling your feelings while also recognizing that you're more than what you feel. As Neff explains, "Mindfulness requires that we not be 'over-identified' with thoughts and feelings, so that we are caught up and swept away by negative reactivity."[5]

Neff is hitting us with the therapist version of "Live laugh love," which is: "Feelings aren't facts." Being underidentified with your emotions is equally problematic; repressing what you feel in the name of mindfulness does not a self-compassionate response make.

Take disappointment, for example, by no means an unfamiliar feeling for perfectionists. Sometimes it seems that everything and everyone falls short. That's because everything and everyone does fall short.

Whatever you want therapy, or your relationships, or a quote, or your kids, or your work, or the car you drive, or the family you were born into, or the family you create, or your vacation, or even just your hair products to give you—whatever you want all these big and small pieces of your life to give you—at some point, they're all bound to fall short. This is inevitable. You will feel disappointed, you will be left unsatisfied, and you will want your life to be a different way than it is.

Disappointment doesn't come because you're doing anything wrong; disappointment is everyone's exact trouble. A self-compassionate response would involve giving yourself permission to feel disappointed while also acknowledging that "disappointed" is not the only thing you feel.

Perfectionists waste so much energy trying to churn their disappointment into something else. We keep asking, "How can I get rid of my disappointment?" The better question is "What else do I also feel?"

How Do You Practice Self-Compassion If You Can't Stand Yourself?

We all need connection. To be disconnected is to be in pain. When someone's in pain, the universal compassionate response is: *You're not alone. I'm here.* Notice that response has nothing to do with the pragmatics of a problem. A compassionate response is not a response that offers a plan or emphasizes a way to control the situation. A compassionate response is a response that offers connection.

Also notice that a compassionate response doesn't pronounce to love or like anyone. This is a critical distinction between self-compassion and self-love.

When you extend compassion to someone else, you're not declaring to that person, *I love you, I like you, I think you're funny, I think you're charming, your hair looks good like that, I feel what you feel with you.* You're only saying the last part: *I feel what you feel with you.* A compassionate response says, *I'm with you.*

Self-compassion is not about forcing yourself to like or love yourself. Self-compassion is a resiliency skill that involves acknowledging pain, holding perspective, and acting with kindness. Even if you're annoying the hell out of yourself, even if you can't stand yourself, you can still do those three things.

Also, self-compassion does not have to be a total personality overhaul to be effective. The amount of compassion you extend to yourself is not commensurate to the amount of healing that will unfold as a result. Giving a little bit of empathy is like lighting a candle in a dark room—that tiny flicker goes a long way to brighten the entire space. Self-compassion can be a feather's-weight more grace to yourself, five seconds, you don't even have to get up.

Trauma-Informed Compassion

What clients whose perfectionism developed as a coping mechanism to childhood trauma come to acknowledge is twofold. First, the control tactics (overachieving, people-pleasing, etc.) that gave them a false sense of power as children are recognized as illusory. They didn't have power as a child; their only resource was a rich imagination.

A child will pretend to be omnipotent, invincible, or superficially perfect because pretending is all a child can do.[6] Retreating into your imagination or otherwise disassociating is adaptive in powerless situations. However, the same responses that were adaptive when you were a child with no power become maladaptive later in life, when you do have power.

The second thing clients come to acknowledge is that their desire was never to be perfect; it was only to be loved. To simply be seen, accepted, and embraced without conditions is what the child, who is now an adult, has been obsessed with—not perfection. If you didn't have a sense of emotional safety growing up, that's what you wanted more than anything. What you thought about and wished for—more than any toy or candy or big house or nice clothes—was love.

Can you take that reality in without needing to blame anyone for it, including your parents? Including yourself? We're not playing hot potato with our pain anymore, remember? There's no agency in blame. Your power lies in practicing self-compassion, then taking ownership over your life now.

The experiences you went through made you skilled at disconnection instead of connection, and now sometimes you have trouble with the latter. That's understandable. That doesn't make you bad. Everybody's got some kind of trouble with something. It's not what happened, it's what you do about it.

Shifting from a model of disconnection to a model of connection is like learning a new language. If you stay committed to a new language, it becomes a part of who you are; it changes you and how you experience the world. It takes time to learn a new language.

Learning a new language is impossibly slow, until it's not. For what feels like an eternity, you experience the new language from the outside in. If you stay committed, eventually you'll experience the new language from the inside out. One night you'll dream in the new language; soon enough you'll be telling jokes.

You stay committed to the language of connection both by practicing self-compassion and by surrounding yourself with people who speak connection fluently.

What If You Still Can't Practice Self-Compassion Even after You Know All the Things?

Let's return to Ava. I talked to her for maybe fifteen minutes after the group session in which she LMB'd me. Together, we reached out to four people in the hope that someone could meet her at the rehab center, stay with her for the night, stay on the phone with her while she walked home, something. Nobody picked up.

I gave her a warmline number and we talked about a few online sober communities she could connect with immediately. I also scheduled a check-in call with her for the next morning. Hoping she could borrow my perspective for the night, I did my best to share my honest view of her, which was deeply positive. She said she'd head home, but I didn't feel confident about that. When I tell you I hated opening that office door without being convinced that she would be okay, *I hated opening that door.*

All five other group members were sitting on the hallway floor waiting for her. Without saying a word, they were saying, "We're with you." The visible demonstration of compassion was a powerful moment for me, one that instantly made me feel better. The moment also proved to be powerful for Ava, one that instantly made her feel worse.

Lodged in shame, Ava could not open herself to any amount of compassion. Not from herself, not from me, not from anyone. She already felt like a lost cause. Now she felt that the group was wasting *more* time on her, which exacerbated her sense that she was a burden to everyone. Already exhausted, Ava became distressed and furious upon seeing the five of them in that hallway. She felt that she now owed them something that she didn't have to give.

Ava did not go home that night feeling good or worthy. She didn't end up taking a hot bath, but she also didn't end up drinking more either. For the rest of the LMB night and for many days that followed, Ava remained disconnected from herself. Self-compassion felt like an out-of-touch luxury, and Ava did not practice it. What she did do was continue to choose connection.

Ava chose connection when she chose to attend group, disclose her alcohol consumption, and stay with me after group was over. Even though she was pissed off by it and didn't speak the whole way, Ava also chose connection by letting a group member walk her home.

The following morning, Ava chose connection again (albeit briefly) when she answered my phone call with "I still feel like shit," then hung up on me. When I called her back, she picked up again and stayed on the call.

None of this connection made Ava feel better in the moment; connecting, in fact, felt perfunctory and useless. When you're not connected to yourself, connecting to others can seem pointless. It's not.

Ava got through her relapse by allowing herself to connect to others without demanding that the connection result in an immediate state of change or peace. Though she hated it at the time, Ava now recalls the moment she saw her group members in the hallway as one of the most loving and connective gestures she has ever experienced in her life. Connection can operate retroactively. Salutary choices that make you feel nothing in the moment can be the very choices that enable you to feel safe, strong, joyful, and grateful later.

Being compassionate with yourself is not a button you push. I know it can be difficult; at times, being compassionate with yourself may feel impossible. You can't control when those times will come or how long they'll last, but like Ava, you can choose connection anyway—you always have the power to choose connection. Just because the connection is falling flat now doesn't mean it won't kick in retroactively later.

Reaching out to someone else doesn't have to be some big dramatic thing—it can be as simple as saying, "You want to stay on the phone and not talk while we watch the same show?" or "Will you bring me some food?" or "Can you send me a bunch of dumb memes today 'cause I need to lighten the mood around here?" Certainly, reaching out can also look like explicitly saying, "I'm struggling, can we talk?" or "I really need help," or "I don't think I can be alone right now."

You can also connect anonymously or more indirectly, joining an app-based community or an online forum, for example. Parasocial relationships are those in which you feel close to a character or public figure whom you don't know but who provides you with a sense of connection, support, and comfort. Morning news programs and talk shows, for example, need hosts who are easy to connect with; that connection is parasocial.

Parasocial relationships are no substitute for real-life relationships, but they are meaningful connections, nonetheless. When you're feeling disconnected, you may find yourself watching reruns, for example. *The Fresh Prince of Bel-Air* is my rerun go-to, but maybe you like *Friends? Grey's Anatomy? SNL?* Research demonstrates that we intuitively gravitate towards reruns when we're feeling down because doing so increases our communal sense of belonging and decreases loneliness; it's the parasocial connection that's comforting us. One study in the *Journal of Experimental Social Psychology* showed that watching reruns of your favorite show "buffers against drops in self-esteem and mood and against increases in feelings of rejection commonly elicited by threats to close relationships."[7] Other examples of parasocial connection include rereading your favorite book, listening to a podcast by a host you adore, or going to the Instagram page of a public figure you're inspired by. That connection counts. Opportunities for connection are all around you.

If you absolutely cannot reach out to someone else, accept someone else's bid for connection, engage connection anonymously or indirectly, or lean on a parasocial relationship, hold still.

What I mean by "hold still" is twofold. First, physically be still for a second. The way this comes out when I'm explaining it to my clients is, "Sometimes you just need to stop what you're doing and lie on the floor." Or spread your hands out palms-down on your desk, a wall, or any flat surface, or simply straighten your posture. Take a breath, be still.

Second, realize that you're in a powerful liminal space.

Liminal Space

Limen comes from the Latin root for "threshold." (I really should've taken Latin.) When you're in a liminal space, you're in a state of transition. You have left one place and you're near the entrance to the next, but you're not quite there yet.

Architecturally, a hallway is a liminal space. Anthropologically, *liminality* is defined as "the quality of ambiguity or disorientation that occurs in the middle stage of a rite of passage, when participants no longer hold their pre-ritual status but have not yet begun the transition to the status they will hold when the rite is complete."[8]

Psychologically, liminal spaces feel like being in two places at once while also being nowhere. Mostly the latter. If you're not aware that liminal spaces exist, being in one can feel like you don't belong anywhere and that you've failed. It doesn't seem like it, but you're right on the precipice of a more consistently powerful version of yourself.

The primary challenge in a psychologically liminal space is to allow yourself to feel empty. In a liminal realm, your emptiness and your potential are the exact same thing. When you block your emptiness from existing, you block your potential from developing. Lao Tzu's famous quote reflecting this truth was the title I gave to the very first blog post I ever wrote, "The Usefulness of a Pot Is in Its Emptiness." Clearly, I did not understand SEO at the time.

You have to have done a lot of grief work to be in a liminal space. Grief is always the admission charge for major transition. You have to let go of the parts of you that you've outgrown, hence, the emptiness.

But we long to feel full, not empty.

"Comfort food," for example, isn't food that makes you feel energetic, lighter, or cleansed; it's food that makes you feel full. Emptiness is not a comfort. Feeling empty can be anticlimactic, dull, and silent. In our triple-screen, Amazon Prime lives, we're understandably so averse to feeling empty that we'll do almost anything to fill ourselves up, even when we know it's hurting us.

Being in a liminal space is like being in a waiting room with no cell reception and nothing to do but flip through last year's magazines. It's relaxing for four minutes *tops*, then you start to squirm. The calm feels unsettling. You need a hit of drama to "fill" your attention; you want something to happen to "fill" the time. Boredom is a good sign that you're in a liminal space.

Liminal spaces are necessary for personal growth. When you're in a liminal space, you have to allow yourself to exist in between dichotomies without putting pressure on yourself to pick a side.

For perfectionists who are losing control and gaining power, this looks like allowing yourself to be in the transition space of no longer feeling that your worth hinges on external validation *and yet* not feeling fully confident that you're worthy of all the love, joy, freedom, dignity, and connection the world could ever offer.

To access power in a liminal space, you need to remember that you're not passively feeling bad, empty, or bored for no reason. You are *actively* choosing to stand firm on the threshold of a boundless, more authentic you. Do not retreat from liminal space. Or as they say in recovery, "Don't give up five minutes before the miracle happens."

In short, just because you can't get yourself to take a hot bath doesn't mean you have to destroy yourself. Reach out. Hold still. As the poet and philosopher Mark Nepo so beautifully puts it:

> Live your worries through,
> and your spirit will wake from its fever,
> and you will want others like soup.

Practicing self-compassion is the opportunity of a lifetime. I regret that this rhymes, but the opportunity is always yours to take because the choice is always yours to make. Meeting yourself with compassion instead of punishment is not a one-and-done choice. You have to make it over and over again for your whole life.

Sometimes, choosing self-compassion will be as easy as settling into your bed after the most exhausting day. Other times, it'll be as difficult as getting out of bed after the most exhausting night. At all times, self-compassion will be worth whatever difficulty or ease you encounter.

7

New Thoughts to Think to Help You Stop Overthinking It

TEN KEY PERSPECTIVE SHIFTS TO
HELP YOU FIND THE SUCCESS YOU'RE
LOOKING FOR IN EVERYDAY LIFE

Being in the game is the prize.

RUPAUL

The way you think is built on cognitive habits. Just like behavioral habits, cognitive habits can be helpful, neutral, or unhealthy. Focusing on problem-solving, for example, is a helpful cognitive habit.

When you're in the habit of problem-solving, you regularly focus your thoughts on useful questions when confronted with a challenge—questions like, "What is the problem, exactly?" "Who can help me understand my choices?" and "What is my goal?"

Overthinking, on the other hand, is a distressing and unhealthy cognitive habit. When you're in the habit of overthinking, you regularly focus on useless, circuitous thoughts when confronted with a challenge. Thoughts like, "That was bad. I can't believe I did that, that was so bad. I wish that had never happened."

Overthinking is a powerless act. Overthinking involves either dwelling on events that have already happened and about which you can do nothing (known as *ruminating*) or worrying about things that haven't happened but could *theoretically* happen, through the lens of a worst-case scenario (known as *catastrophizing*).

When you ruminate, you mistake replay for reflection. When you catastrophize, you mistake worrying for preparation.

Trying to change your thoughts one by one is how you exert control; it takes a lot of energy to control your thoughts because you have to monitor and manage each thought as it enters your mind. Engaging a broadened perspective is how you exercise power. When you make a perspective shift, you automatically see things in a new way, a way you can't unsee. Perspective shifts change your thoughts in one fell swoop.

Broadening your perspective doesn't make your old ways of thinking disappear, nor does it need to. Old ways of thinking can exist alongside new ways of thinking. The point is not to get one brand of thinking to dominate over the other; the point is to stay open enough to understand that your perspective is a choice.

The most powerful perspective shift you could ever make is understanding that you're already whole and perfect. While you may sometimes need medication or coffee or music or therapy or some other kind of ameliorative tinkering to get you thriving, that doesn't mean you're broken; that means you are a human being alive in the world.

The ten perspectives you're about to encounter represent the highest-impact shifts for perfectionists to focus on. Your work in this chapter is to be open to these perspectives; there is no sequel task. Being open is a full-time job.

1. Counterfactual Thinking Is a Cognitive Reflex

Counterfactual thinking is when your brain creates alternative scenarios for events that have already taken place. For example, let's say you're driving through an intersection while another driver runs a red light and crashes directly into your car. You spin out and another car hits you. Ten seconds have passed, and the car accident is over.

You're terribly shaken, but you don't sustain any injuries; you walk away with minor scratches. The fact is that you were in a car accident and you walked away uninjured. A counterfactual thought (a thought that *counters* the fact) might be, *I could have died.*

When the alternate scenario you conjure up is more appealing than the reality, that's called an *upward counterfactual* thought—*If only I would've left work early, I wouldn't have been in that accident.* When the alternate scenario you conjure up is less appealing than the reality, that's called a *downward counterfactual* thought—*I could have died in that accident.* Counterfactual thinking is something we all engage in; it's a cognitive reflex.

According to research, we revert to counterfactual thinking to help us prepare for the future, as well as regulate our mood and behaviors.[1] Thinking about how things could be worse, for example, helps us increase our gratitude for our current situation. Our newfound gratitude serves an important "mood-repairing function" after a negative event (*I could have died, thank God I'm alive*).[2] We're able to make ourselves feel better after a distressing event because our brains have the cognitive power to process the unfolding of an alternate reality. That power is counterfactual thinking.

In some cases, upward counterfactuals can also improve our mood and help us regulate our behavior, particularly when it comes to performance.[3] For example, let's say you lose a tennis match after hitting the ball into the net. You then experience the upward counterfactual thought:

"If only I would've extended the trajectory of my shot instead of trying to be so aggressive and win quickly, I could've won the game." That thought helps increase your motivation to try again because you see where you're making the mistake (you're overindexing on risky shots for the sake of speed) and understand how to correct it (modify your behavior by extending the trajectory of your shots). Even though you lost, you're excited to get back on the court and play more strategically.

You need upward counterfactuals to generate progress because if you can't imagine a scenario that would yield a more desirable outcome, you're not going to try to improve. Upward counterfactuals are only beneficial when they focus on specific alterations (referred to as *specificity*) that you have the power to change (referred to as personal agency) within the context of a dynamic that is likely to occur again.[4]

Specificity and personal agency are the factors linked to increased motivation, not the upward counterfactual thought itself.[5]

For example, the following upward counterfactual thoughts are not beneficial:

"I could've won the game." This upward counterfactual isn't beneficial because it doesn't focus on a specific alteration: it has no specificity.

"If only I would've left work early, I wouldn't have been in the accident." This upward counterfactual isn't beneficial because regardless of the time you leave work, you don't have control (i.e., personal agency) over whether another car crashes into you while you're driving. While it may be true that you wouldn't have been in an accident had you left work earlier that day, the causal inference you're grafting over your degree of personal agency is incorrect. You didn't cause the accident because you left work on time, nor can you prevent future accidents by leaving work early. You're pretending you had control then so that you can pretend you have control in the future. The car accident was a random event that is unlikely to repeat and thus renders upward counterfactual thinking as more likely to do harm than good in that scenario.

Upward counterfactuals also serve a preparative function.[6] You go hiking, and your feet are freezing the entire time. You keep thinking, "If only I would've worn warmer socks." Guess who'll be bringing warmer socks next time.

Counterfactuals can be problem-based or character-based:

PROBLEM-BASED: *If only I had had more ways to adjust for the higher production cost, I could have maintained the profit margin.*

CHARACTER-BASED: *If only I weren't such an idiot, I could have maintained the profit margin.*

Counterfactuals can also be additive (you think about adding something to the scenario to improve it) or subtractive (you think about taking something away from the scenario to improve it).[7]

Subtractive thoughts yield only one solution, which is to remove X. Additive thoughts rely on creative problem-solving, which is a better approach because it yields a greater number of possible solutions (increasing both personal agency and motivation, which operate in tandem).[8]

Note the following subtractive counterfactual thought, underlined below. Also note how seamlessly counterfactual thinking can spur punitive self-talk:

If only I hadn't made that impulsive comment in the meeting, I could've been assigned the lead. <u>I need to stop talking in meetings.</u> I always say the wrong thing. When am I going to learn to shut up in meetings?

Here's an example of an additive counterfactual thought, also under-lined below, with a self-compassionate response:

> *If only I hadn't made that impulsive comment in the meeting, I could've been assigned the lead.* <u>*From now on, I could come to meetings with a specific question or comment in mind, or maybe email my thoughts to the team after the meeting, when I've had some time to process whether commenting would be useful.*</u> *I don't always say the right thing at the right time, but everyone has that problem. Ugh, I'm so embar-rassed; this is such a terrible feeling. What can I do for myself that would help me get through this moment? Oh, I'll text Lisa about it; she always makes me laugh. Maybe I'll stop by the grocery store after work and cook myself my favorite dinner tonight. I'll put on some music when I get home, too, that'll be good. Tomorrow is a new day. It's gonna be alright.*

Research demonstrates that the easier it is for you to imagine the counterfactual scenario unfolding, the more influence the counterfac-tual thought will have over your emotional reactivity in either direction (negative or positive).[9] For example, you feel more grateful for being alive after your car flips over three times in a major accident than if you get into a fender bender because you can more easily imagine how the for-mer scenario could have resulted in your death. Similarly, you're more likely to feel frustrated that you missed the bus when you miss it by twenty seconds as opposed to missing it by fifteen minutes. The outcome is the same in both scenarios (you gotta catch the next bus), but you're not basing your emotional state on the outcome; you're basing it on the inten-sity of your counterfactual thought.[10]

Understanding the psychological principle of *contrast effects* helps clar-ify how counterfactuals impact satisfaction levels.[11] The term refers to the way your perception or experience changes based on whatever informa-tion is most salient to you at the time. For example, if everything in a store is more than one hundred dollars except for one scarf that's thirty dollars, the thirty-dollar scarf seems affordable. A thirty-dollar scarf in a dollar store seems expensive. If you're used to carrying a three-year-old and you hold a six-month-old baby, the baby feels light. If you go on three back-to-back dates with men who are all obnoxious and rude, the next guy who so much as chews with his mouth closed will seem like Prince Charming.

In a notable study from the 1990s, researchers examined counterfactual thinking and contrast effects in silver and bronze medalists at the 1992 Summer Olympics. What they discovered was that silver medalists tend to feel worse than bronze medalists because the most salient counterfactual thought after winning silver is, *I could have won gold*, whereas the most salient counterfactual thought after winning bronze is, *I could have not placed*. As the researchers put it, "Imagining what might have been can lead those who do better to feel worse than those they outperform."[12]

In my work with high-achieving perfectionists, I often highlight the Summer Olympics study to engender a sense of permission (and subsequent self-compassion) over the painful experience of coming so close to what you want, then not getting it. Literal or proverbial second-place winners who share their disappointment with others are often unintentionally admonished for being honest about feeling frustrated. Comments like, "You should be thrilled! Are you crazy? It's amazing that you got this far!" are not helpful in such scenarios.

The sting of silver, as I call it, is real—it hurts. You have to acknowledge the hurt so you can extend self-compassion and move forward. Otherwise, you get stuck in a punitive spiral (*I know I did well. So many people would be thrilled with this result, I shouldn't be feeling disappointed. If I can't be happy now, I'm never going to be happy. Why am I like this? I hate this. I hate myself*).

Therapists often prompt clients to bring awareness to their counterfactual thinking because counterfactual thoughts inform everything: our decision-making, satisfaction levels, sense of personal agency, motivation to try again, and sense of frustration, gratitude, regret, bitterness—the list continues. Counterfactual thoughts influence every aspect of our lives.

Perfectionists who are not aware of their counterfactual thoughts are driving on the wrong side of the road. Because perfectionists are people who, more often than not, notice the gulf between the ideal and reality, perfectionists engage in counterfactual thinking throughout the majority of their lives.

It's not a bad thing to engage in counterfactual thinking. Studies show that upward counterfactuals increase motivation in adaptive perfectionists, who make more specific and additive counterfactuals than maladaptive perfectionists do.[13] Counterfactuals become unhealthy when you don't acknowledge them as a cognitive reflex and when you don't understand that you have the power to get them to work in your favor.

Perfectionists who don't acknowledge that counterfactual thinking is a reflex waste energy trying to force themselves to stop thinking about what might have been. Just as your brain can't help but read a word, it can't help but engage in counterfactual thinking. You don't see individual letters side by side and then decide whether you feel like reading them; you see words and read them simultaneously.

Negative events and counterfactual thoughts unfold in tandem. In fact, you're more likely to experience counterfactual thinking after you fail or hit a setback than during moments when things are successfully proceeding for you without incident.[14]

While you can't control the fact that you engage in counterfactual thinking, you do have the power to exploit counterfactuals to help you increase your levels of satisfaction and motivation.

Counterfactuals operate on a continuum ranging from automatic to elaborative.[15] Automatic counterfactual thoughts are reflexive reactions to an event, whereas elaborative counterfactual thoughts are consciously directed, based on how you decide to experience the situation.

For example, if you reflexively feel the sting of silver, you can choose to elaborate on what you came close to getting or you can choose to elaborate on how far you've come, the skills you've gained, how alive you've felt in the process, the relationships you've developed along the way, the bravado you've demonstrated in working towards your goal, and so forth.

Counterfactual thinking is a way in which your brain initially organizes information. How you construct meaning around that information is up to you.

The reality is that unless you live your life as a big fish in a small pond (boring), you cannot be the best at all things at all times. When you become brave enough to risk failure, you're going to play with some heavy hitters and you're going to lose. The loss is proof that you're not allowing yourself to be intimidated by the risk of unknown outcomes, you're bold enough to go for it, and you're allowing yourself to fail forward. Yes, your reflexes will kick in; that's what reflexes do. You don't have control over your unconscious reactions, but you do have the power to choose a conscious response.

Questions that increase awareness of your counterfactual thought patterns include the following:

Is the counterfactual:

- upward or downward?

- general or specific?

- based on a random event that isn't likely to occur again, or based on a repeating dynamic over which you have personal agency?

- additive or subtractive?

- problem-based or character-based?

- automatic or elaborative?

- easy to imagine happening or difficult to imagine happening?

- spurring compassionate self-talk or punitive self-talk?

You disrupt a counterfactual thought pattern by consciously engaging the alternative. Doing so does not require that you eradicate all negative feelings and thoughts associated with the more dysfunctional counterfactual thought. You're allowed to have a layered experience. You can be disappointed and proud. You can be curious about what might have been and grateful for what is.

As is true for any mental construction based on diametric thoughts and feelings, with automatic and elaborative thoughts, you can choose both.

2. Support Comes in Every Color

Alicia started nodding off in the middle of our sessions, *again*. If you're nodding off in therapy with me, it's not me, it's you. I talked with Alicia about what was going on, and she plainly told me that she was physically exhausted. She had just given birth to her third baby, and she'd been back at work for the past month.

She spoke mostly in five-words-tops sentences at the time: "There are no babies here. No one needs me. You have tea." She closed her eyes and leaned her head back: "I love this couch. I want this couch." I laughed, but she didn't. She left her head tilted back and her eyes closed, then I noticed her hands. They were laid open and still at her sides in a way that made me want to put a blanket on her.

With twenty minutes left in our session, I said: "It sounds like you just really need to sleep. Would it be helpful if I closed the curtains, went to the waiting room, and came back in thirty minutes so you can rest? I spread my sessions fifteen minutes apart. I can write my notes outside while you're in here so we can stretch the time. I'll make sure no one comes in."

I can't describe the expression on Alicia's face.

"What? Yes, yes," she said. I stood up to draw the curtains and when I turned back around, she was already lying down with her eyes shut. For a second, I debated with myself about whether to whisper-ask her to take her shoes off my couch, but I took a deep breath and let it be. I slinked out quietly and knocked on my own office door thirty minutes later.

During our next session, Alicia rushed me through my check-in: "I'm fine. Everything's good. Thank you *so* much. Can we do the sleep thing again?" The following two sessions consisted of Alicia coming in, engaging in increasingly brief check-ins, then taking a nap.

Despite my mixed thoughts surrounding the ethics and efficacy of encouraging Alicia to use her therapy to sleep, I ultimately decided that in the immediate short-term, this was the most helpful way I could offer support. We of course talked about her need to carve out more time to sleep in places other than my office, but for that one impossible month of returning to work while pumping, still bleeding, parenting two other small children, and dealing with a postpartum hormonal landslide, the woman needed rest.

Those sleep sessions, as we affectionately referred to them later, reminded me of the crisis work I used to do, where most counseling sessions would be spent securing housing, registering for food banks, prepping résumés, and so forth. Comprehensive mental health support is dynamic, multipronged, and highly individualized.

Processing your thoughts and feelings is obviously important, and at the same time, sometimes the best thing you can do to support your mental health doesn't look the way you might expect mental health support to look.

I've spent plenty of sessions diving into job searches, helping people set up dating profiles after a tough breakup, reviewing application essays, and doing home visits to help organize the suddenly chaotic spaces of people who are unexpectedly caring for their elderly family members. So much happens in each of our lives, every single one of us. Going to therapy is one way to get mental health support; it's not the exclusive way.

Attending to your mental health is like eating—you need to do it daily. Just like you can't eat a big meal on Sunday and expect it to satiate your appetite for the entire week, you can't go to therapy once a week and expect that single forty-five-minute session to satiate your appetite for mental health.

Here are six specific ways to consider aligning yourself and others with more elastic mental health support:

Tangible support: When you're in a depressive episode, everything can feel hard. Texting back is hard. Falling asleep is hard. Waking up is hard. Brushing your teeth is a victory and washing your face is, well, that's just showing off.

We often avoid reaching out to others in the low, everything-is-hard moments because we feel like, *What can they really say to me to make me feel better? Nothing.* And maybe that's true for the moment; maybe there's nothing anyone can tell you that will change whatever happened (or didn't happen), or change the way you feel. But just because someone can't offer you emotional support doesn't mean they can't come over and clean your kitchen.

Tangible support is practical aid. Committing to stopping by two nights a week to walk your dog. Dropping off a healthy dinner on Thursdays. Babysitting for the same three-hour time block every Saturday. Finding and scheduling a plumber for the leak in the upstairs bathroom. These are examples of tangible support that other people can provide for you.

People want to show up for you, so when they say, "Let me know if I can do anything," *let them know.* Tangible support, especially when it's consistent and scheduled, can do wonders for your mental health.

Tangible support unfolds naturally when you're part of a community, but in this fancy modern world of ours, community can feel like a hard-to-come-by luxury.

If you don't have a circle of people in your life right now who proactively approach you to ask if you need anything, you're not alone. Taking the initiative to ask for support is uncomfortable, but perhaps spending long bouts of time in this one precious life of yours feeling disconnected and stuck is more uncomfortable?

You can rely on the generosity of others, and you can also pay for support. Throw as much money as you can afford to at recruiting consistent tangible support. Hire a weekly housecleaning service, see if any neighborhood kids want to help with pets, or send the laundry out to a wash-n-fold.

Not everything has to be about feelings all the time. Sometimes I can't even think about how I feel, let alone feel how I feel. In those moments, a healthy dinner and clean sheets go a long way.

Emotional support: Engaging in talk therapy, therapy apps, an honest conversation with a trusted friend, a hotline, or a warmline—emotional support includes any outlet in which you can safely express feelings while receiving validation, positive encouragement, and (ideally) an informed perspective. If you think therapy is too expensive or you're too busy to engage in it, remember that helping professionals are highly motivated to help. Most therapists offer sliding-scale rates and hours that accommodate work schedules. It's absolutely appropriate to ask a potential therapist if they operate on a sliding scale, or if they know a great therapist or therapy center that does.

Physical support: I'll tell you something my therapist reminded me of once, "Movement changes your nervous system." I pressed: "What kind of movement? Like, tai chi? I'm not sure what you're suggesting." "Any movement." You know the way the best therapists can say two words, stop talking, and leave you feeling as if they've revealed the key to all of life's secrets in under five seconds? She said it in that way.

It's true that even simple stretching releases endorphins, and don't get me started on the miracle drug that is walking.*[16] Body work, breath work, walking clubs, sports groups, yoga, biking—general physical activity is a great way to support your mental health. There's also physical activity specifically designed to support your mental health, such as Dr. Neff's "supportive touch" technique.

As Neff explains, "One easy way to care for and comfort yourself when you're feeling bad is to give yourself supportive touch. Touch activates the care system and the parasympathetic nervous system to help us calm down and feel safe. It may feel awkward or embarrassing at first, but your body doesn't know that . . . Our skin is an incredibly sensitive organ. Research indicates that physical touch releases oxytocin, provides a sense of security, soothes distressing emotions, and calms cardiovascular stress. So why not try it?"[17]

There are several supportive touch techniques on Neff's website (self-compassion.org); let's review two:

HAND-TO-HEART TECHNIQUE: Place your hand over your chest (touch skin to skin if you can, instead of over your clothes). Breathe deeply. Keep breathing deeply and feel your heartbeat if you can.

HAND-TO-ARM TECHNIQUE: Take your dominant hand and place it on your opposite arm, between your shoulder and your elbow. Brush your hand up and down for some physical reassurance.

---

* If you're a person with a physical disability that prevents you from walking, or someone whose level of mobility is challenged at the moment, know that any activity that gets your heart rate up will benefit your mental health. The National Center on Health, Physical Activity and Disability (NCHPAD) has created a playlist of the top exercise-from-home videos, which can be accessed by clicking an icon on the center's YouTube channel. This playlist for kids and adults includes options for all abilities to help you choose an exercise mode that both works for and is enjoyable to you.

Financial support: This is a delicate space for multiple reasons. Sometimes what we need to get ourselves through a crisis and connect to stability is money. If shame is a moat around the castle of asking for help, the moat widens exponentially when asking for financial help.

On the other side of the coin, there's something about offering money as a means of giving support that makes us feel like we're taking the easy way out. We may think we're not offering "real help"; maybe we're even making things worse by enabling dysfunctional behavior?

Offering financial help is not supportive when you repeatedly offer money to someone who continues to demonstrate that the money you give makes it easier for them to stay stuck in their problem. Every circumstance is different, but there are times in life during which asking for money and allowing ourselves to receive financial support is one of the healthiest, strongest things we can do. Similarly, I assure you that giving money is not a cop-out for offering "real help"; it's a generous and immediate way to provide support.

In addition to the bare basics, we all need the occasional new shirt, maybe a colorful planter pot to brighten up our home, a night out with a friend. Are those bottom-line necessities? No. Am I suggesting we increase consumption to boost mental health? No.

What I'm saying is that all those "little extras" that bring anyone in a position of economic privilege a sense of breathing room, *all of us need those*. There's something very essential about little extras.

Financial stress and mental health are inextricably linked. The word "normalize" is beyond annoying at this point, but let's normalize both asking for money and offering money (within boundaries, of course) as a wonderful way to avail ourselves and others of mental health support. Not just for survival essentials like car payments and tampons, but also for "thrival essentials."

It's not in the textbooks, but the truth is that there are times (for example, when your entire life is falling apart) during which the utility of a mani-pedi far exceeds the efficacious capacity of perhaps more conventional supportive measures.

One way to make it easier for others to support us is to be specific about how having the money would help us manage our stress. Remember, you are allowed to ask, and people are allowed to say no.

Community support: A sense of belonging is a cardinal feature of mental wellness. We need community. Period. Communities don't have to be fancy, officially named, broadcast a mission statement, or anything of the sort.

Communities begin with one person and an invitation to connect. A community is any space in which you can regularly give and receive in ways that are meaningful to you. A community can be a group chat with three people on it, a newsletter you engage with, the regulars at the dog park, a connective Instagram page.

Are there advantages to more formal community settings, like churches and new moms' clubs? Sure. It's also nice to connect to communities that are highly flexible, noncommittal, anonymous, or otherwise non-traditional. The existence of multiple options doesn't mandate that you choose between them—engage in however many communities you want to.

Communities unlock entire worlds—even if you "only" make one genuine connection in a year, that's a big deal! That one person belongs to a whole other community, filled with new people, new information, new places to explore, new recommendations for good food and transformative books, and alternative ways of looking at a situation. But mostly, connection. Engaging in community support and interdependence is one of the greatest ways to attend to your mental health.

Informational support: This can include connecting to people who have gone through what you're about to embark upon, or who can offer you information-based clarity on a particular situation. Informational support can also be gained through independent study, like reading books on a topic or taking an online course. When the information sources you connect to are people, there's less emphasis on needing those people to be emotionally supportive. A few examples:

- You're thinking about freezing your eggs and would like to understand more about what the process entails, so you schedule an appointment with a fertility specialist. You also ask a friend to connect you with two of her work friends who both froze their eggs last year.

- You're considering a divorce and meet with a divorce lawyer or mediator to understand the various options and implications associated with separating.

- You're interested in making a career change into teaching, so you send an email out to your network asking to be put in touch with anyone who's currently in the field.

- You'd like to work on your assertiveness skills, so you buy a workbook designed to teach assertiveness techniques.

If you're in therapy, you can certainly talk with your therapist about IVF, getting a divorce, or pivoting to a teaching career, but your therapist may not have direct knowledge of those processes, and even if they do, that's only one person's perspective.

If you're struggling with your mental health, don't assume it's because there's something wrong with you; assume it's because you don't have the support you need. Going to therapy is never going to get all your needs met. Doing any one thing is never going to get all your needs met.

Remember that support comes in every color. Identify what kind of supports you need and do your best to put them in place.

It's not always possible to get the exact support you need, or even half the support you need, but that doesn't mean you shouldn't try to get *any*. Support doesn't add up; it compounds. Get any amount of support you can and build from there.

Don't do the thing where you resist connecting to support because you feel that you should've mastered your problem by now. You can be very good at something, excel at something, love doing it, know everything you're supposed to do, and *still* parts of it will always be hard.

Human beings need support and connection throughout their entire lives. *Including* when things are going well. *Including* when we already know what to do. Availing yourself of support when you're doing well helps sustain your progress. Progress and growth aside, you don't need a reason to connect to support any more than you need a reason to tap your foot while you sit.

It's been said that flexibility is the cornerstone of mental health; how fitting, then, to demonstrate some flexibility in the kinds of mental health support we reach out for and offer.

3. Maintenance Is a Triumph

Most people operate under the dysfunctional assumption that change is a one-step process that is achieved by stopping something or starting something. For example, if you want to work out regularly, you just have to do it. If you want to quit smoking, you just have to quit.

Reducing change to a one-step process makes change seem easier to enact, which helps us in the short run (presumption of future success motivates us to try) and sabotages us in the long run (we can't figure out why it's so hard to do something so damn simple).

In the 1970s, after studying what made some smokers quit while others struggled, Dr. James Prochaska and Dr. Carlo DiClemente created a five-stage model of change.[18] Starting new habits and quitting old ones represent the fourth stage of change, not the one and only.*[19]

---

* A sixth stage was later added to the model, "termination," in which a person no longer has any desire to return to negative behaviors and no longer has to put any effort into maintaining their change. This is a somewhat controversial stage, particularly in addiction treatment models, so it is sometimes left out.

Prochaska and DiClemente's five-stage model of change reveals one of the best-kept secrets in the world of mental health: just *thinking* about what you want to change without doing a single thing about it is a stage of change.[20]

The notion that simply thinking about what you want to change is a legitimate, critical stage of change is so rational and obvious after the fact (of course you need to think about what you'd like to change and how you'd like to change it before you enact the change). Yet, when trying to gauge our progress, so many of us encounter the following sentiment:

All I do is think about changing X and talk about changing X, but I never do it.

As you can imagine, this statement doesn't exactly roll out the red carpet for a self-compassionate response to enter your mind.

Here's an unlock for anyone (especially procrastinator perfectionists) beating themselves up about why they haven't started changing what they most want to change: not only have you already taken the first step, but you're also probably ready for stage three.

A brief overview of Prochaska and DiClemente's five-stage model of change:

1. **PRECONTEMPLATION:** You're not thinking about changing. You're simply engaging with life and collecting experiences.

2. **CONTEMPLATION:** You begin to encounter repeating thoughts and feelings about that little collection of experiences you've gathered. Some things are working well for you; others are not. You start thinking about whether you'd like to change, how you'd like to change, when you'd like to change, why you'd like to change, etc.

3. **PREPARATION:** By this stage, you've decided that you want to change, and you prepare to enact the change. You might ask around to see how others have successfully made similar changes. You might start ordering books or attending workshops. You might make some purchases

that enable the change (a kettlebell, for example). You might begin announcing to people that you're about to make the change.

4. **ACTION:** The action stage is marked by behavioral changes. This is the stage that most people associate with change because it's the stage that's most visible. If you've made it all the way to this stage, it's taken a whole hell of a lot of mental energy, time, reflection, work, and emotional risk. No matter what happens next, you have much to be proud of.

5. **MAINTENANCE:** A crucial and often overlooked stage. It can take so long to decide on what you'd like to change. After deciding, you have to prepare for the change. After you've prepared, you have to enact the change. By the time you get to the part where you're actually doing the thing you said you would do, it's easy to think the tough work is behind you and you can hit cruise control now. Ironically, the maintenance stage is the one that requires the most support. Regression is a natural part of growth. You will regress, and when you do, you need support around you to remind you that regression and failure are not the same thing. Without support around you after a regression, getting back on track feels like starting over at square one (which it's not). Temporary changes are easy; maintaining change is the real challenge.

Apart from precontemplation, each stage of change requires a great deal of work, attention, time, and energy. Thinking is included in this work.

It's challenging to encounter conflicting thoughts about what you want while weighing those thoughts against your values and goals. Our identities, responsibilities, roles, and desires are fluid and require constant calibration (i.e., thinking). These calibrations take time.

I frequently ask clients, "When you hear someone say, 'These things take time,' what does that mean to you?" The responses I get usually circle around the idea that change is not an instantaneous process: "I know,

Rome wasn't built in a day" or "Change doesn't happen overnight." I follow up with, "Yes, but what does 'not overnight' mean to you?"

I want to know, is my client thinking in terms of days, weeks, months, seasons, or years? For New York City perfectionists, "not overnight" tends to mean "by the next business day," or, if we're in an emotionally generous space, three business days.

When you acknowledge that change doesn't happen overnight, which unit of time do you then default to as a fair reference point? Understand that whatever default time frame you abide by, passing that time frame without moving through all five stages will make you feel like you're failing, even if you're doing everything right.

You can spend years in any one stage of change. The amount of time you spend consciously engaging in whatever stage of change you're in is not a barometer of inefficiency. The amount of time berating yourself for how long each stage took you or is taking you is what's inefficient.

Someone who spent eight years in stage one, for example, might fixate for months on this unhelpful thought: *I can't believe it took me eight years to realize I don't like my job.* We all want to be so efficiently enlightened.

As a perfectionist, you will constantly encounter some version of the question "Am I doing enough?" Beyond using that question as a ringing bell to remind you that your worth is not tied to your output, try to remember that it's not always about the new goals you're able to achieve; it's also about the old goal achievements you're able to maintain—the relationships you keep in wonderful standing, the parts of your job you continue to perform so well, any healthy lifestyle choices you remain committed to.

Whatever the word "success" means to you, obtaining success and maintaining success are two very different things. Included in my answer to the "Am I doing enough?" question is a personal mantra born from the five-stage model of change: *maintenance is a triumph.*

4. Swap "Better or Worse" for "Different"

Every summer, my family spends some time at a tiny beach off North Carolina's coast aptly called Carolina Beach. Most mornings, iced coffee and apple-juice box in hand, my daughter and I walk along the sandy boardwalk before the wood gets too hot to go barefoot. There's a surf shop there that opens early; we like to pop in.

As we enter, the guy behind the register, Clint, nods at the giant blue bowl shaped like a wave. It's full of saltwater taffy. "Go on, that's why it's there," he says. The taffy has melted and come back to room temperature many times over, so we can never get every bit of the wrapper completely off. We eat it anyway.

We spend a good ten minutes in the front of the shop, shaking up snow globes featuring a shirtless Santa in flip-flops, trying on baseball caps, just messing around. In the back of the store, Clint keeps a hermit-crab sanctuary.

Apparently, hermit crabs are high-maintenance creatures. Clint rescues them from owners who mistakenly think they're an easy pet. He makes the hermit crabs little furniture out of wood (miniature sofas, tiny ottomans!).

In attempting-to-be-fancy handwriting, right on the glass of one of the aquariums, a sign reads, "Hermit Crab Real Estate Co." Clint makes the same joke every time about how the hermit-crab housing market isn't thriving, but he can't figure out why. He laughs heartily at his own jokes, which in my opinion is an excellent quality. Carolina Beach is full of people with excellent qualities.

There's a carnival off the boardwalk—it's a small one, but it's a good one. Fresh-caught fish is the daily lunch special, grilled and seasoned to perfection by my husband. You have the sand to yourself at night because nobody's on the beach. There's just a showy moon reflecting off the inky water and that gorgeous wave-crashing sound.

The entire week, we all smell like some combination of coconut sun-screen, bonfire smoke, and the ocean. There's no place in the world I'd rather spend my summer vacation than North Carolina's coast; it's perfect.

Why am I telling you all this?

Because Carolina Beach is not one of the world's premier travel desti-nations, but it is to me.

Many people will rush to tell you how Carolina Beach could never compare to a city like Paris, for example, and they would be right. What's overlooked is this: Paris could also never compare to Carolina Beach.

We make rapid comparisons that our minds automatically plug into hierarchies of first-rate, second-rate, better, worse, etc. Get out of the mind-set of better or worse and get into the mindset of different.

Paris is not better than Carolina Beach; it's different. Carolina Beach is not better than Paris; it's different.

Comparing yourself to others is a maladaptive waste of your energy. You as a person are a whole world of cities unto yourself. You're so dy-namic that you couldn't possibly begin to measure yourself against some-one else, and you do yourself a disservice every time you do. You won't be for everyone; that doesn't mean you need to change.

We get so stuck on what we think we're not, then we compare our-selves into an oblivion:

I'm not as smart as she is, so I could never do what she does. I'm not as hot as them so I could never pursue them. I'm not as funny as all the other people getting up on stage, so I could never get up on stage.

Self-imposed upper limits on what you can and cannot do and who you can and cannot be are control tactics. You're trying to control your vulner-ability to getting hurt.

Keeping your world small is a protective mechanism enacted by the part of you that does not understand that when you're connected to your inherent worth, you have a built-in protection system. Yes, you will fall, and yes, you will feel the fall. But because you know your worth, the fall will not define you.

There's so much subjectivity in whether you're chosen or not, whether you're considered "the best" or not, whether you're even considered "good" or not. It's all so silly; it doesn't mean anything.

What matters is that you're living your life according to your values. There's no point in comparing yourself to others because for one thing, you don't know what's going on in someone else's private world. And for another, no one has the exact same set of values as you do.

Enacting your power looks like compassionately telling the part of yourself that wants to keep your world small the following message: *What hurts me more than falling is not being able to be my full self.*

Whatever you want to do, go out and do that. You're not gonna do it in the same way as someone else did it; that's what makes it valuable. It's not unfortunate that Paris can never be Carolina Beach. Paris is Paris. It's also not unfortunate that Carolina Beach can never be Paris. Carolina Beach is Carolina Beach. The only thing that would be unfortunate is if one city tried to be more like the other, because then it would have to be less of itself.

5. Happiness Is Experienced in Three Stages; So Is Stress

I have no idea what your morning routine is. Coffee? Tea? Snooze button? Do you skip breakfast like I do? What I am sure of is that at some point after you wake up, you're engaging in a psychological activity called *affective forecasting.*

Affective forecasting is when you play psychic and predict your future emotions, something we all do every day.[21] For example, on Saturday morning, you might predict that you'll feel relaxed for much of the day. On the day of a big presentation, you might predict that you'll feel relieved after the presentation is over.

What's important to know about affective forecasting is that it stretches beyond the day you're currently experiencing and into your perception of future events.

If you're going on vacation two months from now, for example, you might predict that you'll be happy on that vacation. Even though you're sitting at your desk not experiencing anything particularly enjoyable, your emotional prediction of your future state engenders happy feelings in the moment. In the research world, happiness based on the prediction of a positive outcome for a future event is known as *anticipatory pleasure*; sometimes it's also called *anticipatory joy*.[22]

Conversely, if you predict that you'll experience negative emotions during some future event (an upcoming speech, for example), your prediction will lead to stress in the moment, even though you're not actively engaged in a stressful task. Feeling stressed based on predictions of future stress is known as *anticipatory anxiety*.[23]

Anticipatory joy and anticipatory anxiety are powerful. The affective direction of your anticipation has been shown to impact memory, motivation, social anxiety, planning, and corresponding emotional states, in addition to impacting the way neural mechanisms in your brain are operating. Researchers Dr. Silvia Bellezza and Dr. Manel Baucells describe the power of anticipation succinctly: "Anticipation is such an important source of pleasure and pain."[24]

In examining the power of anticipation, Bellezza and Baucells note that it's not just the anticipation but the event itself (the vacation or the speech) as well as recalling the event that work together to compose the "total utility" of an experience. In other words, happiness is experienced in three stages: anticipation, event, and recall—Bellezza and Baucells's AER model.

We tend to think of happiness as existing primarily in the event itself, but we can extract so much happiness from anticipating and recalling (reminiscing about) the event.

Anticipation is a critical consideration for well-being because we spend a lot more time anticipating the events of our lives than engaging in them.

You anticipate a date for five days; the date itself lasts three hours. You anticipate a vacation for months; the vacation itself lasts one week. Movies, meals, a kiss, work bonuses, getting together with friends, Saturday mornings—if the ability to pleasurably anticipate these events was taken away from you, how would that alter your quality of life?

In his 2010 TED Talk, "The Riddle of Experience and Memory," behavioral economist and famed psychologist Dr. Daniel Kahneman posed a question to the audience: "What kind of vacation would you plan if your memory of the vacation would be erased?"

Your ability to recall at will the events that made you happy is also a prominent aspect of your well-being. We can create recall cues (framed pictures, displayed mementos), talk about enjoyable moments with others, or privately reminisce—the event doesn't need to continue for you to continue to extract enjoyment from it.

The AER model works in the same way for stress. We often justify agreeing to do things we don't want to do by overindexing on the event aspect of the AER model while minimizing the impact of the other two stages.

For example, we justify agreeing to get coffee with someone whom we don't really want to see by saying something like, "It'll just be half an hour and then I'll leave." No. It'll be the anticipatory anxiety for the week leading up to that half hour, the half hour itself, and then the negative recall of how you felt annoyed and immediately resentful upon sitting down, didn't want to be there, and couldn't believe she said that, even though she always says stuff like that, and that's why you don't like hanging out with her in the first place.

When it comes to agreeing to engage in events we don't want to engage in, there's nothing quick about quick catch-up drinks or quick calls or quick meetings.

The anticipation of a negative event can be so salient that, as author and psychologist Dr. Ramani Durvasula notes, "Often the threat of being hurt and actually being hurt are experienced in the same way."[25] Nothing is happening, and yet you are distressed.

Through intentional planning and intentional recall, you have the power to exploit the AER model to extend the pleasure of positive events. Through increased awareness and the implementation of boundaries, the AER model can also be exploited to minimize and altogether avoid the distress associated with negative events.

6. A Feather's-Weight More Weighs a Lot

Whenever I have a client (and I have been this client myself) who barrels into therapy announcing some major change, how they already feel so much lighter, how the mental shift was *so* easy, how they can't believe that they're suddenly just over them, completely done with sugar, never going to "allow themselves" to be depressed again, and so on, I iron my skirt out with my hands, then take a deep breath.

Sustainable strategies for growth are marked by subtlety, not aggression. Incrementalism—the idea that change faithfully made in small degrees adds up to significant progress—is an example of a subtle approach to growth.

Subtlety is powerful.

The closer subtlety comes to being undetectable, the more powerful the subtlety is. Like effective subtlety, effective healing unfolds without detection. Healing is less often big and bold and more often minute and silent. In hindsight, you can see that the signals of progress were there. In real time, healing feels too slow to count as legitimate growth.

Healing is a series of tiny evolutions, born from ostensibly negligible choices, carried out day after day; it's most often expressed in moments that have no witness other than yourself. These invisible "nothing" moments are where the magic happens.

Healing is an honest acknowledgment made silently in your head—*I'm lonely, I'm ready, I'm scared.* Healing is putting your phone down to rest instead of falling asleep with it in your hand. Healing is giving yourself permission to not smile when you don't feel like smiling. Healing is drinking half a glass of water instead of drinking no water. Healing is feeling your feelings for ten minutes instead of numbing out for three days. Healing is washing the dishes piled up in the sink. Healing is letting yourself cry during the movie. Healing is anything you do when you act on behalf of your most authentic self.

Healing requires an intense amount of work, but healing does *not* require that the intensity of the work be experienced in a consolidated fashion. Motivation, impulse control, support, vulnerability, self-compassion—none of this stuff needs to arrive via freight delivery on your front lawn before you can be ready to heal.

Accessing a feather's-weight more consistently, not perfectly—that's all you need to heal. When it comes to healing, a feather's-weight more weighs a lot.

Incrementalism runs in opposition to the radical trend currently saturating the wellness space: radical self-love, radical forgiveness, radical self-care, radical everything. A radical approach is an extreme approach. While radical approaches to healing may seem ideal for perfectionists who tend to gravitate towards extremes, they often prove to be the opposite.

The notion of radical healing is a precarious one for perfectionists, who tend to attach an immediate expectation of "radical results" to the concept. If positive results don't come in a linear manner commensurate to the output (which they won't, because healing is not a linear process), perfectionists end up feeling like radical failures.

While radical approaches are helpful for a lot of people, keep in mind that they represent only one of an infinite number of ways to heal.

Radical anything sounds bold and sexy—it sounds like the thing cool people do. Meanwhile, incrementalism is not sexy, it's not thrilling, it's not trendy, it's not exciting to talk to other people about ("Last night I drank half a glass of water before bed")—it's not even visible most of the time.

Incrementalism is a little-by-little, inch-by-inch, slowly-but-surely, entirely unceremonious affair. Incrementalism is a hard sell, except that it's so effective.

Healing is boring sometimes; no one tells you that. Amidst the tedium, we look for the shortcut, but I've never seen anyone take a shortcut to healing that worked in real life. Have you? As the expression goes, "Doing the work is the shortcut."

7. The Difference between a Struggle and a Challenge Is Connection

The difference between what we struggle with and what we're challenged by lies not in the task itself, but in the amount of support we connect to as we engage the task. When we're dealing with something that we don't know how to do but we feel we have guidance and that someone understands us, it's a challenge. When we're dealing with something we don't know how to do and feel we have no guidance and that no one understands us, it's a struggle.

Challenges are energizing because, even though we're doing something difficult, we're connected. Connection builds energy. Struggles are exhausting because we're isolated. Isolation drains energy.

It is dangerous to be isolated. Being isolated is not the same as being alone. The latter can be healthy—a form of intellectual, creative, physical, spiritual, or emotional incubation from which you emerge restored and energized. Being isolated, on the other hand, is never healthy.

When you're isolated, whether you know it or not, you don't feel safe. Clients often protest that statement with an explanation that goes something like, "No, I *do* feel safe when I'm isolated. When I'm alone, no one can hurt me."

Feeling "less in danger" is not the same as feeling safe.

Safety requires connection. When you're isolated and you don't feel safe, you make every decision from a posture of defense. Subsequently, your decisions (and your life) become a reflection of fear instead of a reflection of your true, secure, whole, and perfect self.

Let's also clarify that struggle in and of itself is not a virtue-producing experience. I always bristle at the expression "What doesn't kill you makes you stronger." That's not true.

What doesn't kill you might traumatize you to the point of disintegrating your memory recall. What doesn't kill you might push you into addiction. What doesn't kill you might make you suicidal or parasuicidal. What doesn't kill you might lead you to physically or emotionally abuse your children because you don't know how to handle the overwhelming nature of your struggle.

Struggle does not guarantee resilience. A more accurate expression would be "What doesn't kill you forces you into a position where you have to choose between connection or isolation, and choosing connection makes you stronger." (Not as slogan-ready per se, but accurate nonetheless.)

It was never the terrible things that happened to you that made you stronger; it was the resiliency-building skills you engaged to process the terrible things. What doesn't kill you *can* make you stronger, but only if you feel your feelings, process your experience (i.e., figure out what the experience means to you), and engage the protective factors around you—mainly, the power of connection.

Support is not just an exchange of information or aid; support is an exchange of connection.

Fingers crossed, toes crossed, everything crossed—the field of psychology will continue to shift towards the examination of how we thrive as interdependent communities as opposed to how the independent, supposedly pathological person suffers. In this collective tilt towards the sun, instead of asking, "What's wrong with you?" the field will ask, "How can we better connect to one another?" The field will ask the latter question because while struggle doesn't automate resilience, it turns out that connection does.

As Oprah and psychiatrist Dr. Bruce D. Perry point out in their astonishingly informative and inspiring book *What Happened to You?: Conversations on Trauma, Resilience, and Healing,* connection is what builds resilience, not suffering. Connection carries what Dr. Perry refers to as a "buffering capacity" to trauma and stress.

One of the most significant findings in Perry's research is that your "relational health" has more predictive power over your mental health than the adversity you've encountered. Perry defines relational health in this way: "Essentially, connectedness—i.e. the nature, quality, and quantity of connection to family, community, and culture."[26]

What Perry is saying is that it's not the degree of fucked-upness from your past that holds the final say on your ability to be joyful and thrive, it's the quality of connections you build into your life now.

Connection is the ultimate arbiter of mental wellness. When you're disconnected, you can't heal or grow; you can only numb and languish. Connection isn't something that happens to you; it's a choice you make.

You'll encounter challenges throughout your entire life, both unexpected and chosen. As a eudaemonically oriented perfectionist, you wouldn't have it any other way. While challenge is inevitable (and welcomed), struggle doesn't have to be.

Another expression I bristle at: "God doesn't give us more than we can handle." What if that platitude isn't true either? God, life, the universe, intelligent design—whatever you want to call it, the language is not relevant.

Maybe life does give us more than we can handle so that we have no choice but to reach out to one another and connect. Otherwise, we might only connect when it felt easy or instantaneously good. Maybe God never gives us more than we can handle *together.*

8. Simple Isn't Easy

Humans have a special talent for complicating simplicity. We make a spectacle out of simple; it's what we do. Listening, for example, is a simple act. "Listen" is an anagram for "silent," *stop talking.* So many people can't do it.

Not eating when you're not hungry seems simple enough, right? Fifteen out of ten best friends agree, it's incredibly simple to not respond to your ex's lazy/late-night/intoxicated/otherwise shitty "yo" texts. It's very simple to pick a show to watch; we cannot possibly turn the leisurely act of watching TV into a stressful event, could we? Oh yes, we can.

We all know what to do to live better; it's not a big mystery: go to bed earlier, eat five servings of fruits and vegetables a day, hang out with kind people instead of terrible people, take the stairs. We could all dramatically change our lives if we "just" started doing a few simple things regularly, and we know that. And we still don't do them.

The point that doing the right thing is so simple and yet so hard is a universal experience. Whatever simple thing you're working on that you still can't figure out how to do, it's okay. Everyone has a stack of simple things that are hard for them. Simple isn't easy.

As perfectionists set their sights on complicated, ambitious goals, we're also all working on some very, *very* basic goals. If you forget that simple isn't always easy, or you never learned that in the first place, you have no understanding as to why you're having trouble. You expect to do the simple things effortlessly.

When you conflate simple with easy, you don't give yourself a runway of patience or self-compassion to take off from when approaching simple tasks. Additional examples of simple tasks include turning off the TV when you know you need to get some sleep, not yelling, breathing deeply, putting your phone down while you're playing with your kids, and my personal white whale—drinking water.

Without patience or self-compassion, you'll respond to the difficulty of simple tasks with self-punishment: *Why am I like this!? I can't believe I can't do something so simple. I'm the worst. What's wrong with me?!*

Because you're in a punitive space, your thought-action repertoire will narrow, and your negativity will grow.

Because you're not happy about what is, you'll spiral into dysfunctional counterfactual thinking about what could've been.

Because what could've been seems so much more appealing, you'll start to feel like a failure.

Because you feel like a failure, you'll feel justified self-sabotaging any good you previously opened yourself up to because it doesn't make sense to you that good things could fit in your bad, failing, terrible life.

All of this is in your head.

Meanwhile, when you assume simple *should* be easy, you don't give yourself any credit for the simple things that *are* easy for you. Honoring the notion that simple isn't easy not only helps you to be more compassionate with yourself but it helps you to see your strengths.

One of my best friends is great at getting toddlers to eat healthy foods. For a long time, she didn't recognize the value in her skill because her approach is both simple and easy for her—appeal to kids' senses and imagination instead of their logic, make sure they're hungry when they sit down, get them to help make the food, and have fun.

It wasn't until her neighbors began begging her to help them get their kids to eat a healthy dinner that she realized, "Oh, this thing that's so simple and easy for me is really tricky for other people."

At the opportunity cost of exploiting their natural strengths, perfectionists often focus on trying to improve their weaknesses. Perfectionists think, "Once I turn all my weaknesses into strengths, I'll be perfect/ready/better/unstoppable/worthy."

As long as you are a human being, you will always have weaknesses and limitations. Wellness is not about figuring out how to get rid of your weaknesses; it's about accepting your weaknesses so you can deploy your energy into maximizing your strengths.

We've been trained to view mental health through a lens of pathology and deficit: *What's wrong with me, and how can I fix it?* That kind of thinking is on the way out. Thirty years from now, therapy is going to center on the exploration of what's going well and why. Don't wait until the field catches up with strengths-based models to engage the following questions:

What are you easily getting right?

What is the skill set involved?

What would happen if you applied that skill set to other areas of your life?

There's always something going right. No one's getting it right all the time, but more importantly, no one's getting it wrong all the time either. Turn your attention towards your strengths.

But what about gaining insight and self-awareness? How can I strive towards my potential if I abandon my efforts to improve my weaknesses?

Productive self-improvement factors in the law of diminishing returns. When it comes to understanding your weaknesses, basic insight is enough. It's not necessary or useful to delve into the nuance of why you're not good at something. You don't need to write a book of poetry about how your weaknesses were born on a dewy April morning and will always love the smell of cold grass.

Manage your weaknesses with boundaries and support while you focus on maximizing your strengths.

When you have a true passion for something you're not good at, that's not the same as having a weakness; it just means you're a beginner. When you're trying to improve upon that which you hold passion for, you're not hemorrhaging energy because you're being pulled, not pushed. It's different.

Refine the strengths you already possess. Leaning heavily on your gifts is what explodes your potential. Ignoring your gifts while you attempt to triage your shortcomings puts that explosion of potential on pause.

Your gifts are the things that are both simple and effortless for you. We underestimate the value of our gifts because they come to us easily. It's one of the first questions I silently ask myself when meeting a new client: "What does this person do so well, so naturally, so easily, that they don't even realize it's a gift?" I've never met a person who doesn't have a gift.

Being compassionate with yourself about the simple things that are hard for you is a choice you have the power to make. Acknowledging the gifts inside the simple things that are easy for you is also a choice you have the power to make.

9. Energy Management Beats Time Management

Several years ago, I read a life-changing article in *Harvard Business Review* titled "Manage Your Energy, Not Your Time" by Catherine McCarthy and Tony Schwartz. The article discussed how we treat time management as the ultimate key to getting things done while we neglect our health and wellness, thereby draining our energy. What McCarthy and Schwartz pointed out was that the unlock to thriving isn't managing our time; it's managing our energy.

Time scarcity is a top grievance; we all say we want more time. If we just had more time, we could see our friends and family more, exercise regularly, plan the trip, write the book, prep the healthy meals, catch up on sleep, switch jobs, or start dating.

Treating specific units of time as primary drivers in your decision-making is a collective-mentality echo from the Industrial Revolution. Excuse me, are you pulling a lever on a steam engine right now? No. Are you wearing a canvas-colored bleak apron dress right now? No. Are you eating mutton and gruel for dinner next Friday night? No. The Industrial Revolution is over.

You're not desperate to find a spare fifteen minutes, you spent an hour watching trash TV last night before lurking all over Instagram. What you're desperate for is not the time to do it; it's the energy to do it.

As economist Sendhil Mullainathan explains in conversation with fellow economist Katy Milkman, "People who consider themselves 'time-poor' think they're in the business of time management, but actually they're in the business of bandwidth management. Bandwidth operates according to different rules than time."[27]

Mullainathan points out that different activities require varying degrees of mental engagement and that "bandwidth doesn't just switch like time does. You need to think of arranging your time like you might arrange artwork on the wall. "Does this actually fit conceptually next to this thing?" not, "Can I squeeze it in?"[28]

How many times have we had the time to do something but the mere thought of beginning the task elicits that blah sense of *I just can't* defeat? You're defeated because you ran out of energy, not because you ran out of time.

Of course, it's true that we're sometimes legitimately unable to find time, but as celebrated entrepreneur Seth Godin says, "If it's not a reason for everyone in your situation, it's an excuse."

Psychologists have long known that procrastination is not a time-management issue; it's an emotional-regulation issue. When we don't focus on energy management, we've gone through the day with no boundaries and no recovery periods. By the time we get home, we're so knotted up with unprocessed clumps of feelings and little mental ailments of every sort that we couldn't possibly *begin* to untangle them.

We figure the best we can hope for is a little "me time," which bears an eerie resemblance to numbing and avoidance (because it *is* numbing and avoidance). Patterns of numbing and avoidance don't make anyone feel productive, but they especially don't make perfectionists feel productive. This is, in a word, problematic.

Perfectionists love being productive. We vow that we're no longer going to care about or emphasize productivity while simultaneously caring about and emphasizing productivity. Our productivity is the main score board we look up at when determining if we won or lost the day.

How do we change this? We don't.

Productivity is rapidly (and unfairly) becoming the dirtiest word in wellness. Ironically, vilifying productivity is a waste of time and energy. There's nothing wrong with being productive. It feels great to be productive when what you're doing is aligned with your values.

Focusing on productivity becomes dysfunctional when you're striving towards goals you don't care about or in a manner that violates your integrity. Focusing on productivity also causes problems when you use "time" on the x axis and "task completion" on the y axis as the exclusive barometer of your productivity.

Anything you do to protect, save, restore, and build your energy is productive. Productive activities include but are not limited to sleeping, listening to music, lingering in bookstores, taking a bath, washing your car, completing the work assignment, good conversation, cooking, redecorating, watching a movie, getting a manicure, playing basketball, reading, walking, and singing in the shower.

Anything that helps you operate with premium energy is productive. With premium-quality energy, you can access your abilities in a way that "burnt-out you" could never compete with. One hour of premium-quality energy will serve you better than ten hours spent approaching a task while feeling rushed, resentful, disengaged, or exhausted. Half-assing a job for twice the amount of time does not equal a job well done.

Maintaining premium energy is what gives you the stamina for the never-ending task of rising to your potential. It's great that you think about productivity so much; now you get to enjoy being productive in dynamic ways instead of reducing productivity to a task-completion race.

You are not on the earth to complete tasks and then die. You are not a bar graph of output. You are a human being.

You have deep wants, curiosities, gifts, needs, and, yes, work you need to get done. Work you're *excited* to get done. You have so much to give and so much to receive. Giving and receiving is what maintains energy just like inhaling and exhaling maintains breathing.

If you're exclusively focused on output and don't allow yourself to receive anything, you're going to burn out. It's like only exhaling and calling that breathing. You're skipping half the cycle. You need to inhale, *duh*. Especially as a woman, you need to allow yourself to receive (less of an obvious *duh* because of complex cultural imprinting, but still).

Receiving is half the work. Receiving is productive.

Don't worry about getting so lost in your leisure that you won't return to your work. You're a perfectionist; the drive within you to excel is compulsive, so you won't be able to help returning to your work.

Enjoy the fact that what's initially so hard about being a perfectionist is the same quality that makes it so great to be a perfectionist later. You do not have it in you to chill and do the bare minimum. Imagine the nicest person you know trying their hardest to be nasty and mean. They're still being considerate, right?

Sleep, make some art, work, have sex, walk through the park in the fall—productivity is anything that energizes you without hurting you. What energizes you without hurting you? How might your life change if you did more of that?

10. Closure Is a Fantasy

"I just want closure." I've heard those words said so many times. I always ask the same question in response: "What does closure look like for you?" Every answer is different, but a common thread binds them: the desire for closure reveals a fantasy.

Closure is a fantasy wherein you can bookend remnant confusion with bricks of logic so that everything makes perfect sense. Closure is a fantasy wherein all pain can be justified and all suffering exists for a righteous reason. Closure is the fantasy that you get to pick which feelings are attached to which memories. Closure is the fantasy that you can catalog your pain, put it in the emotional version of alphabetical order, and then have it stay organized. Closure is the fantasy that you can always exfoliate away the rough surface of an experience to reveal its reassuringly pure and glistening core.

Closure is also about the fantasy that you can no longer be penetrated by the pain, that you are officially done having to deal with something, that your proverbial therapy paperwork is red-stamped HEALED.

When we say we want closure, what we really want is control. Understandably, we want to hold our past, our connections, our traumas, our memories, and all the attendant emotions on our own terms. If we go one level deeper, when we say we want closure, what we're really saying is that we're grieving.

Grief is a word that's used interchangeably with bereavement, but grief is not exclusively about the physical death of a person. You grieve whenever you have to let go of something that you're not ready to let go of.

The demand for closure is an expression of cognitive perfectionism. Seeking a complete list of reasons "why" is an analytical approach to grief. You can't apply analytics to grief. You can't perfectly understand grief.

Before I started practicing, I believed that everything happens for a reason. I don't believe that anymore. Sometimes, not only is there not a perfect answer for "why," there's no answer at all.

Focusing on the need for closure is a way for us to both delay and process our loss. Another way to process loss is to move through the part where you try to control your pain and into the part where you access your power.

Power in grief involves allowing diametric states to coexist. Our desires and experiences as human beings are regularly diametric. We want freedom and security, indulgence and moderation, spontaneity and routine. We want everyone to be treated equally, and we also want status. We want to connect deeply to those around us, and we also want everyone to leave us alone so we can look at dumb shit on our phones in peace.

Our relational experiences can also be diametric. A parent can both neglect us and love us. A colleague can be met with both appreciation and distrust. We can feel so relieved upon leaving a relationship and miss the person still. These aren't contradictory experiences; they're whole experiences.

I don't like it when people say things like, "Your freedom is on the other side of your fear." There is no other side. Mental health is not a door you walk through; it's also not a staircase, or a checklist, or anything designed to be completed.

Experiences swirl around in spheres. When you demarcate healing with midway points and finishing lines, you make healing a race and something that ends. Healing is neither. Spheres have no sides.

Wanting closure is about wanting to take a whole experience and reduce it down to one static piece. One story that doesn't change. One predominant theme. One overarching sentiment. It's a shared myth floating around in our collective bobbleheads—that healing means you streamlined your internal world so that everything is clean and explainable.

Healing is less about establishing resolution and more about being able to center yourself in the parts of your life that remain unresolved. Yes, sometimes you can take what's shattered and piece it back together into a mosaic that's even more beautiful than it was before it broke. When you can do that, I'm hand-on-my-heart thrilled for you. Your life will feel like you're living inside of art.

At the same time, not everything is a "teachable moment."

Some moments are devastating, retching, abominable, horrible. Period. We don't need to transmute every uncomfortable emotion into something shiny and useful.

We are coming dangerously close to operating under the notion that being upset for more than a few hours means you're unhealthy. It's somewhat surprising to me that we haven't turned crying into a disorder.

There are so many events in life that we don't stand a chance at achieving closure with. It's important to let people hurt, not only in especially painful moments but also in everyday life.

Beyond external events, there's the closure-less experience of navigating the complex, ever-changing *internal* world of our identities, desires, perceptions, and passions—all of which are *supposed* to twist and turn and writhe around doing who knows what for who knows how long.

We put such pressure on ourselves to know exactly who we are and what we want in every moment; it's okay for some things to be fuzzy. People who identify with having "so many issues" are often just people who don't have immediate or perfect closure on the ever-evolving experience of being human.

You think you have "issues" because you're told grieving is only supposed to happen during certain occasions in life. We grieve in every season. Moving in the direction of your potential requires a perpetual loosening of your grip, a constant letting go.

We're all grieving something all the time.

It's only natural to want perfect closure; it's also only natural to not get it. If you're fixated on closure, it's because you're hurting. You think closure will be the thing that takes away your hurt, but it's self-compassion that will prove to be your salve. Give yourself permission to hurt.

Holding space for your difficult, probably diametric experiences looks like allowing your painful emotions to exist without trying to cookie-cut them into heart and star shapes. Pain isn't supposed to be cute.

Your pain does not need a makeover; your pain needs permission to stay unkempt. Difficult emotions need to be allowed to lie there like a brick. They're feelings, not who you are.

You can want closure and still choose power. Power amidst the desire for closure is about recognizing that you don't need something to close; you need something to open. You need opensure.

People who heal are not the anointed ones who've figured out how to tie up all the loose ends; they're the ones who've pulled the string on something new.

Your curiosity knows what you need to open yourself up to. Curiosity is the unsung hero of mental health. Curiosity is strong; it can pull you out of anything.

When you can't transmute your pain into something beautiful and it just hurts, you can still have that "living inside of art" feeling if you remember that the point of art is not to be beautiful but to rouse a sense of connection within the person who's encountering the art.

The point of art is to move you. Being moved by art looks like standing still and realizing that your internal world is so much more alive than you remember it being before you encountered the artwork.

Art is designed to be experiential. Any description of an artwork is an immediate reduction of an artwork; that's what makes it art. Grief is the same way. Nobody fully understands art or grief because neither allows for perfect closure.

Art is a closure-less experience, and we love that about art. We love that we can't put our finger on what exactly it is about a paint stroke or a movie or a melody that draws us in. There's no accounting for the way in which art seems to move and change each time we look at it, even though we know it's been left physically untouched.

Grief is also a closure-less experience, and we hate that about grief. We hate that we can't put our finger on what exactly it is about the subject of our grief that keeps drawing us in. Neither can we nail down the way grief seems to move and change each time we look at it—one moment it's a soft memory, the next a bitter wince.

The impossibility of closure within art is the very quality that makes art invaluable. If you think I'm about to tell you that art and grief are both priceless experiences with which one decorates life, no. I'm not that kind of therapist—also this isn't therapy; this is a book.

I'm inscribing a link between art and grief to pull a string. To offer an entrance into something new. To allow exploration without destination.

Exploration doesn't need to culminate in bullet-pointed certainty about anything. Thoughts and feelings don't need to operate with an itinerary. It's okay to hold something for a long time, look at it, turn it over, feel it, think about it, turn it over again, talk about it, write about it, and then look up and say, "I don't know." It's okay to not have closure.

Part of why we love movies with a "Hollywood ending" is that they delight us with the fantasy of closure. It's the immediate gratification of closure that puts the "feel-good" in feel-good movies.

Immediate gratification is amusing, but you need only look at last year's Oscar nominations for Best Picture to see that what we most value in a story is not perfect closure—it's meaning. Meaning is what transcends entertainment we like into art we love. The same is true for the stories of our own lives. We're not fulfilled by discovering perfect closure; we're fulfilled by discovering meaning.

Once you connect to your power, which is found in the self-defined realms of connection and meaning, you may be surprised at how little you care about closure. Maybe closure becomes something that no longer matters to you at all, a superficial desire completely satiated by watching a rom-com.

No matter what anyone else does or does not do, no matter what does or does not happen, you're the one who has the power to decide what you open yourself up to next.

When someone's connected to their power, they don't need closure. They don't need one more post-breakup talk to "officially for real this time" clear the air with their ex, they no longer resent people who are living freely, they no longer wish they could stop thinking about the person who died—they've let go of trying to control the past. When you understand that closure is a fantasy, you have all the closure you'll ever need.

<u>Whenever you can, remember:</u>

Counterfactual thinking is a cognitive reflex.

Support comes in every color.

Maintenance is a triumph.

Swap "better or worse" for "different."

Happiness is experienced in three stages; so is stress.

A feather's-weight more weighs a lot.

The difference between a struggle and a challenge is connection.

Simple isn't easy.

Energy management beats time management.

Closure is a fantasy.

New Things to Do to Help You Stop Overdoing It

How can we expect someone to give up a way of seeing and
understanding the world that has physically, cognitively, or
emotionally kept them alive? None of us is ever able to part
with our survival strategies without significant support
and the cultivation of replacement strategies.

DR. BRENÉ BROWN

I was expecting Kait for an in-person session but she FaceTimed me
instead: "Hey! Hope it's okay that we do a virtual session today, really
busy day."

Kait's face was smushed and framed into what looked to me to be the
face cradle of a massage chair. "Kait? Are you getting a massage right now?"

KAIT: Yeah, you're on speaker.
ME: I'm confused.

KAIT: I was thinking about what you said, about prioritizing restoration. I figured this is more efficient. Mental and physical restoration, consolidated.

ME: I'm not comfortable with this.

It's not that perfectionists are bad at restoring; it's that they're horrible at it. Restoration is the eighth wonder of the world for perfectionists, a fascinating paradox replete with so many more questions than answers: *How do I know if I need to restore? How do I restore? How much do I restore? When should I restore? What's an appropriate marker I can use while I'm restoring for me to gauge how well my restoration is going? What's supposed to happen after I restore? What if what's supposed to happen doesn't happen, then what happens next?*

Restoration presents a unique set of challenges for perfectionists. Engaging in some harmless downtime, for example, doesn't feel harmless to a perfectionist—it feels like a risk wrapped up in pressure: *Okay, I am going to walk outside on my lunch break and I am going to return relaxed. This better work.* I know this is a blasphemous thing for a therapist to say, but that's not how you're supposed to feel.

The reason perfectionists struggle with restoration is twofold. One, needing restoration initially feels like failing to perfectionists. Perfectionists interpret the experience of being tired as if they did something wrong and need to correct for their error.

If you want to render a perfectionist speechless, inform them that the CDC recommends spending approximately one third of the day asleep. It continues to be a head-spinning truth for perfectionists to accept: a significant amount of rest *every single day* is required for human beings to function—we can't believe it, we can't get over it.

Two, restoration requires decompression. Decompressing involves taking the pressure off, not piling it on—that's what decompression means, a reduction in pressure. Perfectionists are bad at decompressing because they thrive on pressure.

The reason you can't relax while you're watching TV, for example, is because you're secretly clocking the ratio between the time you're spending on the activity and how restored you feel. If the ratio isn't churning fast enough, you get the sense that you're wasting your time and being unproductive; you start feeling more frustrated than you did before you started "relaxing."

Applying pressure to alleged leisure activities does not a leisure activity make. So how do you restore if restoring requires decompression, but you thrive on pressure?

Think of decompression as "passive relaxation." When you decompress, you're releasing, you're letting go, you're emptying out. Some examples of passive relaxation might include watching TV, scrolling through Instagram, taking a nap, that kind of thing. Perfectionists become unnerved during passive relaxation *unless* they're able to incorporate play into their lives.

Yes, play.

Play is another word that's best left described, not defined. My favorite description of play comes from *the* play theorist, Dr. Brian Sutton-Smith, who said that the opposite of play isn't work; the opposite of play is depression.

If you're like most of my clients, you do not like the idea of "playing," so let's agree that we'll instead be using the phrase "active relaxation."

When you actively relax, you're filling yourself up; you're renewing yourself through an activity that holds meaning for you. Some examples of active relaxation might include rowing, walking, cooking, indulging in your favorite part of your job, going to a party, painting, dancing, writing, making a playlist, attending a lecture, gardening, organizing, and getting dressed up.

Decompression = passive relaxation = emptying yourself out

Playing = active relaxation = filling yourself up

Restoration = passive relaxation + active relaxation

Restoration is a two-phase process. You empty yourself out, you fill yourself back up. It's not straightforwardly iterative, but you can't skip a phase. Without allowing yourself decompression cycles during which you empty yourself out, there's no room for what you're trying to fill yourself back up with to fit—your restoration falls flat.

If you only decompress, you end up feeling lazy, vaguely gross, and empty inside. If you only actively relax, you end up feeling like you're trying hard to restore but your efforts just end up causing you more stress.

The combination of decompression and playing is essential for perfectionists (it's essential for everyone, but other people don't equate passive relaxation with failure like perfectionists in a maladaptive space do, so restoring isn't as complicated for them).

Examples of active relaxation for each type of perfectionist:

INTENSE PERFECTIONISTS: expressing aggression in healthy ways, like playing sports or exercising

CLASSIC PERFECTIONISTS: paying meticulous attention to detail, like taking an hour to style a single shelf on a bookcase

PARISIAN PERFECTIONISTS: doing something that helps them feel connected to themselves or others, like making a care package or going on a walk with their thoughts

MESSY + PROCRASTINATOR PERFECTIONISTS: engaging in pursuits that can be begun, continued, and finished in one sitting, like cooking a meal, or the glorious trifecta that is writing a thank-you note, addressing the thank-you note, and putting the thank-you note in the mailbox all in the same day.

Perfectionists also resist restoration because they think restoration is defined exclusively through physical rest (i.e., sleeping or "doing nothing"). Perfectionists don't like "doing nothing." Regardless of what the wellness world tells you, you don't need to figure out how to enjoy doing nothing to be healthy.

It's okay if doing nothing is boring for you. Just as there are different iterations of support *in addition* to emotional support, there are different iterations of rest *in addition* to physical rest.

For a long time, for example, I was confused as to why I love cheesy action movies so much. I'm a hopeless romantic for one. Also, loving bro-ey, frat-tastic, artistic-integrity-level-zero action movies doesn't track with my affinity for the richness of stories. The nuance, the history behind the nuance, the details you notice without noticing you're noticing, every idiosyncratic thing about storytelling—I love it and want it all. I could listen to stories all day long. Then I realized, "Oh, I already do listen to stories all day long and as much as I love my work, I need rest from it, too."

Action movies give me emotional rest from the emotional labor I invest into being a psychotherapist. To empty out and decompress, I don't need more stories, I need to watch inanimate objects blow up while no one talks to me. Bring on the flimsy character development. Dialogue optional. An hour and a half of explosions and car chases is like going to a spa for me.

We need all kinds of rest, and we restore for all kinds of reasons other than being physically tired. Different types of rest help us restore our creativity, integrity, empathy, clarity, humility, spirituality, motivation, confidence, sense of humor, and more.

Rest is not a four-letter word (classic perfectionists, kindly put your *well technicallys* away). Rest is not an option or a preference. Like water, rest is a need.

Our categorical models of mental illness propel the false notion of "healthy" as a prize you win, then get to keep and put on display, like a trophy on a shelf. Being healthy is not a static coordinate in space that you land on, plant your flag in, and conquer. The sustained energy required to attend to your life in a consistently conscious manner (which is the way adaptive perfectionists operate) is a type of athleticism.

Restoration is a repeating requirement for living consciously. You can make progress without restoration, but you can't sustain it without restoration. When perfectionists commit to restoration, the dividends are endless.

What happens when each type of perfectionist takes time to restore?

Restored Parisian perfectionists come to understand that it's not that you want to be perfectly liked by all people at all times; it's that you have a live-wire understanding of the power of connection. Connections validate us.

Needing validation from others is pathologized in the pop-psychology world. The truth is that human beings need to be seen, heard, and understood by one another. Validation becomes especially critical when you're part of a marginalized group or you've been singled out and actively invalidated.

Needing validation is not a reflection of insecurity; it's a central mode of connection. Healthy people need validation. Everyone needs validation. It's okay that you need validation; what's not okay is for you to employ external validation as a primary source of self-worth.

When they're not restored, Parisian perfectionists use people-pleasing as a shortcut to connection. People-pleasing doesn't work as a bridge to connection because it disconnects you from yourself. You might get across to the other person, but you've left your true self on the other side of the bridge.

Being "the cool girl" is a euphemism for a woman who represses both the feeling and expression of anger. When you're restored, you more easily remember that anger and frustration are healthy, natural, and informative. You become more accepting of conflict. You focus on enjoying the people, projects, and communities that are welcoming and easy for you to connect with.

Healthy connections don't require you to sublimate yourself—you remember that when you're restored. Connections that require performance become unappealing to you.

You still seek validation, but you do so in a healthy way, by enjoying experiences that validate you for who *you've* decided you want to be. You also strive to validate others in healthy ways. Perhaps most importantly, you validate yourself.

You own your sense of belonging before anyone reinforces it for you. When you walk through the door and don't know you're worthy, external validation says, "You're performing well for now, so you can stay here for a while." When you walk through the door and *do* know you're worthy, external validation says, "Welcome home." As long as you don't need it to walk through the door and know you belong, there's nothing wrong with enjoying a warm welcome.

Instead of trying to coach yourself into not caring about what other people think, you recognize that caring is a wonderful quality and direct that shiny quality of yours towards people, places, and projects that reciprocate the high-quality connection you're offering.

You stop wasting your energy on those who are unable or unwilling to connect with you. You stop trying to be popular. You focus on pleasing yourself.

Restored messy perfectionists come to understand that it's not that you're too disorganized to follow through or that you need the middle of the process to be perfect, it's that you're trying to avoid loss.

Every choice you make involves a loss. You cannot live in all the cities, you cannot marry all the people, you cannot accept all the offers, you cannot give life to all the ideas.

Accepting the opportunity cost that comes with choice is painful. The shortcut you take when you're not restored is pretending that you can bypass that pain, operating as if your enthusiasm can both abrogate tedium and be a stand-in for commitment.

The work you have the energy to engage in when you're restored is using your enthusiasm to recruit the support you need. You learn what boundaries are and how to implement them. You take an inventory of your values and decide what you want to commit to and what you don't. You understand that because present loss triggers past loss, the work of pursuing your potential is more emotionally weighted than you may have initially assumed it to be.

From a restored place, you have the bandwidth to be compassionate with yourself about what you're letting go of. You stop pretending that you can be in twenty-six places at once, and then you stop pretending that you can be in fifteen places at once, and then seven, and then two.

Once you stop burning through your internal resources trying to resist loss, you're able to redirect all that neon energy of yours towards one clear path. You reap all the benefits of being committed to that which you hold passion for, mainly the joy of watching what you love take shape, expand, and change you for the better.

Restored procrastinator perfectionists come to understand that it's not that you want the start to be perfect; it's that you want faith that you're going to be okay even if you fail. Like messy perfectionists, procrastinator perfectionists also experience a sense of loss; the loss just hits at a different stage in the process and for a different reason.

Loss for a procrastinator perfectionist is not about mourning opportunity cost, as it is for messy perfectionists. For procrastinator perfectionists, the loss is anticipatory: *What if this thing I want doesn't work out? Then who will I be? Then what will I have?*

The shortcut you take when you're not restored is placating your fear by running towards the false security of a guaranteed outcome. You get into scarcity mode and try to hedge the loss. You think, *I'll take this job I don't really want and then at least I'll be guaranteed to have X.*

Whether it's applying for the job, finding a partner, trying to get pregnant, or even smaller-scale changes like redecorating a bedroom or taking a trip, it's hard when a vision exists in a perfect state in your mind because ushering that dream into the real world feels like you're endangering it, like you're taking a baseball bat to something you love.

From a restored place, you can see that your vision isn't collapsing when you allow it to enter the real world, nor is it failing just because it doesn't look the way you expected it to look. The vision changes because it's growing, and it's growing because you gave it life.

Restored procrastinator perfectionists learn to take action not because they feel assured that everything will work out in their favor but because they understand that being ready and being in control are two different things. Understanding that you have little to no control over the world around you is liberating; it opens you to step into your life now instead of waiting until you have more control.

Taking intentional action and then allowing space for whatever happens next to unfold is metamorphic, particularly if you're not used to doing that. Living out their desires in real time, restored procrastinator perfectionists become so much more of themselves; they feel animated, excited, present to the good in their life. Procrastinator perfectionists still encounter the exact same fear, but with the energy to face their fears, they're simply not as intimidated.

Restored classic perfectionists come to understand that it's not that you need perfect order or organization, it's that you revere function and beauty. The underbelly of your reverence is that you wish you could erase dysfunction. You wish you could erase all the things in this world that threaten the beauty of it. From a restored place, you hold a deeper understanding of your perfectionism, as well as the ideal wishes propelling it.

The shortcut you take when you're not restored is siphoning away anything that seems chaotic or dysfunctional and burying it under structure.

Chaos isn't the same as dysfunction; the latter is avoidable, while the former is not. From a restored place, you can tell the difference. You accept, maybe even embrace, that a certain degree of chaos is natural and good.

You relieve yourself of the responsibility to compensate for the external dysfunction that you have no control over, and so you gain the energy to encounter your internal world. You let yourself feel the sadness or undesirable feelings you were previously trying to cover up with all your organizing and perfecting. You realize how full of empathy you are.

You attend to the parts of yourself that need your own loving care. You make room for the chaos life brings. You make room for the chaos inside yourself.

You still love planning, you still love organizing, you still love making it beautiful—but you do it because you want to, not because everything will fall apart if you don't. You operate from a well of desire, not a pit of desperation.

Your life may or may not look the same on the outside, but on the inside, much has changed. You stop working to curate a programmed experience. You allow yourself open access to all that you think and feel. You allow yourself to be free.

Restored intense perfectionists come to understand that it's not that you need the outcome to be perfect; it's that you want to matter—to others, to the world, and to yourself. You focus on being a human being as opposed to being a "value add."

The shortcut you take when you're not restored is using goal attainment as proof that you're a "value add"—to the world, to your kids, to your friends, to your job: *Look what I did. Look at all I do. Tell me I matter.*

You fire the expression "value add" from your vocabulary.

When you're not restored, the more you achieve, the more pressure you feel to top your achievements, lest your "value add" expire. Because you can't achieve fast enough to keep up with the insatiable need for external validation, you get fixated on efficiency in a way that not only engenders *inefficiency* but also isolates you.

The counterfeit need to achieve becomes urgent, so much so that you abandon your real need for connection. You perpetually address your life from a future state: *I'll connect with my kids after I finish X. I'll start dating after I finish X. I'll focus on my health after I finish X.*

When you're restored, you're strong enough to hold the understanding that you matter now, and your life is now. You continue to work hard while also prioritizing meaningful connection—with others, yes, but even more so with yourself.

You give yourself permission to be supported.

You allow yourself to be flexible because when you're rested, it's easier to remember that your way is not the only way. You have the energy to be compassionate with yourself in the moments when you still scream, stew, or hold on to aggression because you have compassion for the part of you that wants so badly to feel important, the part of you that doesn't know you're already important.

Regressing into negative patterns still happens when you're restored, but it happens less often, you're conscious of it faster, and you have the energy to make swift and meaningful repair attempts.

Restoring yourself doesn't inoculate you from making mistakes. Nothing inoculates anyone from making mistakes. Old mistakes, new mistakes, some creatively hybrid version of old and new mistakes—no matter how adaptive or healthy we become, we will all continue to make mistakes.

The work *every* perfectionist has the energy to engage in when they're restored is that of finding the strength to define success on their own terms—on their own timetables, honoring their own values, with their own metrics for achievement. Perfectionism represents the natural, innate, and healthy human impulse to align with our whole, complete selves. A restored perfectionist understands that it's not that you long for some external thing or for yourself to be perfect, it's that you long to feel whole and to help others feel whole.

Prioritizing your restoration is essential for managing your perfectionism. As discussed, every perfectionist is both a maladaptive and an adaptive perfectionist. You need a heavy rotation of positive coping skills and restoration strategies at your disposal because you already have a heavy rotation of negative coping skills and burnout strategies at your disposal.

As you grow, your needs will change, and you'll need to tweak your solutions to accommodate those changes. What worked six months ago might begin to glitch; that's fine. It's okay if a solution stops working. We grow out of solutions just as we grow out of our problems.

Solutions stop working because you're changing and the environment around you is changing, which is what's supposed to happen. You're not doing anything wrong. Nothing is breaking. Change is natural. Everything is changing in every moment. We're always being called upon to let go of something, hence the screen-saver grief that comes with being human.

The important thing to remember is that there are always multiple solutions to any one problem.

This chapter is designed to help you incorporate restoration into your daily routine through eight specific tools. If you press all the buttons at once, it will jam the system. Going on a restoration blitz is not going to help you.

I offer multiple approaches to restoration because healing is not a one-size-fits-all situation, and as the saying goes, nothing that works works all the time. The idea is to pick up one tool that suits you more than the rest, that you think you'd find to be the most enjoyable, and start there.

Pay attention to your instincts as you read through the following strategies. Notice what you're curious about. If something grabs at you, grab back.

Know that you can pick nothing and simply engage in the second stage of change. This is not a "thirty days to a better you" moment. We're not doing that here.

It's okay to think about changing off and on for a while without behaviorally doing anything; that's how personal development begins.

Conscientiously processing your internal experience is just as productive as tangible representations of productivity. You're here to work smarter, not harder. You're a perfectionist; you already work hard enough.

Lastly, restoration is a highly individualized process. Only you know what you need, how much you need, and when you need it. It's possible you may be getting your restoration just right. If you feel energized and restored, make note of what's enabling that and consider continuing to do what you're doing without changing a thing.

You have the power to incorporate the eight restoration tools below into your routine at any time, to any degree you choose. The first tool is the reframe.

1. Reframe

My mom tells me that my first word was "bird," but I'm convinced that it was "reframe" and that she just wasn't in the room when I said it. The reframe is every therapist's best friend; we use this tool as reliably as clients look at their phones in the waiting room.

Clinically referred to as a *cognitive reappraisal*, a reframe is when you shift the language around a concept or an event to enable a more helpful perspective.

For example:

A lot of us (consciously or unconsciously) interpret asking for help to mean that we're incapable of doing something well on our own, which makes us feel inadequate, scared, and less likely to ask for help.

Here's the reframe: *Asking for help is a refusal to give up.*

Thinking about asking for help as a refusal to give up makes us feel strong, determined, empowered, and *more* likely to ask for help.

Reframes are powerful because one of the best ways to change the way you think is to change the way you speak. For example, replacing the word "time" with the word "energy" helps reframe the way you conceptualize your schedule by reinforcing Mullainathan's notion of bandwidth management from the last chapter:

INSTEAD OF: How does my schedule look tomorrow? Will I have the time to meet with her?

TRY: How does my schedule look tomorrow? Will I have the energy to meet with her?

While discussing the mental health of veterans, Prince Harry noted that he prefers the term "Post-traumatic Stress Injury" to "Post-traumatic Stress Disorder."[1] As the former army captain explained, conceptualizing PTSD within the framework of an injury as opposed to that of a disorder helps us to understand that, just like when we incur a physical injury and take steps to heal our body, we can incur psychological injury and take steps to heal our mind. Reframes that recognize the fluidity of mental health move the field in the right direction.

Reframes don't just help you shift the way you see your own life; they can also help shift the way you see the lives of others. For example, many people describe women who don't have children as "childless." When "less" is used with a word, it implies that something is missing: thought*less*, penni*less*, home*less*, direction*less*, meaning*less*.

Women who elect not to have children are not operating at a deficit. Not only do some women not want kids; some women are also completely, joyfully fulfilled by not having kids. These women are not avoiding a full life, they're not "missing out," they're not secretly hurting, and they're not going to regret not having children. Consider the perspective change we invite when we describe women who don't want children as "child-free."

Let's look at other examples of reframes as they pertain to mental health.

INSTEAD OF: attention-seeking behaviors

TRY: connection-seeking behaviors

INSTEAD OF: defense mechanisms (*Ugh, they're being so defensive.*)

TRY: protective mechanisms (*Oh, they're trying to protect themselves from getting hurt.*)

INSTEAD OF: I don't know what I want.

TRY: I'm reimagining what's possible for myself.

INSTEAD OF: I never did well in school.

TRY: I'm not a classroom learner.

INSTEAD OF: I gotta fake it 'til I make it.

TRY: I give myself permission to lead with the burgeoning parts of myself.

INSTEAD OF: I have anxiety.

TRY: I have excess anxiety.

INSTEAD OF: I have so much baggage.

TRY: I have a rich history of experience.

INSTEAD OF: I have to . . .

TRY: I have the chance to . . .

INSTEAD OF: I'm experiencing a painful breakdown.

TRY: I'm experiencing a painful breakthrough.

INSTEAD OF: disorder

TRY: reaction / syndrome

INSTEAD OF: I'm sorry I'm such a mess.

TRY: Thanks for your patience with me.

INSTEAD OF: symptom management

TRY: healing

INSTEAD OF: I'm bipolar.

TRY: I'm managing bipolar disorder.
(You are not your mental health disorder.)

INSTEAD OF: She's bipolar.

TRY: She's managing bipolar disorder.
(Other people are not their mental health disorders.)

INSTEAD OF: patient

TRY: client

INSTEAD OF: I need advice.

TRY: I need counsel.

INSTEAD OF: What do I need? What am I feeling?

TRY: What does [your name here] need? What is [your name here] feeling? (Research supports the notion that speaking to yourself in the third person, while it may feel silly, can create a perspective shift that allows you to better regulate your emotions and focus on what you need. Clinically referred to as self-distancing, the practice of reflecting on your situation in the third person can be helpful because it generates psychological distance between you and your experience. You know how it's so much easier for you to know exactly what your bestie should do about all their problems, and yet your problems feel so complicated and unsolvable to you? The psychological distance between you and your best friend's experience is what makes it easier.[2])

INSTEAD OF: I'm such a perfectionist. It's so annoying, I know!

TRY: I have a strong and clear vision.

INSTEAD OF: I'm a recovering perfectionist.

TRY: I've learned how to make self-compassion my default emotional response. / I've stepped into my power. / I now understand that trying to find balance is like trying to find a needle in a haystack that didn't have a needle in it to begin with.

Let's talk about reframing "I don't know what to do."

I was trained to respond to that statement, frequently asserted by clients, with a simple and genuine question: "Is that true?"

It turns out that most of the time we *do* know what to do; we just can't imagine doing it. When a client says, "I don't know what to do," and they mean it, what I hear is that they're open to trying a new strategy.

Acknowledging that you need a new strategy is hard. It takes courage to recognize that something's not working instead of pretending that it'll work if you try harder and force it, or that it will somehow magically fix itself if you ignore it.

To avoid the difficulty of initiating a new approach, people play the passive "wait and see" strategy out until the dysfunction culminates into a crisis, then they busy themselves with the urgency of triage.*[3] After the crisis is contained, you still have to develop a better strategy.

Recognizing that you don't know what to do is a signal of awareness, yet *I don't know what to do* is often experienced as a helpless thought. Consider reframing it as one of the most powerful thoughts you can have.

I don't know what to do precedes support-seeking actions, as well as other helpful thoughts like, "Maybe I should get another perspective . . . Whom can I ask for help . . . I want to talk to someone who's been in this position before . . . What are my instincts telling me?"

I don't know what to do is also a sign of openness, humility, and flexibility. The stronger people's narcissistic tendencies are, for example, the less likely you are to ever hear them utter the words "I don't know what to do."[4]

INSTEAD OF: I don't know what to do.

TRY: I'm ready for a new strategy now.

Reframes give new meaning to the admonition to "watch your language." Watch how reframing your language reframes your perspective.

Reframing is not a denial or a minimization of the difficulty associated

---

* Trauma also causes us to delay conscientiously attending to dysfunction.

with whatever you're reconceptualizing. A reframe acknowledges your initial perspective while also acknowledging that your perspective is one perspective, and multiple perspectives exist.

In a tripartite study of perfectionism (which compared adaptive perfectionists, maladaptive perfectionists, and non-perfectionists), adaptive perfectionists scored highest on their ability to reframe. Maladaptive perfectionists scored highest on their attempts to suppress and control negative emotions.[5]

Reframing is a skill, and skills can be learned. To begin practicing the skill of reframing, ask yourself the following question: "What's another way to look at this?" If you can't think of another way yourself, ask around.

The most classic reframe is to note that a glass half empty is also a glass half full. An additional reframe is to note that it doesn't matter how full the glass is if you know how to turn on the tap. There are always multiple perspectives, and there are always multiple solutions.

2. Explain and Express

Therapists are trained to listen for what's *not* being said as much as we're trained to listen for what *is* being said. How do you hear what someone isn't saying? There are lots of ways, one of which is to hold the distinction between explaining and expressing.

Explaining is telling someone what happened, what is happening, or what you think will happen.

Expressing is telling someone how you feel about what happened, how you feel about what is happening, or how you feel about what you think will happen.

For example: *I'm moving in three weeks* is explaining. *I feel scared* is expressing. *I feel scared because I'm moving in three weeks* is explaining and expressing.

If you overexplain and underexpress, you don't connect to the entirety of your experience. You intellectualize a lot, you talk *around* the issue, but you don't actually "go there."

Exclusively explaining makes people feel disconnected from themselves. You might know what happened, but you don't understand how you feel about it or what it means to you, which in turn makes it difficult to know what to do next.

The other side of the communication coin is that if you overexpress and underexplain, you don't give your emotions a way to evolve into insight. You're going around in circles talking about how you feel, but without anchoring the feelings in the explanation of "who, what, when, where, and why," no story can be formed.

When there are no logistical landmarks within your emotional experience, it's disorienting. You might know how you feel, but you don't know why you feel that way. Without explaining, you can't find patterns or triggers; nor can you develop sustainable solutions. You just keep swimming laps in a pool of feelings.

We construct meaning by talking about what happened *and* how we feel about it. Explaining and expressing is what therapists mean when they say, "We need to process this."

Classic and intense perfectionists tend to overexplain and underexpress, or only express themselves in one-dimensional ways (an intense perfectionist who only expresses anger, for example, or a classic perfectionist who only expresses patience).

This abbreviated communication mode can leave others feeling disconnected from both types of perfectionists. While others may understand what the intense or classic perfectionist does or does not want to have happen, they may experience difficulty connecting on a level that isn't based on logistics.

Being in any type of relationship with an intense or classic perfectionist who doesn't express can feel like you know a lot of facts about the person, but you don't know anything about who they really are.

Conversely, messy and Parisian perfectionists tend to overexpress and underexplain. Others may understand how both types of perfectionists feel, in addition to having a strong sense of who they are deep down, but there's a great deal of confusion about what these two types of perfectionists want, need, or are thinking.

My friend Pippa told me a funny story about her former boss. A Parisian perfectionist through and through, Pippa's boss had to fire one of Pippa's colleagues, Lee (obviously not the funny part).

Lee had a general sense that she was going to get fired, so when she was called into her boss's office, she thought, *Okay, here it comes.* Lee came out of the meeting . . . confused.

The Parisian perfectionist boss focused on expressing her genuine fondness for Lee; she recounted memories of traveling for work together, acknowledged Lee's many strengths, and even invited Lee to dinner. The problem was that the boss forgot to *explain* to Lee that she was, in fact, fired.

Upon Lee's return to her desk, Pippa anxiously asked what happened. Lee's response: "I think I just got fired, but I'm not sure? We're definitely getting dinner next Friday."

Nobody gets the balance between explaining and expressing perfectly right all the time, and nobody needs to. The point is to increase your awareness about how your communication style is being experienced. You want to grow more aware of not only how others are experiencing your communication style but also how you yourself are.

In your own self-talk, have you been doing a lot more explaining than expressing? Did I get that backwards, and you're doing a lot more expressing than explaining? To increase clarity in communication, consider adopting these scripts in your own self-talk as well as in your discussions with others.

For Messy and Parisian Perfectionists:

- What I'd like to have happen is [name the action].

- I need you to [name the action].

- I want you to stop [name the action].

- What's going to happen now is [name the action].

- I need help with [name the task] in the next [identify a time frame].

For Classic and Intense Perfectionists:

- I've been feeling less and less [name the emotion] lately.

- I enjoy feeling [name the positive feeling you enjoy], and when [name the action] happens, I feel more [repeat the positive feeling you enjoy].

- I don't like feeling [name the undesirable emotion], and when [identify the event] happens, I feel more/less [repeat the undesirable emotion].

- I miss feeling [name the emotion], and I'm trying to get that feeling back.

- I want to feel more [name the emotion] and less [name the emotion].

- This matters to me because [share meaning].

Procrastinator perfectionists can fall anywhere on this spectrum (as is true for anyone). If you're not sure whether you'd benefit from doing more explaining or more expressing, read over the two lists again and identify which list seems harder to you. The harder list is the one you'd benefit from practicing more.

Alter the above statements into questions when you notice people over- or under-explaining/expressing and you'd like to understand more about their experience.

3. Hold Opinions, Not Judgments

Judgment catalyzes punishment. When you judge yourself as "bad," you believe you deserve bad things (i.e., a punishment). But how do you not judge yourself if you did something that you already know better than to do, or, frankly, if you did something that was obviously not a smart thing to do?

The way to sidestep judgment is to hold opinions instead.

The difference between an opinion and a judgment is that an opinion reflects your thoughts and perspective, whereas a judgment reflects your thoughts and perspective alongside an analysis of your worth as compared to that of others. For example:

Opinion: Eating high fructose corn syrup drives inflammation, disrupts metabolism, negatively impacts mood, and contains no nutritional benefit. I want to avoid all those negative consequences, so I will avoid eating high fructose corn syrup. *Avoiding high fructose corn syrup is better than consuming it.*

Judgment: Eating high fructose corn syrup drives inflammation, disrupts metabolism, negatively impacts mood, and contains no nutritional benefit. I want to avoid all those negative consequences, so I will avoid eating high fructose corn syrup. *Avoiding high fructose corn syrup is better than consuming it, so I'm a better person than you are because you consume high fructose corn syrup and I don't.*

We associate being judgmental with holding a sense of haughty superiority over others, but the more common form of being judgmental comes from holding a shaky sense of inferiority *under* others.

Being a judgmental person is bidirectional.

You may identify other people whom you deem to be smarter, hotter, more patient, funnier, healthier, and otherwise more successful than yourself. Transmuting your opinion into a commentary on the other person's worth, you consciously or unconsciously conclude that the other person is a better human being; thus, they're more worthy of goodness than you are. When you do that, you're being judgy.

For example, you judge your colleague to be more attractive and smarter than you are, so it makes sense to you that she's in a happy and fulfilling relationship. You think, *Well, of course she found love.* The sub-text of your thought is *She's worthy of love.* The subtext of the subtext of your thought is *I'm not as worthy of love as she is.*

Whenever we judge others, we create separation between us and "them." Whenever we judge ourselves, we create separation between the parts of ourselves that we think deserve goodness and the parts that we think don't.

When we judge ourselves in either direction (as better than or less than), we make our worth conditional and set ourselves up for shame. The more you meet others with nonjudgment, the more you enable that attitude towards yourself, and vice versa.

One of the components that makes therapy so helpful is the therapist's nonjudgmental perspective. A good therapist can get in your head and see the exact same situation, minus the judgments and assessments of self-worth that you're grafting onto the scenario.

The subtraction of judgment alters everything about the way you per-ceive a situation, including what the problem is, which solutions are available, and what you deserve.

I always delight in seeing former clients' names pop up in my inbox and hearing an update on how things are going. So often I receive a note along the lines of "You're the voice in my head on a bad day." Whenever I recognize patterns in my work, I get curious. For a while, I engaged the sentiment with "Could I ask what stuck with you?"

Occasionally it was a single statement I had made, but I discovered that what clients were saying is that they've learned to approach their lives and their mistakes without judgment. What they're hearing isn't anything I ever said to them; it's their own fresh, judgment-free perspective—they just chose me to do the voice-over work.

4. Strike When the Iron Is Cold

Esteemed psychiatrist and writer Dr. Irvin Yalom wished that all therapists and clients would read his book *The Gift of Therapy: An Open Letter to a New Generation of Therapists and Their Patients*; I share in that wish.

One sparkling gem from Yalom that travels beyond the therapeutic process and into everyday life is his recommendation to "Strike when the iron is cold."[6]

The context within which Yalom offered this advice concerned giving feedback to clients about their negative behaviors when they're behaving differently. For example, the best time to bring up a client's tendency to take a stance of victimhood is during a moment when the client is engaged in a more empowering narrative.

The concept of striking when the iron is cold applies well to multiple contexts. At work, in your parenting, in your relationships, and most importantly, with yourself—don't try to resolve the negative issue at the height of the negative issue.

Remember Ava from the LMB moment in chapter 5? The reason I didn't flood her with buzzwords and behavioral theories and TED Talk links and book recommendations in the moment she started crying was that the iron was too hot; Ava wasn't in a place where she could sift through and absorb a bunch of high-level interventions.

Striking when the iron is cold is about consciously choosing the moment when the intervention, feedback, or appeal for connection is most likely to be received.

Applying this principle to your perfectionism looks like recognizing that the moments when you're in the most adaptive space are the best moments to actively manage your maladaptive perfectionism.

It sounds counterintuitive: *Why would I need to address the maladaptive aspects of my perfectionism if I'm not in a maladaptive headspace?* Because mental health is fluid and contextual. You will be in a maladaptive headspace sooner or later, guaranteed.

When you're upset, your interventions with yourself are significantly less likely to be received because your stress response is activated. Your nervous system is flooding your body with stress hormones like adrenaline and cortisol. These hormones make your brain interpret information in a markedly different way than it would if you felt calm and centered.

When you're doing well, show up for the future you that's having a hard time. Forge and reinforce protective factors around yourself. Create routines that restore your energy—find an exercise buddy, read books that teach and inspire you, go to therapy, nurture healthy habits, "broaden and build" your life.

If religion is connective for you, find a home church now, start attending Shabbat dinners now, engage in puja wholeheartedly now, try your best to prioritize your Jummah prayer now. Honor the tenets of whatever you believe in when you feel strong, not just when you've been crying for nine hours and your mascara's giving you Alice Cooper eyes.

If you know your mood is negatively impacted in the winter, book a trip somewhere sunny well ahead of time instead of trying to compare flight costs when you're feeling depressed and listless during an icy night in February.

You strike when the iron is cold because that's when you have the most energy, patience, and optimism, not to mention a solutions-oriented mindset.

Prevention is the golden child of all the wellness strategies. Exploit moments of your highest functioning to broaden your repertoire of positive coping mechanisms and align yourself with support in every color. Having support in place, even if you never use it, can be curative in and of itself.

5. Ask for Help

For so long, I honestly believed that whatever I accomplished didn't count if I had to ask for help along the way. I used to never ask for help, for anything, from anyone.

At twenty-four, I went through an abrupt breakup with a boyfriend I lived with, and instead of asking my friends if I could stay with them, I responded to an ad—*on Craigslist*—for the first available apartment my dog and I could move into that night. It was a month-to-month single room in a three-bedroom apartment. When I tell you the occupants of the other two bedrooms were literally the sketchiest men in Los Angeles . . .

The guy who owned the apartment was named Dax and drove a piece-of-shit convertible with a vanity license plate that read "Daxtasy." Calling that a red flag is like saying the core of the earth gets kinda hot sometimes. In not-at-all-shocking-whatsoever news, he stole my security deposit.

For the month I lived with him, Dax brought women home almost every night and had loud, terrible-sounding sex that was like listening to a ten-minute-long car accident. In the mornings, the smell of sticky whisky and stale cigarettes hit me the second I opened my bedroom door. I'd go to the kitchen to make coffee and there'd be remnants of cocaine all over the counter. I hated being in that apartment; I especially hated showering and sleeping there. I can't explain my choices other than to say I thought I was being "strong."

Even though I was aware that I was putting myself in clear danger, I remember feeling so proud of myself for doing it all on my own. At the time, doing things without anyone's help was my greatest source of pride. It's so sad, but the risk involved and the point that most people would've asked for help made me feel more proud of myself. Pride can misguide us in dangerous ways.

It's easy to mistake isolation for independence and being stubborn for being strong. Never asking for help was like laying lead on top of my potential. The Daxtasy situation was a particularly stark example of my misguided sense of independence, but there were so many other big and small instances of having to be hit with this lesson over and over again before I learned:

Not only is it okay to ask for help, the strongest people are the ones who connect to support.

At this point in my life, all I do is ask for help. There is not *one person* in my life from whom I haven't repeatedly asked for help in some form or another.

Asking for help looks like this:

"Can you help me with [thing you need help with] by [way the person can help you]?"

Asking for help is both a very simple and a very hard thing, especially for high-functioning perfectionists. Just because you can function well doesn't mean you aren't hurting. It never ceases to amaze me how put together and relaxed some people can appear on the outside, while on the inside, they're "ambulatory and breathing"—to use a phrase by Dr. Harriet Lerner. Dr. Karen Horney echoed the sentiment: "For the analyst it is a source of never-ending astonishment how comparatively well a person can function with the core of himself not participating."[7]

The gift of a crisis is that it's a call to action; something is visibly wrong, and a crisis demands that reparative action be taken immediately. People act swiftly in a crisis. In the absence of a crisis, accessing support is often postponed or altogether ignored.

For high-functioning perfectionists, the siren will never sound, the lights will never flash. When your suffering is invisible to other people (and when you're adept at keeping it that way), you need to be the one to fire the flare.

Somewhere along the line, we got it in our heads that being healthy and strong means that we've finally figured out how to not need anything from anyone. *We have that exactly backwards.* Being healthy and strong means that we've finally figured out we could use help from everyone.

Life involves loss and confusion for every human being; we're not supposed to go through those alone. Human beings are not meant to be isolated any more than we're meant to navigate through adulthood crawling on our hands and knees.

We're all interconnected, and we all need one another. We don't just need one another occasionally; *we need one another all the time*. It's hilarious how much we need one another and how much we operate as if we don't, and by hilarious, I do mean tragic.

You don't have to be in dire straits to ask for help; you can just want things to be a little easier. And if you don't want things to be a little easier, may I ask what exactly you're trying to prove?

6. Set Boundaries

Operating without boundaries invites dysfunction. You cannot rise to your potential unless you know what your boundaries are, you know how to communicate them, and you know what to do if your boundaries are violated.

A boundary is a limit imposed for the purpose of protection. To protect your time, energy, safety, and resources, you decide what is and is not okay with you—those decisions are your boundaries. For example, to protect your time and energy, you decide that you don't respond to emails after 6:00 p.m.

Boundaries have also been described as the place where your responsibility ends and another person's responsibility begins. Writer, activist, and founder of The Embodiment Institute, Prentis Hemphill, describes a boundary as "the distance at which I can love you and me simultaneously."

Asserting boundaries activates boundaries. If you're not asserting your boundaries, you don't have boundaries; you have ideas about what your boundaries *could* be.

Some boundaries are nonnegotiable and fixed; for example, "I don't get in the car with someone who's been drinking." Other boundaries require regular calibration because they're based on shifting needs.

For example, there may be some days or seasons during which you need to incubate, be alone more, do less, say no. You tighten your boundaries in those moments. Other days or seasons you might need to roam free, be with people more, take on more projects, say yes. You widen your boundaries in those moments.

There's a lot I want to say about boundaries, but I have to put boundaries on my section on boundaries lest this book get swallowed whole by the topic. Fellow psychotherapist Nedra Glover Tawwab picks up where I'm leaving off with her elucidating and practical book *Set Boundaries, Find Peace: A Guide to Reclaiming Yourself.*

7. Sleep

Prioritizing sleep is a grossly neglected mental health intervention. We pour an astounding amount of money, energy, and time into managing our mental health, all while neglecting a primary driver for mental wellness—sleep.

Dr. David F. Dinges is the chief of the Division of Sleep and Chronobiology at the University of Pennsylvania's Perelman School of Medicine. As Dinges notes, "People have come to value time so much that sleep is often regarded as an annoying interference, a wasteful state that you enter into when you do not have enough willpower to work harder and longer."[8]

Sound familiar?

We don't think of sleeping as an activity, and we certainly don't think of sleeping as being productive, yet sleep is one of the most productive activities you could possibly engage in. The neuroprotective aspects of sleep, for one, are extensive.

Sleep does for your brain what hydrating does for your skin—sleep makes your brain glow. There's a network of vessels in your brain called the *glymphatic system*.[9] The glymphatic system's function is to clean your brain, and the system goes to work as soon as you go to bed.[10]

As researchers Dr. Jolanta Masiak and Dr. Andy R. Eugene explain, "The glymphatic system acts to flush out the cellular trash in the body just like a plumbing system would do."[11] When you don't get enough sleep, it's like not flushing a toilet inside your body. Guzzling a ton of coffee the next day is like spraying a bunch of air freshener in a bathroom with a broken toilet; it ain't gonna cut it. You'll just be heavily caffeinated and tired at the same time, just like your bathroom would smell like air freshener and "unflushed toilet" at the same time.

The more you consider the staggering amount of emotional and physiological regeneration that occurs during sleep, the more difficult it becomes to think of sleep as unproductive. While you sleep, you consolidate memories and clear synaptic space to learn new things the next day.[12] Your body deploys the cellular equivalent of thousands of tiny hands to repair all your muscles, including your heart.[13] You stabilize your metabolism and endocrine function, the latter of which helps you regulate your emotions (i.e., you have fewer mood swings).[14]

In a remarkable study examining the immunity-enhancing effects of sleep, two groups were given a vaccine for hepatitis A. The vaccine was administered to both groups at nine in the morning. One group slept through the night after receiving the vaccine; the other group was kept awake through the night and didn't sleep until 9:00 p.m. the following day. One month after the vaccine was administered, both groups were tested for antibodies to hepatitis A. The group that got a full night's rest after receiving the vaccine had almost *double* the number of antibodies than the group that didn't sleep the night after receiving the vaccine did.[15]

Have you ever wondered why you sometimes get ravenously hungry even though you just ate? It might be because you're not getting enough sleep. Leptin is an appetite-suppressant hormone that rises dramatically in your sleep (presumably to stop you from waking up because you're hungry). Studies have shown that leptin levels are dependent on sleep duration, and that sleep deprivation lowers leptin levels by around 19 percent. The people in the leptin studies who were sleep-deprived reported being approximately 24 percent hungrier after waking up than those who received adequate sleep.[16]

What's more, that 24 percent increase in cravings took the form of, as the researchers described, a "preference to high carbohydrate foods (sweets, salty food, and starchy foods) . . . craving for salty food increased by 45%. This suggests that sleep deprivation may affect eating behavior favoring nonhomeostatic food intake (food intake driven by emotional/psychological need rather than caloric need of the body)."[17]

The leptin studies help explain why the CDC has long been campaigning for the public to go to bed already, citing sleep deprivation's close link to obesity and type 2 diabetes.[18]

Tragedies such as the space shuttle *Challenger* explosion, the *Exxon Valdez* oil spill, and the American Airlines flight 1420 crash have all been directly and officially linked to sleep deprivation.[19] Prolonged sleep deprivation does horrible things to your mind and body, which is why sleep deprivation is used as a method of torture in warfare.

Is your depression causing you to lose sleep, or is your disrupted sleep causing you to slip into a depression? While difficulty sleeping has historically been understood to be a common symptom of underlying psychological distress (which it definitely is), more current explorations of sleep's intimate connection to mental health *also* view sleep as having a more causal, direct role in the development and perpetuation of mental illness.[20]

One of the most salutary mental health interventions I ever gifted myself with cost me four dollars and twenty-nine cents. I'm confident that the dramatic increase in sleep that followed my purchase of a box of earplugs from the drugstore saved me from multiple depressive episodes over the last two decades.

There is no rule stating that significant advances in personal growth need to involve deep excavations into the bedrock of your psyche amidst your twisty, sweaty, dark night of the soul. Our mental health is best honored through practical action. Breathing deeply, walking, sleeping—these are *highly* efficacious mental health interventions.

In his book *Why We Sleep: Unlocking the Power of Sleep and Dreams*, Dr. Matthew Walker identifies alterations to noise, light, and temperature as excellent starting points to optimize your sleep environment. Sleeping with a fan blowing on you, wearing earplugs, using white-noise machines—any sleep intervention is also a mental health intervention.

Rough nights, spotty months, hard seasons—we all have "bad" mental health moments. If all you do in a "bad" mental health moment is work to stabilize your sleep, you'd be doing a whole hell of a lot.* Optimizing your sleep preemptively is a protective measure for your mental health, too. Your body will step in and do so much of the work of healing for you if you give it the chance.

I don't know what did or did not happen for you today or what it's been like to be you lately. I don't know if you're in a bad moment, a good one, or if you're living in the gray. What I do know is this: no matter what's happening in your waking life, part of you heals in your sleep.

8. Do Less, Then Do More

Sometimes the number one thing you need to do is less. Do less, fall back, say no, stop. The more you learn to listen to your instincts and set your intentions, the more clarity you'll gain on what you care about and what you don't. Not giving energy or time to that which you don't care about is as brilliant as restoration strategies get.

Do you know what you care about and what you don't? Most people aren't clear on what their values are. Remember Lena from chapter 4, who wanted to figure out how to be her average self without feeling like a loser? What we discovered in our work together was that Lena was pursuing culturally sanctioned values that didn't reflect those of her authentic self.

---

* I'm not saying that stabilizing your sleep is a panacea, but it is an immediate and efficacious way to promote mental wellness and enable other efficacious mental health interventions to be more easily accessed and received.

After we examined the choices she was making in her life, looking at where she spent her time and energy, it became apparent that Lena was pursuing the following three values above all else: money, rank, and speed.

"But that's not what I value—I swear!" She said it like someone who had just been framed.

Taking time to clarify your value system is one of the greatest gifts you can give yourself. Lena didn't want to stop trying to excel; she wanted to stop trying to excel in areas that held no meaning for her.

Whatever you value, consciously or not, you're going to pursue with full force; as a perfectionist, you won't be able to help it. To the best of your ability, get clear and intentional on what your most deeply held values are.

After Lena identified her true values, it made it so much easier for her to make decisions in her everyday life. Excelling at what she cared about and abandoning what she didn't care about became an energizing, enjoyable thrill.

Take a look at the list of values below. Do any stand out to you as important? Not important?

Loyalty	Cleanliness	Curiosity
Artistry	Pleasure	Fun
Connection	Punctuality	Status
Health	Privacy	Gathering
Family	Joy	Restoration
Money	Surprise	Safety
Integrity	Solitude	Beauty
Service	Freedom	Gratitude
Speed	Friendliness	Humor
Honesty	Celebration	Adventure

Most values sound good on paper, but which ones do you care-care about? What's missing from the list? Remember that you're allowed to value whatever you want.

Invest less in what you don't value; invest more in what you do value.

You are the person who decides what you will and will not do with your life. Take firm ownership over your decisions. When you accept responsibility for the decisions you make, you position yourself to be less resentful.

Resentment is a barrier to joy. The energy of resentment is dense and heavy; it's stones in your pocket and bricks in your bag. You cannot run fast and free while you're carrying resentment.

A control mindset grasps onto resentment. When you don't understand that you have the power to validate your own experiences, values, and choices, you use resentment as a dial to try to control how much validation you get:

Can't you see how real my pain is, look at how resentful I am!

We use resentment as a bid for validation, and we also use resentment to avoid the awesome task of taking responsibility for our lives:

The more I resent you, the more it proves it was your fault, which means you're the person who should fix this, not me.

A power mindset registers resentment as a signal to explore how much energy you are devoting to a person, a narrative, or a task. Your power then invites you to recalibrate your energy expenditure however you see fit.

Taking ownership of your choices reduces resentment because when you accept the role as the leader of your life, you feel more entitled to say yes to what you want more of and no to what you want less of.

Whether you can *enjoy* a life full of more of what you want is another matter, and the subject of the next chapter.

9

Now That You're Free

And the day came when the risk to remain tight in a bud
was more painful than the risk it took to blossom.

ANAÏS NIN

Thus far, you've learned that being a perfectionist is part of who you are and that making an enemy out of who you are happens to be the opposite of healing. You've learned that your perfectionism is a gift—that you are a gift. You know that we'll all continue to have Target parking lot moments, that simple isn't easy, and that there's power in your presence. You can see support in full color, and you can see that judgment is bidirectional. You know that you honor a process through acknowledgment and celebration and that you're the one who chooses whether failure is filed as an event or an identity. You've learned about the retroactive power of connection and the loopholes we cite to deny ourselves compassion. You know all about counterfactual thinking, liminal space, the fluidity that is mental health, the fantasy that is closure—the list continues. Suffice it to say, in the past eight chapters, you've covered a lot of terrain.

After you finish this book, you'll continue to cover all kinds of terrain, new and old; a lot happens in life. Even in the most outwardly uneventful life, quiet riots from within abound. Moving forward, you know that you're going to make mistakes, but you also know how to release yourself from the punitive patterns that once corralled your potential. You have what you need to lead a self-defined life. This is the Dorothy moment, where you see you've had the power all along—you just had to learn it for yourself.

The Dorothy moment is not enough for perfectionists.

Perfectionists push. We think, *That's nice that we've had the power all along, but what does that mean? What comes next?*

Realizing your power means that you're free. What comes next is learning how to enjoy your freedom.

Enjoying freedom isn't a given. We can know we're free and still feel trapped. When we feel trapped, we experience freedom as a technicality: *I know I'm technically free to do what I want, but I could never actually do what I want.*

When we can only experience freedom in illusory glimpses, what's imprisoning us still?

Martyrdom is always a good place to start troubleshooting. Giving up your life to make someone else happy doesn't make that person happy—we know this already. Love from a martyr is the blood-money version of love; it doesn't feel good to receive it. The only people who are happy to receive offerings from martyrs are narcissists.

The sacrifice of one's own pleasure marks the difference between service and martyrdom. Pleasure is an interesting string to pull. Examining the areas of your life in which you are sacrificing pleasure will lead you to a direct understanding of the conditions you place upon feeling joyful and free.

Giving yourself permission to feel joy now is the ultimate marker of successfully managing perfectionism. Perfectionists mired in maladaptive patterns heal by committing to self-compassion as a default response to pain and then letting joy into their lives.

Self-compassion primes joy because it invites pleasure; you're no longer punishing yourself by restricting pleasure until you've "earned" the right to feel good. Without self-compassion or pleasure, joy is elusive. It's very hard to feel joy when you hate yourself, for example.

Not that you need to hate yourself to electively restrict joy from your life; perfectionists do it all the time. Maladaptive perfectionists are perpetually on some version of a joy diet.

- The low-calorie version: *Sure, I'll have a little joy, but just a taste, because I'm working really hard on X project right now.*

- The intermittent-fasting version: *Thank you, but I only allow myself joy for the half hour before bed.*

- The paleo version: *I only consume joy from a single source, my children.*

Joy is healthy in any amount. Like the air you breathe, you never have to worry about having too much joy. Restricting joy is profoundly unnecessary.

It's not that perfectionists are consciously trying to restrict joy; perfectionists are consciously trying to restrict pleasure. We restrict pleasure in misguided expressions of responsibility, the irony being that when it comes to your mental health, restricting pleasure is an irresponsible decision. From a clinical perspective, sacrificing your pleasure is not a virtue; it's a serious risk factor.

"Enjoy" means you are "in joy," not outside of joy looking in, not intellectualizing joy. Joy is a feeling. To feel joy, you need to give yourself access to pleasure.*

We think of pleasure as a superfluous, hedonic piece of our lives, but pleasure is central to our sense of aliveness and personhood. Pleasure is a serious mental health issue.

---

* Anhedonia (the inability to feel pleasure) is a common symptom of depression. I don't mean to imply that anyone struggling with anhedonia or the reduced ability to feel pleasure is choosing that experience for themselves. I'm addressing those who make the choice to actively deny themselves pleasure in the name of responsibility.

When clients describe their depression to me, the description is a direct commentary on their ability to access pleasure. Pleasure is so intrinsically linked to clinical depression that the *DSM* identifies a loss of pleasure as one of the two *core* diagnostic criteria for a major depressive episode.

If pleasure is an afterthought for you, you are in danger.

Let's clarify the difference between immediate gratification and pleasure. Both feel good in the moment, but pleasure also feels good in the anticipation of the pleasurable event and in the recall of the pleasurable event. In contrast, immediate gratification can produce excess anxiety before the event (*I hope I don't "give in"*) and induce guilt after the event (*I wish I hadn't done that*).

Pleasure isn't loaded; it's a direct, joyful satisfaction—the pleasure of holding the door open for someone, the pleasure of toiling over work you love, the pleasure of laughing, the pleasure of listening to someone learn how to play the piano, the pleasure of smelling fresh dirt while you weed the garden. Yes, dirt can bring you pleasure. Pleasure does not require any justification whatsoever.

As women, we're taught that we need to justify our pleasure, and the justification better be damn good. Accordingly, pleasure seeking is relegated to the bottom of our to-do scrolls, assuming it makes the list at all. Women wrestle so much with the mastery of immediate gratification that we don't even give ourselves the chance to graduate to our pleasure.

Eating, for example, can be considered one of the most basic, most pleasurable acts in life. But the diet industry has pillaged the American woman's psyche such that taking simple pleasure in eating is something that's seen as a naughty indulgence.* The point of food for women is not to enjoy it, unless you're *really* in the mood to be "bad" and "cheat."

---

* We refer to the diet industry as a subsidiary system, as if "diet foods" are in one aisle of the grocery store and "regular food" is everywhere else. In the US, the diet industry is the food industry. That's how pervasive diet culture is.

Women are supposed to use food to fuel their bodies for maximum stamina—so that we can balance more tasks and take care of more people while also managing our weight. Hence why there's such a strong market for meal bars that taste like chalk mixed with your grandmother's lipstick.

Women's relationship to eating food is a microcosm of what happens when pleasure is pathologized. When eating is designed to be a functional act instead of a pleasurable act, there's no point in consciously asking yourself, "What do I want to eat?" The question instead becomes, "What am I supposed to eat?" When you conflate pleasure with sin outside the context of food, there's no point in asking yourself, "What do I want to do?" The question instead becomes, "What am I supposed to do? How am I supposed to be behaving?"

Without pleasure, our lives become performative. We perform in ways we think will make us happy instead of trusting ourselves to explore what feels good and right. This generic-at-best formula for satisfaction leads to depression for one thing, and it also leads women to conflate being selfish with experiencing pleasure: "Well, it made me feel good, so it was selfish." No. It made you feel good, so it was pleasurable.

The more you deny yourself access to pleasure, the less you can access your instincts about what you need and when you need it. Returning to our diet culture example: this is why so many women can no longer tell whether or not they're hungry. The basic instinct of sensing your own hunger and satiation is lost, buried under a pile of other people's directives about how to do something as simple as eating food.

When you put your desire on mute, you also mute your intuition. This forces you to rely exclusively on your thoughts—you *think* you're hungry all the time, and you can't stop eating. Or you *think* you're not hungry all day until you find yourself ravenous in your kitchen after work, swallowing muffins whole and tearing through hundred-calorie snack packs with your teeth.

In the United States, pleasure is not a value that's emphasized. Immediate gratification, yes. Pleasure, no. Hard work, efficiency, grit, and independence are the values we emphasize, and those are wonderful values to hold. At the same time, you do have to ask yourself, *What's the endgame here? Efficiency for what?*

This is your life, and you're not going to be alive forever. At some point, you're going to die. While you're alive, do you want to be "not depressed," or do you want to feel joy?

Pleasure is everywhere. We can delight in the pleasure of our children's company, the pleasure of getting clean, the pleasure of piling in a car with friends, the pleasure of watching a film, the pleasure of calling a movie a film, the pleasure of noticing the moon in the daylit sky. None of that has anything to do with efficiency.

Joy and efficiency have very little in common—if they went on a blind date, it would be thirty-five minutes of immediately forgettable small talk and would end with a corporate handshake. Joy and pleasure, on the other hand—they'd close out the restaurant.

"Cheat days," "treats," "rewards," the dog-clicker language we attach to women's pleasure is appalling. Every day in the summer, I get a cup of plain frozen yogurt with Oreo crumble toppings and walk around New York City for at least twenty minutes. The yogurt is fresh and tart, the Oreos taste like a sleepover, and the sun glows warm on my bare skin. All the people I pass look so interesting that I almost want to stop every single one of them so they can each tell me their entire life story—it's all such a pleasure.

My frozen yogurt is not a treat, it's not a reward, it's not me being "naughty" or "bad"—I did not steal the frozen yogurt. Eating frozen yogurt in the summer sun is just a part of my day.

When you make your access to pleasure conditional (a "treat" for being good), you're communicating to yourself that whether you deserve to feel good lies in direct proportion to your performance, not your existence. A pleasure-conditional mindset can rapidly metastasize into polarizing experiences of self-worth for anyone, particularly for perfectionists who are already prone to dichotomous thinking.

INSTEAD OF: I'm going to allow myself a treat of chocolate because I've been good this week.

TRY: I want chocolate, so I'll eat it.

We don't take the "I want it, so I'll do it" approach because we don't trust ourselves. We think we'll want too much. We'll eat all the chocolate and then we'll eat more "bad" foods. We'll get wasted, binge-watch TV for a year, quit our jobs, become even more reckless, and then cease to function. We're secretly nervous that if left to our own devices, we'll spin out of control, hurt everyone around us, and then go crazy. Wherever could we have gotten that idea?

Women "going crazy" is a dangerous trope that clinical psychology has a dark history of reinforcing. As scholar Rachel P. Maines writes, hysteria was one of "the most frequently diagnosed diseases in history until the American Psychiatric Association officially removed the hysteroneurasthenic disorders from the canon of modern disease paradigms in 1952."[1]

Hysteroneurasthenic?

The reason people binge on immediate gratification is not that they want too much. The reason people binge on immediate gratification is that they're burnt the fuck out.

Pleasure is an energy source. Taking pleasure in our lives sustains us. Taking pleasure out of our lives destroys us. Immediate gratification is not a substitute for pleasure. There is no substitute for pleasure.

Perfectionists get scared that they're going to lose their competitive edge if they let in too much pleasure and get "too happy." Look at the successful people you admire; joy *is* their edge.

There's no greater competitive advantage than loving what you do and taking pleasure in your life. The research is clear on this, the irony of prioritizing efficiency over joy is that joyful people get more done in the long term because they don't burn out.[2]

Replete with the energy-giving joy that comes from leading a pleasurable life *and* equipped with the powerful drive to excel that a perfectionist doesn't even have to try to cultivate, your motivation explodes. Your pleasure could never bury your drive; your depression could, though.

If pleasure invites joy into our lives, how do we invite pleasure into our lives?

The more you trust yourself, the more pleasure you allow yourself to experience.

When You Don't Trust Yourself

When you don't trust yourself, you move through life trying to memorize the right thing to do instead of trusting yourself to know it. You interpret setbacks as failures because you don't have the security to operate from a wider perspective.

You *need* what you're doing right now to work out (a relationship, a job, a creative project) because if the thing doesn't work out, you don't trust that you'll figure out a way to pivot and succeed regardless. You live with an attachment to a future outcome that generates chronic excess anxiety and you call that anxiety "hope."

It doesn't feel good to not trust yourself. And what does everybody tell you to do in those moments? Love yourself, *of course.*

Loving yourself is touted as a cure-all. Let's get clear on something— self-love is not a panacea.

Thinking that self-love is the answer to every single one of our internal woes, we practice self-love faithfully. We go to therapy, we get enough sleep, we put lotion on our legs before bed, we assert boundaries, we speak kindly to ourselves, we do all the things. *So why do we still feel locked out of joy?*

No matter how much you love yourself, if you don't trust yourself, you meet your gestures of self-love with low-key suspicion and hesitation.

It's like a relationship in which one partner has cheated on the other. The non-cheating partner can receive all the roses and proclamations of love that the cheating partner could ever offer, but the roses are received with resentment and the loving proclamations sound hollow and eye-roll-worthy until trust is restored. You can love someone deeply and not trust them at all. Trust and love are sold separately; they should really put that on the box.

You can't enjoy relationships in which trust has gone bankrupt; your relationship with yourself is no exception.

When You Do Trust Yourself

People who trust themselves allow themselves to adopt the role of "expert" in their own lives. Like all experts, those who develop trust with themselves move with confidence, not certainty.

It's important to know that even the people who diligently commit to accessing their intuition and connecting to support still make mistakes and encounter ambiguity about what the best course of action is. You don't have to have all the answers to be an expert; that's not what makes someone an expert.

Experts are people who stay committed to both informed and experiential approaches in their domain of expertise. Your domain of expertise is your own true self. It's okay if you're not positive at every moment about how to be you; you're constantly changing, so how could you be permanently sure? It's okay if what you thought was the right answer shifts as you gain more information and experience being you.

Listen closely and near constantly, you'll hear experts say things like, "There's no one right answer," or "The reality is, it varies." Situations can be complex, and there's rarely one clear, right path. Acknowledging the layers and paradoxes within our lives, the smartest people in the world are the ones who say, "I don't know" the most.

There are three main myths about what trusting yourself looks like.

1. *If you trust yourself, you can let yourself do whatever you want whenever you want.*

    People who trust themselves trust themselves because they're honest with themselves. More specifically, they're honest about what they need to restrict themselves from or altogether avoid. We think that the more we trust ourselves, the fewer boundaries we'll need; the opposite is true. The people who trust themselves the most are the ones who honor their boundaries the most.

2. *When you trust yourself, you don't need outside counsel or guidance.*

    Seeking counsel is a time-honored tradition in leadership. Authority figures who refuse to seek counsel signal both arrogance and insecurity. When you trust yourself to lead your own life, not only are you secure enough to hear other people's perspectives, you're secure enough to actively seek out those perspectives.

3. *Trusting yourself means you make fewer mistakes.*

    Mistakes are a part of learning and taking risks. When you trust yourself, you're not trying to prove anything. You may take more risks, which may mean you make more mistakes.

    Trust engenders curiosity and openness. When you trust yourself, you focus on being curious about what you need instead of being suspicious about who you are.

    For example, if you notice you've been numbing out all week beyond a level you're comfortable with (too much TV/drama/food/shopping/alcohol/work/whatever) and you *don't* trust yourself, you think, *Here I am once again, ruining it all. I knew this would happen. Am I ever gonna be able to get it together? Am I just eternally damaged?*

    When you don't trust yourself, you're waiting to catch yourself in a mistake so you can pounce on your own certainty about how unworthy of trust you are. You get petty. You become fixated on your mistakes, and you keep a tally of those mistakes.

In contrast, when you notice you've been numbing out all week beyond a level you're comfortable with and you *do* trust yourself, you think, *Huh, I've been numbing out so much, there must be something I need that I'm not getting. I wonder what that is. I wonder who could help me figure that out.* When you trust yourself, there's no tally of mistakes. There's no pettiness. There's generosity in self-compassion and curiosity, followed by action to better support yourself.

Healing is not about figuring out what to do; it doesn't matter if you know what to do if you don't trust yourself to do it. Healing is about learning to trust yourself.

Trust Is a Choice, Supported by Action, Built over Time

Trusting yourself is not something that happens to you; it's a choice you make and support through action. No matter what you achieve or how well you perform, you will not trust yourself until you choose to trust yourself.

Accolades don't deliver self-trust. You can rise all the way to the tippy-top-teetering tier of your field. Without trust in yourself, you'll be as insecure at the top as you were before you started the climb.

Be wary of the need to prove to yourself that you trust yourself via some big bold move you're not ready for (impulsively quitting your job, for example). When you act with boldness to prove trustworthiness, the boldness backfires. Trust cannot be rushed.

For example, I've worked with a lot of clients dealing with the aftermath of an affair where trust has been racket-smashed into the dirt. It's never *ever* the big bold action that reestablishes trust. The person who has been betrayed does not give a shit about a room filled with two hundred roses. The person who has been betrayed wants their partner to do simple, seemingly little things consistently for a long time, like call when they say they will call and be where they say they will be.

You don't have to grand gesture yourself. Any size action that is aligned with your values will help you rebuild trust with yourself. Think of it like this: if you knew that someone had hacked into your bank account and stolen twenty-five dollars, wouldn't that bother you as much as if they'd stolen seventy-five dollars? It's not the dollar amount that breaks your confidence, it's the gesture of stealing anything. Period. Similarly, it's not the "dollar amount" that rebuilds your trust; it's the gesture of honoring your values to any degree. Period.

But you don't understand. I have very good reasons not to trust myself.

We all have very good reasons not to trust ourselves. We've all betrayed ourselves badly, repeatedly, shamefully, and knowingly. Show me someone who hasn't abandoned themselves, and I will show you a child. As we grow into adults, our world opens and we make mistakes. Ignoring your own needs and deserting yourself is a universal mistake.

Paradoxically, the people who trust themselves the most are usually the people who have betrayed themselves the most profoundly, but then made the decision to walk themselves home—inch by inch—to their authentic selves.

Your self-destructive patterns are the least interesting thing about you; why are you allowing them to lead your identity? Is the damaged version of who you are really your whole story? Are you not bored with this narrative yet?

Excitement lies in the much bigger story you're not sharing about who you really are. The worth that's piled up inside you, waiting to be scooped up like a heap of riches in a cave—the latent gifts and desires within yourself that we both know you can feel.

You know why you're not leading with that part yet? The part where you stake claim to what you really want? Because you don't trust yourself to live up to that version of your story.

As Marianne Williamson so eloquently puts it:

> Our deepest fear is not that we are inadequate. Our deepest fear is
> that we are powerful beyond measure. It is our light, not our dark-
> ness that most frightens us. We ask ourselves, "Who am I to be
> brilliant, gorgeous, talented, fabulous?" Actually, who are you not to
> be? You are a child of God. Your playing small does not serve the
> world. There is nothing enlightened about shrinking so that other
> people won't feel insecure around you. We are all meant to shine, as
> children do. We were born to make manifest the glory of God that
> is within us. It's not just in some of us; it's in everyone. And as we
> let our own light shine, we unconsciously give other people permis-
> sion to do the same. As we are liberated from our own fear, our
> presence automatically liberates others.

When you're ready to face your fears, you don't ask yourself what the
worst thing that could happen is; you ask yourself what you truly want.

The First Step in Trusting Yourself

This is the question to start with when it comes to trusting yourself:
What do I want?

"What do I want?" is an extremely basic question, and yet it can elicit
a deer-in-the-headlights reaction: *What do you mean? Can you explain the
question?* The question is, What do you want?

I understand that you're grateful for all that you have; do you understand that it's okay for you to want more? Do you understand that your
desires are not pathological?

There's a voice inside you that's always there. It tells you what feels
right and what doesn't. It tells you what you need, what you desire, and
where your true pleasure lies. To adapt to your truest self, you need to
listen to your intuitive voice. Anytime you ask yourself what you want,
you invite your intuition to speak directly into the microphone.

Let the sound of the words hit the air as you say it out loud, *I want* ___.

Once you've identified what you want, thinking and speaking about yourself in a manner that supports the idea that you are a person who can get what you want proves to be a whole other animal. There can be a deep reluctance to honor the intuitive knowing you hold inside: that you're capable and worthy.

Contrast that with the ease with which we as women can list our inadequacies. When it comes to identifying our faults, we reflexively shoot from the hip all day long and into the night. We memorize and broadcast our perceived flaws like a bunch of bored waitresses reciting the specials.

Rebecca didn't have a deer-in-the-headlights response to the *What do you want* question. An intense perfectionist, she gave her answer in a burst of efficiency.

ME: I want you to close your eyes.

REBECCA: I'm not closing my eyes but go ahead.

ME: I'm going to ask you a question, and before you answer the question, I want you to describe any images that come to your mind, any images at all.

I asked Rebecca to describe images because I've noticed that's how a lot of people first encounter what they intuitively want—visually. An emblem of their desire appears long before there are clean words to articulate it, almost like a waking dream.

REBECCA: Got it. Let's go. Ask me the question.

She reminded me of a tennis player in ready position, eager to sprint to any spot on the court.

ME: What do you want?

REBECCA: A cactus.

I heard the immediacy with which Rebecca answered before I heard her response. And I began to respond to that immediacy until I stopped myself and listened to her answer.

ME: Let me slow you down. The point of this is—wait, did you say a cactus?

REBECCA: I see a cactus.

ME: What do you think that means?

REBECCA: Oh, I already know what it means. I think about cactuses all the time—on my way to work, in meetings, in the shower. I want to be in the warmth. I need the sun. I want to live somewhere bright, somewhere hot, somewhere cactuses grow. Is that the point of this exercise, because if so, I think we should move on to the next part.

It was the dead of winter. I tilted my head towards the window, featuring a beautiful view of Manhattan's skyline against a white fog.

ME: It's not very hot here.

REBECCA: I know, and I hate that. I loved New York when I first moved here, but it's lost its appeal for me. I want to move to LA. I feel like myself there. Everything's easier there.

ME: You never mentioned any of this before.

REBECCA: Yeah, well it's not like I'd actually go.

ME: What stops you from moving to LA?

REBECCA: We don't have offices there.

ME: But you don't even like your job.

REBECCA: That's not the point.

Rebecca had no romantic attachments in the city, no kids, no pets, and she was renting. Some of her family and friends lived in New York, but most were spread across the country. She was in a unique financial situation, too. She'd paid off her student loans and debts, and after living well below her means for years, she had a seriously sizable nest egg. She was able to pick up and leave, and yet she stayed.

ME: Rebecca—

REBECCA: I know. I already know everything you're about to say, but you can't just rearrange your whole life because you want to be in the sun.

ME: Who told you that?

REBECCA: What are you talking about?! Nobody told me that. It's the way it is. You can't just run around doing whatever you want whenever you want.

ME: Of course not, if doing what you want is hurting yourself or some- one else. But in this case, *not* doing what you want is hurting you. You're depressed, and what you're telling me is that you intuitively know that being in a sunnier environment where it's easier for you to feel like yourself is what you want. I'm so curious about what would happen if you started taking some trips out to LA. Are you curious, too, or am I alone in that?

REBECCA: No, I'd love to spend more time there. When the plane lands in LA, it feels like something has physically lifted off me. I talk to people there, strangers, and it's nice. I'm a different person there. I feel freer.

ME: What does it feel like when you land in New York?

REBECCA: Like a funeral.

ME: That's strong language; you really don't like it here.

REBECCA: I hate it here.

ME: You described a sense of entitlement earlier, that it's not okay to feel free to "run around doing whatever you want." Do you ever wonder what makes you feel so entitled and free to run around doing all the things you *don't* want to do?

Rebecca took a long pause (long for her, at least).

REBECCA: I don't like this conversation.

ME: I'm not asking you to like it.

REBECCA: Well, what are you asking me? What do you want me to say?!

ME: You feel free to do what you *don't* want all the time. I'm asking you to seriously consider whether that's where you'd like your sense of entitlement and freedom to remain.

In subsequent sessions and in a somewhat clandestine way, Rebecca shared with me that she'd begun imagining the details of her LA home— a gray stone path over uncut grass leading to the front door. Her vision was widening. Encouraging the pleasure of envisioning her home, I told Rebecca about my love of front doors, likening them to the quirkiness of custom mailboxes.

REBECCA: What do you mean?

ME: Every door is so different—

REBECCA: No, about the mailboxes.

ME: Well, you know, you can pick your own mailbox if you have your own house. It's not like the communal mailboxes here.

REBECCA: You can pick your own mailbox? People do that?

ME: Yeah, some people do.

With that, Rebecca embarked on finding the perfect one. She took inexplicable pleasure in googling mailboxes. She'd occasionally text me screenshots of her favorites, and I'd text back with cactus and sun emojis. We discussed how her pleasure was informing a much deeper desire. How the mailbox was coming to represent something intangible but critical.

One session, before I thought we'd even begun, while she was taking off her coat, Rebecca asked me if I thought two hundred dollars was too much to pay for a mailbox, if she really loved the mailbox. "You found the perfect mailbox?" I asked. "I found the perfect mailbox," she said.

This was a watershed moment for reasons neither of us could articulate but for which we nonetheless shared a clear understanding. "Show me right now," I said as we remained standing next to her hung-up coat.

Rebecca scrolled around for a second and then handed me her phone. I recognize how bizarre this sounds, but seeing the mailbox she chose was like looking at a picture of a newborn baby. It was perfect. "Oh, Rebecca," I said. "I know," she replied.

It took Rebecca two years to move to LA. As all of us do, she struggled with feeling entitled to "go around doing whatever she wants." She spent a lot of energy defending her decision to an imaginary council in her mind. Rebecca also struggled with bouts of clinical depression, which made it harder to feel brave and bold and to trust herself. But! Hard is not impossible. She did it.

Rebecca got to the Golden State by allowing herself to entertain her desire within the framework of an impending reality—something that was going to happen—as opposed to treating her desire like it was a fantasy that could never be real.

As so many intense perfectionists do, Rebecca got tripped up on process perfectionism. She felt like every step was taking far too long. The time it was taking her to "just move" broadcasted her fears about being a failure. For example, it took her four months to reach out to a real-estate agent, which displayed the following fear-based message on the marquee of her mind: *See how long it's taking you just to get started? If you really wanted this, you would have done it by now. You're never going to do it. You're just distracting yourself with this silly fantasy. Get back to work.*

There was a moment when Rebecca had to decide if the fact that it took her four months to reach out to a real-estate agent meant that she was no longer worthy of going to California in her lifetime. Punishment or self-compassion—I'll never forget that moment. I'll also never forget the call I got from her when she started receiving junk mail at her new house. I was in session, so she left a message: "I have mail! It says, 'Current Resident.' *I'm* the current resident! I live here!"

Sustainable change unfolds on such a granular level, so microscopically, for so long. When you're in the middle of the change, you don't realize how much you're changing. Inevitably, there are moments of discouragement when you don't think you're changing at all. Then, a single visible moment stacked upon thousands of invisible ones bursts through.

It's easily one of my favorite parts of my job, the way clients announce to me that the shift they've been working towards consistently for months or years has "somehow" occurred. As if by magic. As if I would be surprised. It's the giddy shock of the "suddenly moment."

"Suddenly" something happens that makes you realize that the goal you've been working on has become a reality. Maybe the "suddenly moment" hits you when you overhear a stranger on the bus talking about the app you built and you're like, *Oh my God, that's my app. I really built an app!* Maybe you're at dinner with your new wife and the waiter asks, "Do you or your wife have any food allergies?" and you're like *Oh my God, I have a wife. We really got married!*

The "suddenly" list is endless. The point is that you're experiencing something that previously was almost impossible for you to *even imagine.* This experience cannot happen without you earnestly asking yourself, "What do I want?"

All that said, there are times in life when you're so lost that you honestly have no idea what you want because you don't know who you are. Lost moments can be the most powerful moments of your life.

The Greatest Form of Power

Zero-gravity, raw, utterly "lost" moments beckon for surrender. Surrender is the ultimate loss of control and the greatest form of power. Surrendering is not conceding to defeat. Surrendering is conceding to potentialities beyond your imagining.

To surrender is to affirm that you are not alone. When you surrender, you acknowledge that there is a force other than you at work, and because that force exists and you also exist, connecting to that force is possible. To surrender is to invite that connection forward.

The force you connect to doesn't have to be God or any proxy of God;

you don't even have to name it. It can be whatever makes the sun come up or the alchemical properties of laughter. In secular terms, God is wherever you find meaning, and prayer is communing with that meaning. If you find meaning being out on the ocean, then getting on a boat is a form of prayer for you.

Surrender is a prayer that says, "I'm open." It's not uncommon to arrive at the point of surrender after being broken open. It doesn't matter how you arrive at the point of openness. What matters is that you understand that being open is powerful.

Surrendering creates an openness wherein you welcome that which was previously not possible for you to understand, hold, or be.

When you surrender, you're not asking for anything, you're affirming connection to that which exists beyond your individual self. When you're disconnected from anything beyond your individual self, you operate against a panic.

You think it's all up to you, and in the thick of that impossible pressure, you feel that you must control everything. Because it's not all up to you and you can't control everything, you fail.

When you lose control and don't surrender, what you're left with is immutable failure. There's nothing for the failure to transmute itself into because you don't believe in anything other than your individual self.

When you lose control and do surrender, what you're left with is possibility. The possibility arises because in the process of surrendering, you let go of the narcissistic notion that you are the all-knowing being who can figure out every answer to every question and thereby control the universe at large.

A 2017 study explored differences in well-being between adaptive perfectionists, maladaptive perfectionists, and non-perfectionists. While adaptive perfectionists reported the highest levels of meaning in their lives, maladaptive perfectionists reported the highest levels of *searching* for meaning.[3]

You don't need to believe in divine providence or anthropomorphic metaphysical labels for your life to have meaning, but you do need to believe in something. Without believing in anything, we can't produce meaning. Without meaning, we struggle.

Finding Meaning

What penetrates us with meaning doesn't have to be steeped in gravity or righteousness. You can believe in the power of eye contact, the importance of public libraries, or being the one who always brings the good snacks. Meaning is an equalizing affair; the lightest touch seeps just as deep.

You have the power to assign meaning to whatever you choose. You also have the power to take what's meaningful to you and bring it to life through personal policy. For example, if you believe that eye contact has the power to validate others and you find meaning in that, then you enact a policy of making eye contact with each human being you encounter instead of transactionally existing among others, and your life becomes more meaningful. If you don't know what's meaningful to you, ask yourself this question: What's sum is greater than the whole of its parts? Music, for example, is a sequence of notes played at a particular cadence. If you believe a song is more than a sequence of notes played at a particular cadence, then music holds meaning for you.

Meaning transforms something literal into something figurative.

When you connect to something meaningful, you get perspective and purpose, but you don't get control. You want to make something? You don't get to control whether others like it. You want to love someone? You don't get to control how safe they are at all times.

It's terrifying to bring more meaning into your life. There's no special hat trick for making the fear disappear. Remember that most of what you're afraid of exists only in your mind, then let the paper tigers roar.

Invite meaning anyway. A person who understands that they can use their everyday life to animate what's meaningful to them is a person who is in touch with their power.

An Imperceptible Shift

When you don't give yourself the chance to animate what's meaningful for you, you set yourself up for a death-by-papercut life in which you never get to be your real self in the world. You never get to be free.

You feel as if you're living behind glass, as if you can only be yourself in private. It doesn't feel awful every day, that's the most dangerous part. Experiencing freedom on a technicality feels familiar, routine.

You can live your whole life that way, politely being less. Pretending you're not powerful and calling that modesty.

Curtailing your power and presence is not a reflection of modesty, humility, or anything of the sort. Leading with your strengths while also recognizing that every human being has a talent for something—that's what modesty is. Understanding that whatever it is that you want to accomplish or whomever it is that you want to become, you need so much help and collaboration from other people to get you there—that's what humility is.

The sun hits your skin differently when you're no longer behind the glass. The difference is subtle, but the subtlety is everything. As you adapt inwardly, the shift you experience will be subtlety imperceptible to anyone but you. At least at first, only you will feel it, only you will know. Letting yourself delight in that private shift is both a pleasure and a gift unto yourself.

If you keep denying yourself pleasure, you're signaling to yourself that you're not to be trusted with power and that you need to be controlled.

In a control mindset, pleasure is a distraction. You don't have time to feel good when you're operating within a scarcity model that demands a continual supply of externally validated worth. You start intellectualizing joy, making an excellent plan to be very happy later.

In a power mindset, you allow yourself to delight in your world now, today. Not because you earned it or because you feel like being "bad" or "naughty," but because you are alive.

If pleasure invites joy and trust invites pleasure, what invites trust?

Self-Forgiveness

If you're trying to rebuild trust with yourself, it behooves you to take an inventory of past versions of yourself that may need your present-day forgiveness. Rebuilding trust and forgiving yourself sounds like a slog, but it doesn't have to be. You can begin renewing trust and forgiveness in the next few minutes because trust and forgiveness are not binary.

You can trust yourself a little, a lot, somewhere in between, most days, not at all, or implicitly. Same with forgiveness. You can forgive yourself a little, a lot, somewhere in between, most days, not at all, or unconditionally. As the saying goes, forgiveness is not a line you cross, it's a path you walk on.

If you don't trust yourself implicitly or forgive yourself unconditionally, that's fine. The notion that you have to love yourself and forgive yourself and trust yourself 100 percent in every category of your life before you can consider yourself healthy or healed is ludicrous.

For example, women are constantly told "Love your body" because of the mistaken idea that loving yourself "doesn't count" until you love the way your body looks. While well intended, directives to love your body are a continuation of the centering of women's bodies as their primary (mandated) route to happiness. Perceived to be the most impressive indication of confidence, loving your body is billed as the highest-flying flag of mental health for women. Loving your body and loving yourself are synonymous statements in the wellness world.

Loving yourself doesn't hinge on loving your body. Loving yourself and loving your body are not the same thing, because you are not your body. You can like your body, appreciate your body, dislike your body, or not think about your body that much at all. You can also love your body and hate yourself.

We think loving ourselves "doesn't count" until we love our bodies. We think forgiving someone "doesn't count" if we still feel occasional resentment towards the forgiven. We think trusting ourselves "doesn't count" unless we can be locked in a room with our Achilles' heel person or habit and know with certainty that we won't engage. None of this is true.

You have the power to choose to examine forgiveness and trust through a nonbinary lens instead of an all-or-nothing lens. In Dr. Harriet Lerner's myth-smashing, breakthrough book, which should be required reading in every high school, *Why Won't You Apologize?: Healing Big Betrayals and Everyday Hurts*, she spotlights a couple she was counseling through an affair, Sam and Rosa.

Ultimately, the couple decided to stay married and reached out to Dr. Lerner again several years later regarding an issue they were having with one of their kids. At the end of that session, Sam unexpectedly turned to Rosa and asked her if she'd forgiven him for the affair. Rosa's response: "Ninety percent. I forgive you for having the affair, but I will *never* forgive you for the time that you slept with her in our bed when I was out of town."

In Dr. Lerner's words, "Rosa forgave Sam 90 percent and that was enough for them to move forward in their marriage . . . I suspect Sam respected his wife more for continuing to claim her 10 percent. Maybe, over many years, the 10 percent of non-forgiveness would lessen, or maybe not. In any case, Rosa knew she was on solid ground not to forgive everything."[4]

Just like other-forgiveness, self-forgiveness does not need to be 100 percent for you to move forward.

Perfectionists encounter significant resistance when it comes to self-forgiveness. Self-forgiveness threatens our heightened sense of accountability, and (more simply) we don't know how to forgive ourselves. What does forgiveness look like, exactly? What are we even supposed to be for-giving ourselves for?

Maybe you have nothing you need to forgive yourself for, I don't know. What I do know is that if you've stepped outside of your integrity, ignored your instincts, neglected your desires, or otherwise dismissed your true self *without acknowledging that those things happened*—that's a problem. It's a problem because resentment is a placeholder for the unac-knowledged.

Resentment is heavy. If you want to be light enough to be uplifted by joy, you have to let go of the things that weigh you down.

But how?

According to Dr. Lerner, "The word *forgive* is much like the word *re-spect*. It can't be commanded or demanded or forced or gifted for no rea-son at all."[5] Dr. Lerner goes on to note that when people say they want forgiveness, what she hears is that "people just want the burden of their anger and resentment to go away. Words or phrases like *resolution, detach-ment, moving on,* or *letting go* may better describe what they seek."[6] Apply-ing that language to self-forgiveness may initially seem problematic—how do you detach or move on from yourself? You don't.

You detach, move on from, and let go of the idea that your worth as a human being is connected in any way to the number of mistakes you've made in the past. Entertain the notion that who you are in this moment is not defined by previous versions of yourself.

Self-forgiveness is about being able to reserve some room in your iden-tity for a new adaptation of yourself to appear. Whether it's big or small, giving yourself some blank space on the canvas is a generous offering and a sign of real openness.

Forgiveness also looks like responding to the you who's showing up now, not the you from the past (keeping in mind that "one hour ago" counts as the past).

We've all heard that gratitude increases your joy, but that's only half true. Gratitude *can* increase your joy, *but only if you've forgiven yourself enough to let joy in*. Don't think of gratitude as the key to joy. Gratitude is a gas pedal for joy; self-forgiveness is the key that turns everything else on.

To be clear, forgiveness does not automate trust. Are there not people in your life whom you've forgiven and no longer harbor resentment towards, but whom you also don't allow to get close to you because you don't trust them at all? Love, trust, forgiveness—none of them offer any guarantees on the others.

To recap: forgiving yourself releases resentment and invites a clean surface on which to rebuild trust with yourself. Trusting yourself invites the allowance of pleasure. Taking pleasure in your life invites joy. None of this invites certainty.

Certainty

Certainty isn't real. Therapists continually witness certainty being upended. Sometimes everything a person thinks is true about their life changes in the span of ten months, ten hours, or even ten seconds.

When you're connected to yourself and you're present, you don't need certainty. When you trust yourself, you understand that no matter what changes *around* you, there are a thousand right paths to the true self *within* you.

We want there to be only one right way to be ourselves because we think that will tell us something about who we are. If we know that what we're *doing* represents the right choice, then we can know if *we're* right or wrong. On a deeper level, this emotionally charged logic translates to our incessant need to verify our worth—if what we do is the good thing to do, then we are good. We also want what we do to be who we are because defining who you are outside of what you do is arduous work.

If we lose weight, we want that to mean we're healthy. If we stop drinking, we want that to mean we're responsible. If we give to charity, we want that to mean we care. If we have sex, we want that to mean we're comfortable with our sexuality. If we're good at being liked, we want that to mean we're worthy of being loved. If we get into a top-tier school, we want that to mean we're smart. If we're pretty, we want that to mean we're confident . . .

We grip onto an endless array of unconscious attachments about the ways in which our relationships, appearance, and achievements define who we are and what we're worthy of.

You are a human being. You are not what you do or what you have or who you're with or what you look like. You are an expansive, powerful, large, ever-changing force in the world, like an ocean—not some tiny forgotten room in an old run-down house. The larger you allow yourself to be, the easier it is to find your way back to yourself.

If you think of yourself as the small room, you'll look for the one door that'll get you into the room. If you think of yourself as the ocean, you'll know there are a thousand places you can dive in from. The former feels anxiety provoking: *What if I can't find the door?* The latter feels like an empowering adventure: *Where should I jump in from today?!*

You're in a control mindset when you fixate on finding the one right person, the one right job, the one right house, or the one right life. There is no one right way to be who you are. There's no "one right door" to enter before you get to you any more than there's one right place to dive into the ocean.

Even when you do know with absolute certainty that someone or something is definitely "it," you change. People change, jobs change, passions change, cities change—everything changes. Adaptive perfectionists cycle through change vigorously because we love pushing ourselves to grow, and you can't grow without changing.

Change is scary because we think it requires us to rearrange ourselves such that we have to find the one right way all over again. Change is a lot less scary when you stay in touch with the notion that you are large, not small, so of course there are a thousand paths to yourself.

What Trusting Yourself Looks Like in Real Life

In the rom-com version of life, change is sweeping, sequential, and accompanied by an upbeat soundtrack. Someone's always standing in an elevator with a cardboard box looking sad, then the magical musical montage happens.

First come the scenes where the person is falling face forward into their bed after a long hard day of starting over. Then come the scenes where they step on some gum or some dog poo, maybe they spill their coffee all over themselves or they miss the bus—the point is, they "persevere."

Then, before the catchy song is even over, they're standing in front of a mirror making needless adjustments to their amazing outfit with a gorgeous, self-satisfied grin. They got a shiny new life full of everything they wanted in less time than it takes me to clean my retainer. That's not how change works.

Trusting yourself looks like taking a month to secretly pick a mailbox for a house you don't yet own, without being able to explain why the task is both pleasurable and important (while also feeling vaguely embarrassed about it the whole time). Trusting yourself looks like finding the courage to override the constant temptations to minimize the small but meaningful steps you're taking to honor your intuition. Trusting yourself looks like depersonalizing setbacks. Trusting yourself looks like realizing that just because the thing you felt so certain about changed, that doesn't mean you were wrong, made a bad choice, or have faulty intuition.

When you're in an adaptive space, you allow what's perfect for you to change because you know that the perfection is coming from inside of you. What was so funny about Rebecca's move is that she never bought a mailbox. When she found the right house for her, she said the mailbox it came with was "already perfect." The sense of perfection she was projecting onto the mailbox reflected her internal alignment with a decision that she knew was right for her. Rebecca felt like her full, whole, perfect self when she moved to LA; her internal state colored the way she experienced her external world.

When you're in a maladaptive space, you're not connected to your wholeness (perfection), so you try to outsource perfection. Your world becomes superficially perfect while you're miserable on the inside.

If you're out of the practice of asking yourself what you want, and aren't we all at some point, trusting yourself looks like being brave enough to ask yourself that question in the first place, *then believing your own answer.* Your most authentic life probably won't look the way you were expecting it to look. Trusting yourself looks like giving yourself permission to enjoy and embrace the surprises that come.

Lastly, trusting yourself looks like knowing that even though living the way you want to is taking you so much longer than you thought and it's not looking the way you thought it would, you can do it—and, in fact, you are already doing it.

In writer Holly Whitaker's beautiful words, "We are always, forever doing the things we imagine in our hearts. We have always started long before we even realized we started. The gestation periods can be long and un-notable; the blocks are the path. If you are feeling like you aren't doing it, or like you're waiting for the real work to begin, please remember in this moment, you are doing it. There is no other way through to it than the way you have gone, are going . . . You *are* doing it. This is it."[7]

It Will Take Time

What you think will take six months *tops* somehow takes five years. Life enters the room. It's okay—life enters the room for everyone. Personal development doesn't happen in a vacuum and the challenging circumstances we face are real.

You can't instantaneously leave your job when you need money and health insurance. We have kids who need stability and good school districts. We have astronomically high student loans and medical bills. We have loved ones struggling with addiction (perhaps we are the loved ones struggling). We have time constraints, genetic predispositions, bad credit, bad housing markets, a history of trauma, excess anxiety, depression, that thing that keeps happening with our back.

Again, so much happens in every single person's life.

What you want will continue to present as intangible for a significant, probably painful amount of time. Remember that your worst day of actively working towards what you want in this life is going to be better than your best day of a life in which you are denying yourself your truest desire.

Easy Come, Easy Go

There will always be other people around you who seem to be able to "decide and do" while you have to grind away slowly. People with less obligation, less intense mental health struggles (for now), more money, more privilege, more resources, more connections, and so on. Wanting to move across the country when you're taking care of an aging or sick parent, for example, is a very different experience than wanting to move without having to consider that kind of familial obligation.

The people who do it "instantly" have their own struggles to contend with. As appealing as it may seem to be able to generate immediate results, there are costs associated with getting what you want quickly. As Dr. Tal Ben-Shahar puts it, "Talent and success without the moderating effect of failure can be detrimental, even dangerous."[8]

Those who get what they want with minimal to no effort miss the opportunity to cultivate the strengths and skills required to sustain success. While there are exceptions to every rule, the adage "Easy come, easy go" applies well here.

Needs Are Not Wants

A great leap occurs in conversations about how we struggle but then find resilience. What we leap over is the distinction between whether we're struggling to survive or thrive. *What do you want?* may be a basic question, but it's not as basic as *Are your fundamental human needs being met?*

When we think of basic human needs, we think of physical needs: food, water, shelter. Humans have basic psychological needs, too: dignity, emotional safety, liberty—these are not wants.

We can't rise to our potential while our basic needs go unmet. And whenever fundamental human needs go unmet, trauma is not far behind.* It's an oversimplification, but I can sum up trauma in four words: trauma is a block. You don't remove the block that trauma creates by removing yourself from the traumatic situation; removing yourself only stops the bleeding. Stopping the bleeding is not the same as healing the wound.

In systemic trauma, you can't remove yourself from the situation because the situation is the culture. Dismal access to quality health care, exposure to cycles of violence, geographical isolation from community care, living in poverty, living under white supremacy, racism—these chronic psychosocial stressors are examples of systemic traumas.

We resist thinking of ourselves as traumatized because it feels like taking a passive stance of victimhood. On the contrary, it's empowering to understand what's happening, why it's happening, and what we can do about it.

You remove the block that trauma creates by acknowledging that trauma has occurred (or is occurring), learning to recognize its pervasive effects, and incorporating trauma-sensitive intervention strategies into your healing.

---

* For better or worse, the word *trauma* has become a ubiquitous way to describe hardship. Because you are the one in charge of assigning meaning to your world, only you can say whether an experience was traumatic for you.

Adopting a trauma-informed approach when our basic needs have gone unmet helps us to externalize the source of the dysfunction we experience. In other words, it's not you; you're not broken, you're not bad, you're not too far gone. You're walking through trauma in the dark. You have the power to turn on the light.*

Helping ourselves and others create the lives we want requires community care.

Community Care

Community care is about fostering interdependence; you allow yourself to both help and be helped by the community at large. On a macro level, community care looks like operating with an understanding of the social determinants of health (SDOH) and then integrating social care models into multidisciplinary realms (primary-health-care delivery systems, urban and regional planning, gerontology, education policy, etc.).

Examples include ride-sharing and public-transit programs that offer travel vouchers for doctor appointments or visits to elderly care facilities, telehealth platforms that democratize access to therapy, and educational institutions that incorporate SDOH subject matter into their core curriculum.

On a micro level, community care looks like creating communication pathways for shared childcare pools or elderly monitoring (which can be as simple as a group text between three neighbors), community fridges, toy swaps, book swaps, groups that meet monthly to revitalize the neighborhood, potlucks, block parties, and so on. Being a good neighbor is community care—it can be as simple as changing your neighbor's hard-to-reach lightbulb because you have a ladder and they don't, or offering to

---

* The best book I've encountered on what trauma is and what to do about it is *What Happened to You: Conversations on Trauma, Resilience, and Healing* by Oprah Winfrey and Dr. Bruce D. Perry. It's written as a conversation between the two authors and includes lots of storytelling, so it's easier to digest than one might initially assume it to be.

babysit for a new mom, or dropping off food for a family who you know is going through a crisis.

Community care also looks like spending your privilege and moving, as author and activist Brittany Packnett Cunningham writes, "toward solidarity and not charity."

Perhaps the best definition I've heard comes from Dr. Maya Angelou, who said of engaging in community care: "In doing so, your life is enlarged. You belong to everybody, and everybody belongs to you."

Expect Resistance

There's no shortage of psychoanalytical jargon describing the human inclination to push away from that which one most deeply desires. I prefer the simple term "resistance."

Expressions like "You're your own worst enemy" and "Get out of your own way" allude to the self-sabotaging nature of resistance: we internally fight against what we know is right for us.

All human beings encounter resistance; it's as natural as sneezing. You want to get out of that relationship you know isn't right for you? Expect resistance. You want to advance to the next level of your career, which you know in your bones you're ready for? Expect resistance. You want to write a book, start a company, stop smoking, connect more meaningfully with your kids, create art, breathe deeply, go to bed earlier, mail a letter, eat a salad, do anything that's not explicitly self-destructive? Expect resistance.

Artist extraordinaire Steven Pressfield describes resistance well:

> Resistance is an impartial force of nature, like gravity . . . The apparition of resistance is by definition a good sign, because resistance never appears except when preceded by a dream. The dream arises in our psyche (even if we deny it, even if we fail to or refuse to recognize it) like a tree ascending into the sunshine. Simultaneously

the dream's shadow appears—i.e., resistance—just as a physical tree casts a physical shadow. That's a law of nature. Where there is a dream, there is resistance. Thus: where we encounter resistance, somewhere nearby is a dream.[9]

The bigger the dream, the bigger the shadow (the more resistance there is). Resistance is a good thing; it means you're on to something real. There's no need to personalize the fact that you encounter resistance. Resistance is an inextricable part of growth, one that doesn't stop once you become "healthy."

No matter how good you get, no matter how far you advance, no matter what you do to evolve, resistance mutates itself alongside your growth. While there are endless examples of resistance, at the core, resistance for perfectionists involves resisting your inherent worth.

The remedy to resistance is not discipline; it's pleasure. Pleasure is an antidote for so much. Find what brings you real pleasure and you will find your way home to yourself.

My Greatest Pleasures

Listening is one of my greatest pleasures. I listen all the time—in grocery store lines, on the subway, in museums. I can't help it. I don't want to help it.

I waitressed in high school (this was in North Carolina), and my very Southern boss would regularly threaten to fire me because I kept sitting down at customers' tables. The customers would get going talking to me, and before I knew it, we'd be sitting together. I'd look up to see my boss attempting to telepathically communicate with me across the room via bulging eyes.

He'd head-gesture me into the kitchen and as soon as we passed the threshold of those swinging doors, he'd lecture me with that sweet Carolina drawl: "One more time, girl, you do that one more time and you're fired." I always did it "one more time," I didn't realize I was doing it, and I did get fired.

After college, I moved to London and worked at a tiny jewelry store in the Fulham Broadway tube station. Through listening, I learned that wearing jewelry is about wanting to feel something and gifting jewelry is about wanting to express something. Each time a customer came in, whether they knew it or not, so much of what they wanted to feel or express walked in with them. People just told me things, intimate things, especially when no one else was in the shop. Nervous British men were my favorite customers; they were either very much in trouble or very much in love or very much both—and nervous British men do not stop talking.

Bartending was a great job for listening, obviously, and I also loved working as a "coat check girl"—I got to listen to all the ways people say goodbye to one another. I've loved every job I've ever had because I found a way to listen in every job I've ever had. You can only imagine my joy when I became a professional listener for a living.

In addition to the thousands upon thousands of hours I've clocked as a psychotherapist, I've been listening my whole life. While the net of my listening is wide, what's caught in it is small. I've found that every want can be distilled down into one: *connection*.

We get so swept away in our efforts to uncover the meaning of life, drunk on existentialism. It's so simple: *all people want is connection.* It's connection that brings joy and meaning to our lives—that has always been the case and will always be the case.

In my millions of moments of listening, I want to tell you what I've never once heard:

"I miss the way she maintained her wedding weight throughout our entire marriage."

"I knew we'd be fast friends when she was able to buy a house before she turned thirty."

"There was something about the industrious impression that washed over me when I looked at their résumé, and I realized in that moment that I had to have them on my team."

"Now that she's out of the house and off to college, I savor the memories of my daughter getting good grades and always dressing appropriately."

"I'm so inspired by the fact that he went through his entire acting career without a single flop."

"I'd give anything for one more day with her, as long as her hair looked right and she was being funny."

"What most drew me towards her was the way her arms always looked so sculpted in her Instagram photos."

The external achievements you're working on that you think are going to certify your belonging with others: the career moves, the body, the fill-in-the-blank achievement before fill-in-the-blank age? I say this with all the love in my heart: *nobody cares.*

All people care about is you, and you are not a composite list of your perceived accomplishments and failures in life. The energy you bring into the room with you is more valuable than anything you could ever do.

We love to preface conversations about energy with disclaimers: "I know this might sound woo-woo/weird/mystical/hippie, but . . ." There's nothing woo-woo about empathic accuracy; it's part of our interconnectedness as a species. We feel eyes on us from across the room, and we turn. We can cut the tension with a knife because, even though tension is invisible, we can feel the energy of it. We're all connected to a degree so immense that our minds cannot comprehend it.

Acknowledging that we can feel one another's energy doesn't mean we have to start burning incense, shake tambourines, or move into a treehouse. Acknowledging that we can feel one another's energy helps us understand how much power there is in our own energy.

Spend a few years walking with people through their grief and you will discover how little we care about the material. We care about one another's presence. We all just want one more joke in the break room, one more long dinner, one more walk together, one more bath-time, one more holiday morning in our pj's. If you somehow got that "one more" moment with someone you've loved and lost, you would experience every second of it as total perfection. The moment would be perfect because you would be present.

Acutely aware that the moment was a gift, you'd savor the sweet mundanity of it all. A clear understanding of the enormous chasm between matters that hold primary versus secondary importance would instantaneously crystallize for you. You would feel whole. Compassion and forgiveness would be effortless. Joy would flood every part of you.

Those "one more" type of moments happen every day, a hundred times a day, with the people who are still physically in our lives now, and with ourselves; we're just not present for them. Everything you need to be present, you already have. Everything you need to be powerful, you already have. Everything you need to enjoy your life, you already have.

The work of self-acceptance requires you to accept your flaws and limitations, yes; it also requires you to accept your wholeness. There's perfection inside you, there's completeness, and there's freedom. There's a place where your mistakes can't touch who you are and where the past simply does not fucking matter. That indestructible part of you in a den deep inside, what some people might call God, there's nothing you can do to break that part. If you can connect to that place inside yourself, you will connect to your power.

Connecting to your power is not a static task; it is your life's work. We all lose control over and over again, and we all have the same choice to make. We either fight to regain the illusion of control, or we work to align with our power.

The choices you make moving forward belong only to you. Will you choose self-punishment or self-compassion? Absence or presence? Performance or freedom? Isolation or support? Resentment or forgiveness? Suspicion or trust? Immediate gratification or pleasure? Planning joy or joy now?

Will you choose control or power?

Remember, you'll forget. You're going to get distracted. You have to go online and pay that outstanding lab bill from the bloodwork you did at last month's checkup. You have to call the party decoration store because if you don't have balloons at the birthday party, no one could possibly have fun. In your distracted or altogether absent state, you will make the wrong choices.

You'll have moments where you forget everything in this book; that's fine. I'll have moments where I forget everything in this book and I wrote the damn thing. Don't build your story from the part where you forget; build your story from the part where you remember.

AFTERWORD

I had a waking dream. You and God were in it.

You approached God's door, which was ajar. As you knocked, you entered. You came with flowers and sweet confections in your hands. God saw you and beamed. "Come in, come in! How wonderful it is to see you!" God was telling you the truth.

God noticed the beautiful flowers and cheerful candies you were holding. God said, "You brought gifts! Thank you, you didn't have to do that." God was telling you the truth again.

You beamed back at God and said: "I know I didn't have to. I wanted to." You were telling the truth, too.

Then you found a place to sit. It was right beside God, and you made yourself at home.

AUTHOR'S NOTE

Human beings are dynamic creatures whose identity is not static. As Deepak Chopra puts it, "Identity is, at best, provisional." I offer the identities of the five types of perfectionists (and of "perfectionist" itself) to invite awareness around patterns of behaving, thinking, feeling, and relating to oneself and others.

Whether you are or are not something is a binary way of thinking. While binary logic can be helpful in certain circumstances, it is otherwise too simplistic to apply to human beings with consistent accuracy.

Are we perfectionists or not? The identity stamp doesn't matter. I wrote this book to serve as a connection to your true self, no matter who you are or how you choose to define yourself.

Labels are not who you are. Labels represent our desire to contain our experiences with some degree of reliability. Carl Jung's fundamental personality conceptualization of introverts and extroverts; Alfred Adler's concept of the universal "inferiority complex"; Elliott Jaques's notion of a "midlife crisis"; John Bowlby's four attachment styles; Gary Chapman's five love languages; Adam Grant's givers, takers, and matchers; Gretchen Rubin's four tendencies; Susan Cain's sanguine or bittersweet orientations—these are merely a few of the infinite number of ways to categorize the extraordinary experience of being human.

As with the five types of perfectionists, all of these labels are inherently limited intellectual constructs. They are offerings, not the truth. They're someone else's ideas, someone else's interpretation of patterns, someone else's attempt to name what they saw. None of these categorizations mean anything unless they mean something to you.

Healing is a highly individualized process and never looks the same for two people—not in pace, not in method, not in the language that ends up resonating; we each heal in our own unique way. What you most need, only you can know.

In case no one's told you recently (or ever), you are the best expert on your life, your motivations, your desires: whether or not you have a problem, the depth of your capacity, what defines you, whether you're a perfectionist or not, whether that's a good thing or not, what you need to do or not do about it—these are your decisions to make.

Dethrone the idea that anyone else could ever begin to instruct you on how to be who you are. As well-intentioned as others may be, as ever-bursting with love or credentials or authority or experience that others may be, you are the one who knows.

Letting go of control doesn't automatically transmute into power. Sometimes letting go of control means that you just handed the control off to someone else. Giving control to someone else is another way to deny your power. Don't let anyone, including me, tell you who you are. You tell other people who you are—that's power.

As an individual work, this book represents my observations, my experiences, my perspective, my bias. I'm not presenting my ideas and theories as the final word on the matter. I don't believe there could be a final word on the matter.

I wrote this book as a conversation starter. My hope is that these pages spark deeper discussions about what perfectionism is, how it influences us, how we can influence *it*—and more broadly, how we can integrate facets of our mental wellness and mental illness together to achieve mental health.

There are several critical pieces of this conversation that have not been addressed within this book, including the relationship between perfectionism and eating disorders, socially prescribed perfectionism in people of color as a response to white supremacy, the origins of perfectionism in psychological literature (which position perfectionism as one of the most positive forces at work in the psyche), the limitations of perfectionism research, and so forth.

I've published an extended author's note section on my blog for the purpose of addressing these points and continuing the conversation we just started. I invite you to read on at katherinemorganschafler.com, where you'll also find a dedicated page for mental health resources.

In the words of every therapist ever, let's keep talking about this.

ACKNOWLEDGMENTS

It is in a very particular order that I first thank my clients. Amidst so many other lessons, it was you who taught me that there's no line between helper and the person being helped; there's only connection. If I'm working with you now or if I've ever worked with you, know that I'm always in your corner. I'm better by serious measure for having crossed paths with you and I will forever be grateful that out of all the therapists you could've chosen to work with, you chose me. I wanted to write a book to honor the work we did together; the ways you trusted me, helped me, schooled me, shaped me. I always knew I would fail at this endeavor, but I had to try. I hope I failed you well.

Rebecca Gradinger. If Marianne Williamson could see us now! RG boot camp is no joke, but oh how it's prepared me for this moment. Your developmental edits were critical not just in getting this project off the ground but in helping me find my authority as a writer. Is there a better gift a first-time author could possibly receive? It's such a pleasure to find myself standing in the long line of those who have told you: this book would simply not exist without you. One day we will agree on the same thing, *at the same time*, and on that glorious day we will release doves over NYC's skyline. Until then, please accept my most heartfelt thank-you for making my dreams come true. Additional thanks to Kelly Karczewski, Elizabeth Resnick, Veronica Goldstein, Melissa Chinchillo, Yona Levin, Victoria Hobbs, and Christy Fletcher for running the show so seamlessly from behind the scenes.

Niki Papadopoulos. Thank you for saying yes to this project during a moment in history when it was hard to say yes to, like, getting coffee. You're a tonic, the most wonderful teacher, and a fabulous editor. I don't know where all that wisdom comes from, but I suspect it's hard won, and I thank you for sharing it with me. As is true for most people who better the lives of others simply by being themselves, you'll never understand how much you helped me.

Team Portfolio! I gave you a Word document and you gave me a book! The opportunity to write *Perfectionist's Guide* has been one of the greatest of my life; every single person at Portfolio only enhanced the experience. Kimberly Meilun, thank you for explaining everything to me ten thousand times, for your editorial eye, and for continually reminding me that I had extra support if I needed it. Sarah Brody, thank you for this gorgeous cover that I'll cherish always. In case you hate me, our relationship has nowhere to go but up! Margot Stamas, Amanda Lang, Mary Kate Skehan, and Esin Coskun, your collective enthusiasm and brilliant strategy impressed me from minute one. Thank you for championing this book forward as if it were the only one on your list. The copy editors, proofreaders, managing editors, design and production teams: Plaegian Alexander, Nicole Wayland, Lisa Thornbloom, Megan Gerrity, Meighan Cavanaugh, Jessica Regione, Caitlin Noonan, and Madeline Rohlin—to have such careful, perfectionistic, thoughtful attention poured over a project that is so close to one's heart and mind is a feeling like no other. Thank you for making this book sing. Adrian Zackheim. Thank you for turning all the lights green for me, for giving me more time when I needed it, and for making yourself so available to me. Especially because you're in the business of saying "no," thank you for such an enthusiastic, "yes." It's been an honor to work for you and your outstanding team.

And Seth Godin. There were many reasons to choose Portfolio, but you were my favorite reason. Thank you for saving me from a life of politely being less. And Leah Trouwborst. Thanks for going to bat so hard for this book. Parallel universe you and me are totally hanging out right now.

To my first readers and earliest supporters:

Jean Kilbourne. Reading your book as a teenager was one of the best things that ever happened to me. Your support and encouragement back then felt like magic. Your support and encouragement now feel so full circle I could cry. Lori Gottlieb. You make lifting others up look easy and effortless, but I know it requires a lot of energy. Thank you for sending some of your precious energy straight to me. I think about your generosity all the time. Susan Cain. I have no words for you (I could think of a couple songs though). I will say that when I emerged from the solitude of writing this book, your cheering was one of the first sounds I heard. The memory of receiving your support is such a joyful one; I'll never forget what that felt like. Deepak Chopra. You're perfect, but you already know that. Thank you for being open to me, for being open to everything. Nothing but love. Holly Whitaker. You're an extraordinary talent and I love watching you go. Thank you for your instant support. Dr. Bruce Perry. From the bottom of my heart, thank you for your work. I honestly can't get to the part where I thank you for being one of the first people to read and support this book. Dr. Tal Ben-Shahar. As if I weren't impressed enough with you already, there you go being wide open to multiple perspectives and encouraging more dialogue on perfectionism. It's so energizing to see leaders who walk the walk. Michael Schulman. Your artistic integrity, friendship, and enthusiasm have been so uplifting. Thank you for always entertaining my early morning texts, and for making me feel like a real writer on that walk around the reservoir. Ashley Wu. The pandemic took away so much, but I'll always remember that it brought me closer to you. Thank you for creating the physical space wherein this book sprang to life, and for the game-changing, tremendous amount of support you offered in helping spread the message of this work.

Special thanks to Dr. Brené Brown. You're a fortress of boundaries and no one could get to you to deliver a note from me along with this book, which made the therapist in me smile the biggest smile. In short, your work makes me a better therapist and a better human being. Thank you.

It's been my extraordinary luck in life to have attended schools at the same time that these brilliant minds were teaching: Dr. Anika Warren, Dr. Ruth T. Rosenbaum, Dr. Dacher Keltner, Dr. Derald Wing Sue, Dr. Donna Hicks, Dr. Pei-Han Cheng, Naaz Hosseini, Dr. Elizabeth Fraga, and my neuroscience professor from Berkeley whose name I can't remember but who taught neurochemistry via haikus. To each of you: you had a profound impact on my life, my work, and this book. To be in your presence was an education unto itself.

I'd like to acknowledge the leaders in my field who paved the way for this book through their research, writings, and teachings: Dr. Brené Brown, Dr. Tal Ben-Shahar, Dr. Gilad Hirschberger, Dr. Clarissa Pinkola Estés, Dr. Bruce Perry, Dr. Harriet Lerner, Dr. Barbara Fredrickson, Dr. Randy O. Frost, Dr. Simon Sherry, Iyanla Vanzant, Dr. Serena Chen, Dr. Samuel F. Mikail, Dr. Gordon L. Flett, Dr. Paul L. Hewitt, Dr. Joachim Stoeber, Dr. Kristen Neff, Dr. Irvin D. Yalom, Dr. Mary Pipher, Dr. Maya Angelou, Dr. Heinz and Dr. Rowena Ansbacher, Dr. Karen Horney, Dr. Carl Rogers, and of course, Dr. Alfred Adler.

Pippa Wright, thank you for being the first person in the world to buy this book. Lindsay Robertson and Kelsie Brunswick, thank you for helping to get this whole thing started. Thank you to Carla Levy, Courtney Maum, Emma Gray, Dr. Robbie Alexander—and to my research assistant, fact-checker, and endnote citation angel of mercy Kassandra Brabaw.

Melba Remice, any chance I get to publicly thank people, your name will be shared. Lily Randall and Monica Lozano, same.

Bringing a book from inception to publication is, to say the least, hard. Thank you to the incredible friends who rushed to help me through this process when I asked, and even when I didn't ask. Reshma Chattaram Chamberlin, Ben Simoné, Carola Beeney, Dr. Rabia de Latour, Alex de Latour, Natalie Gibralter, Anna Pitoniak, Maya Gorgoni, Thomas Lunsford, Ashley Crossman Lunsford, Shelby Lorman, Christine Gutierrez, Maya Enista Smith, Ty Laforest, Vanna Lee, and Arielle Fierman Haspel. Mary J. and Jeanne, I love you forever. Craig, you're my favorite but don't tell anyone.

Peter Guzzardi, the guardian angel of this book! Thank you for meeting me straight from the airport and telling me you get it. Your friendship during this moment in my life feels fated. I can't wait for all the collaborations ahead.

Dr. Maureen Moomjy, Dr. Carol Aghajanian, and the entire nursing staff at Memorial Sloan Kettering (especially the one blonde nurse from Ireland whose name I forgot but whose kindness on a particularly difficult day I will never forget): thank you for your excellent care while my life spun out of control. And a deepest, endless thank-you to my beautiful and brilliant therapist, and to all my supervisors.

I write about the power of parasocial relationships in this book. It's a resource I tap into all the time and one I especially needed during the pandemic, when I wrote much of this work. Thank you to the bevy of artists and public figures who helped hold me up during that moment. To name only a few: Jada Pinkett Smith, Dax Shepard, Monica Padman, Mandy Patinkin and Kathryn Grody (your shared Instagram page is my happy place), Glennon Doyle (duh), Abby Wambach (double duh), Francesca Amber, Taraji P. Henson, Gayle King, Laura McKowen, Sarah Jakes Roberts, Malcolm Gladwell, Will Smith, Linda Sivertsen, Robin Roberts, Jonathan Van Ness, Bradley Cooper, Megan Stalter, Regina King, and of course, Oprah (the duh of all duhs). To each of you: I hope you never underestimate the power behind the connection you offer. Thank you for your art and your help. Your positive impact lingers.

Liz Gilbert. If only you could've seen me working out while eating doughnuts while listening to *Big Magic*—you would've been damn proud. You made my fears portable. I'm so glad you happened to the world. And to the energy that picked me to write this book, thank you for picking me. Sorry I was mad at you at first.

Shannon, Lauryn, and Lisa. So it turns out being flanked by angels makes for a pretty great life! Thank you for making everything feel cozy, hilarious, and perfect—especially in the moments when life has been the opposite of those things. Where I would be without you three, I cannot fathom. What an eternal blessing, to never have to fathom that.

Oleshia, Jayme, and Marissa: you are loved, adored, and perfect in every way. I must've done something really, *really* good in another life to get to know each of you in this one.

To my parents: thank you for giving me the world and love and grit and freedom. I feel I got the best of both of you, and I thank God for you both. Richard. I imagine you in a crisp, white shirt, drinking steaming espresso early in the morning, getting ready to have a good day. I love you. Caroline. My best friend and greatest inspiration. Thank you for always going first. Your light is so bright it lit the path for me—oats 4eVr. Alexander. The kindest person I know. You elevate everything and everyone in your orbit. How lucky I am to be in your orbit. Je t'aime.

Pam, Scott, Jono, Maia, and Rhoda: thank you for loving me through my many adaptations.

Michael. You've been my greatest champion throughout this many-years-long process and you're a true partner in every realm of life. Thank you for the tremendous amount of love and support you surround me with every day. Even if you never figure out what you want for dinner, I'll love you forever. You're perfect.

Abigail. Well. It is no coincidence that I became obsessed with writing a book about perfection the second you and your little dimples hit the scene. I've been operating with a joy bias since I met you. Strawberries taste sweeter, music sounds better, the world is brighter in every possible way. I love you past all the numbers and letters, past all the things no one even invented a name for yet! You're the one who taught me that we can grow as much through joy as we can through suffering—even more so. Then even more still. Then more again. As you love to say, "Again! Again!"

Lastly and most critically, thank you to whoever oversees thesaurus.com. On the cold, dark days when I was alone at my desk looking up complex words such as "the" and "seemed," thesaurus.com was always there for me. You are the unsung hero of the literary world and anyone who says otherwise has not written a book.

NOTES

Chapter 1: Expect to Be Graded on This

1. Adler, Alfred. *The Individual Psychology of Alfred Adler: A Systematic Presentation in Selections from His Writings*. Edited by Heinz Ludwig Ansbacher and Rowena R. Ansbacher. New York: Harper Perennial, 2006.

Chapter 2: Celebrating Your Perfectionism

1. Ashby, Jeffrey S., and Kenneth G. Rice. "Perfectionism, Dysfunctional Attitudes, and Self-Esteem: A Structural Equations Analysis." *Journal of Counseling & Development* 80, no. 2 (April 2002): 197–203. https://doi.org/10.1002/j.1556-6678.2002.tb00183.x.

2. Kanten, Pelin, and Murat Yesıltas. "The Effects of Positive and Negative Perfectionism on Work Engagement, Psychological Well-Being and Emotional Exhaustion." *Procedia Economics and Finance* 23 (2015): 1367–75. https://doi.org/10.1016/s2212-5671(15)00522-5.

3. Chang, Yuhsuan. "Benefits of Being a Healthy Perfectionist: Examining Profiles in Relation to Nurses' Well-Being." *Journal of Psychosocial Nursing and Mental Health Services* 55, no. 4 (April 1, 2017): 22–28. https://doi.org/10.3928/02793695-20170330-04.

4. Larijani, Roja, and Mohammad Ali Besharat. "Perfectionism and Coping Styles with Stress." *Procedia—Social and Behavioral Sciences* 5 (2010): 623–27. https://doi.org/10.1016/j.sbspro.2010.07.154; Burns, Lawrence R., and Brandy A. Fedewa. "Cognitive Styles: Links with Perfectionistic Thinking." *Personality and Individual Differences* 38, no. 1 (January 2005): 103–13. https://doi.org/10.1016/j.paid.2004.03.012.

5. Kamushadze, Tamar, et al. "Does Perfectionism Lead to Well-Being? The Role of Flow and Personality Traits." *Europe's Journal of Psychology* 17, no. 2 (May 31, 2021): 43–57. https://doi.org/10.5964/ejop.1987.

6. Kamushadze et al. "Does Perfectionism Lead to Well-Being?"

7. Stoeber, Joachim, and Kathleen Otto. "Positive Conceptions of Perfectionism: Approaches, Evidence, Challenges." *Personality and Social Psychology Review* 10, no. 4 (November 2006): 295–319. https://doi.org/10.1207/s15327957pspr1004_2.

8. Suh, Hanna, Philip B. Gnilka, and Kenneth G. Rice. "Perfectionism and Well-Being: A Positive Psychology Framework." *Personality and Individual Differences* 111 (June 2017): 25–30. https://doi.org/10.1016/j.paid.2017.01.041.

9. Grzegorek, Jennifer L., et al. "Self-Criticism, Dependency, Self-Esteem, and Grade Point Average Satisfaction among Clusters of Perfectionists and Nonperfectionists." *Journal of Counseling Psychology* 51, no. 2 (April 2004): 192–200. https://doi.org/10.1037/0022-0167.51.2.192.

10. LoCicero, Kenneth A., and Jeffrey S. Ashby. "Multidimensional Perfectionism in Middle School Age Gifted Students: A Comparison to Peers from the General Cohort." *Roeper Review* 22, no. 3 (April 2000): 182–85. https://doi.org/10.1080/02783190009554030.

11. Rice, Kenneth G., and Robert B. Slaney. "Clusters of Perfectionists: Two Studies of Emotional Adjustment and Academic Achievement." *Measurement and Evaluation in Counseling and Development* 35, no. 1 (April 1, 2002): 35–48. https://doi.org/10.1080/07481756.2002.12069046.

12. Afshar, H., et al. "Positive and Negative Perfectionism and Their Relationship with Anxiety and Depression in Iranian School Students." *Journal of Research in Medical Sciences* 16, no. 1 (2011): 79–86.

13. Hewitt, Paul L., Gordon L. Flett, and Samuel F. Mikail. *Perfectionism: A Relational Approach to Conceptualization, Assessment, and Treatment.* New York: Guilford Press, 2017.

14. Tolle, Eckhart. *A New Earth: Awakening to Your Life's Purpose.* London: Penguin, 2016.

15. Tolle. *A New Earth.*

16. Aristotle. *The Metaphysics.* Edited by John H. McMahon. Mineola, NY: Dover, 2018.

17. Ryan, R. M., and E. L. Deci. "On Happiness and Human Potentials: A Review of Research on Hedonic and Eudaimonic Well-Being." *Annual Review of Psychology* 52, no. 1 (2001): 141–66. https://doi.org/10.1146/annurev.psych.52.1.141.

18. Ryan and Deci. "On Happiness and Human Potentials."

19. Paul, A., Arie W. Kruglanski, and E. Tory Higgins. *Handbook of Theories of Social Psychology.* Los Angeles: Sage, 2012.

20. Grant, Heidi, and E. Tory Higgins. "Do You Play to Win—or to Not Lose?" *Harvard Business Review*, March 1, 2013. https://hbr.org/2013/03/do-you-play-to-win-or-to -not-lose.

21. Bergman, Anthony J., Jennifer E. Nyland, and Lawrence R. Burns. "Correlates with Perfectionism and the Utility of a Dual Process Model." *Personality and Individual Differences* 43, no. 2 (July 2007): 389–99. https://doi.org/10.1016/j.paid.2006.12.007.

22. Chan, David W. "Life Satisfaction, Happiness, and the Growth Mindset of Healthy and Unhealthy Perfectionists among Hong Kong Chinese Gifted Students." *Roeper Review* 34, no. 4 (October 2012): 224–33. https://doi.org/10.1080/02783193.2012.715333.

Chapter 3: Perfectionism as Disease, Balance as Cure, Women as Patients

1. Borelli, Jessica L., et al. "Gender Differences in Work-Family Guilt in Parents of Young Children." *Sex Roles* 76, no. 5–6 (January 30, 2016): 356–68. https://doi.org /10.1007/s11199-016-0579-0.

2. Van Natta Jr., Don. "Serena, Naomi Osaka and the Most Controversial US Open Final in History." ESPN, August 18, 2019. https://www.espn.com/tennis/story/_/id /27408140/backstory-serena-naomi-osaka-most-controversial-us-open-final-history.

3. Matley, David. "'Let's See How Many of You Mother Fuckers Unfollow Me for This': The Pragmatic Function of the Hashtag #Sorrynotsorry in Non-Apologetic Instagram Posts." *Journal of Pragmatics* 133 (August 2018): 66–78. https://doi.org/10.1016 /j.pragma.2018.06.003.

Chapter 4: Perfectionism Up Close

1. Ciccarelli, Saundra K., and J. Noland. *Psychology: DSM 5*, 5th ed. Boston: Pearson, 2014, 681.

2. Ciccarelli and Noland. *Psychology*, 241.

3. Ciccarelli and Noland. *Psychology*, 768.

4. Ciccarelli and Noland. *Psychology*, 768.

5. Ciccarelli and Noland. *Psychology*, 679.

6. Ciccarelli and Noland. *Psychology*, 679.

7. Ciccarelli and Noland. *Psychology*, 679.

8. Ciccarelli and Noland. *Psychology*, 682.

9. Brown, Brené. *I Thought It Was Just Me (but It Isn't): Making the Journey from "What Will People Think?" to "I Am Enough."* New York: Avery, 2008.

10. Horney, Karen. *Neurosis and Human Growth: The Struggle toward Self-Realization.* London, 1951. Reprint, New York: Routledge, Taylor & Francis, 2014.

11. Hewitt, Paul L., Gordon L. Flett, and Samuel F. Mikail. *Perfectionism: A Relational Approach to Conceptualization, Assessment, and Treatment.* New York: Guilford Press, 2017.

12. Covington, Martin V., and Kimberly J. Müeller. "Intrinsic Versus Extrinsic Motivation: An Approach/Avoidance Reformulation." *Educational Psychology Review* 13, no. 2 (2001): 157–76. doi:10.1023/A:1009009219144.

13. Bergman, Anthony J., Jennifer E. Nyland, and Lawrence R. Burns. "Correlates with Perfectionism and the Utility of a Dual Process Model." *Personality and Individual Differences* 43, no. 2 (July 2007): 389–99. https://doi.org/10.1016/j.paid.2006.12.007.

14. Horney. *Neurosis and Human Growth.*

15. Carmo, Cláudia, et al. "The Influence of Parental Perfectionism and Parenting Styles on Child Perfectionism." *Children* 8, no. 9 (September 4, 2021): 777. https://doi.org/10.3390/children8090777.

16. Green, Penelope. "Kissing Your Socks Goodbye." *New York Times*, October 22, 2014. https://www.nytimes.com/2014/10/23/garden/home-organization-advice-from-marie-kondo.html.

17. Flett, Gordon L., Paul L. Hewitt, and American Psychological Association. *Perfectionism: Theory, Research, and Treatment.* Washington, DC: American Psychological Association, 2002.

18. Stone, Deborah M. "Changes in Suicide Rates—United States, 2018–2019." *Morbidity and Mortality Weekly Report* 70, no. 8 (2021). https://doi.org/10.15585/mmwr.mm7008a1.

19. Yard, Ellen. "Emergency Department Visits for Suspected Suicide Attempts among Persons Aged 12–25 Years before and during the COVID-19 Pandemic—United States, January 2019–May 2021." *Morbidity and Mortality Weekly Report* 70, no. 24 (June 18, 2021): 888–94. https://doi.org/10.15585/mmwr.mm7024e1.

20. "Facts about Suicide." Centers for Disease Control and Prevention, January 21, 2021. https://www.cdc.gov/suicide/facts/index.html.

21. "parasuicide." APA Dictionary of Psychology, n.d. https://dictionary.apa.org /parasuicide.

22. McDowell, Adele Ryan. "Adele Ryan McDowell." Adele Ryan McDowell, PhD, 2022. https://adeleryanmcdowell.com.

23. Heilbron, Nicole, et al. "The Problematic Label of Suicide Gesture: Alternatives for Clinical Research and Practice." *Professional Psychology: Research and Practice* 41, no. 3 (2010): 221–27. https://doi.org/10.1037/a0018712.

24. Tingley, Kim. "Will the Pandemic Result in More Suicides?" *New York Times Magazine,* January 21, 2021. https://www.nytimes.com/2021/01/21/magazine/will-the -pandemic-result-in-more-suicides.html.

25. "Firearm Violence Prevention." Centers for Disease Control and Prevention, 2020. https://www.cdc.gov/violenceprevention/firearms/fastfact.html#:~:text=Six %20out%20of%20every%2010.

26. Preidt, Robert. "How U.S. Gun Deaths Compare to Other Countries." CBS News, February 3, 2016. https://www.cbsnews.com/news/how-u-s-gun-deaths-compare-to -other-countries.

27. Dazzi, T., R. Gribble, S. Wessely, and N. T. Fear. "Does Asking about Suicide and Related Behaviours Induce Suicidal Ideation? What Is the Evidence?" *Psychological Medicine* 44, no. 16 (July 7, 2014): 3361–63. https://doi.org/10.1017/s0033291714001299.

28. Freedenthal, Stacey. "Does Talking about Suicide Plant the Idea in the Person's Mind?" Speaking of Suicide, May 15, 2013. https://www.speakingofsuicide.com /2013/05/15/asking-about-suicide.

29. Smith, Martin M., et al. "The Perniciousness of Perfectionism: A Meta-Analytic Review of the Perfectionism-Suicide Relationship." *Journal of Personality* 86, no. 3 (September 4, 2017): 522–42. https://doi.org/10.1111/jopy.12333.

30. Hewitt, Paul L., and Gordon L. Flett. "Perfectionism in the Self and Social Contexts: Conceptualization, Assessment, and Association with Psychopathology." *Journal of Personality and Social Psychology* 60, no. 3 (1991): 456–70. https://doi.org/10.1037 /0022-3514.60.3.456.

31. Klibert, Jeffrey J., Jennifer Langhinrichsen-Rohling, and Motoko Saito. "Adaptive and Maladaptive Aspects of Self-Oriented versus Socially Prescribed Perfectionism." *Journal of College Student Development* 46, no. 2 (2005): 141–56. https://doi.org /10.1353/csd.2005.0017.

Chapter 5: You've Been Solving for the Wrong Problem

1. Hewitt, Paul L., Gordon L. Flett, and Samuel F. Mikail. *Perfectionism: A Relational Approach to Conceptualization, Assessment, and Treatment*. New York: Guilford Press, 2017.

2. Morin, Amy. "How to Manage Misbehavior with Discipline without Punishment." Verywell Family, March 27, 2021. https://www.verywellfamily.com/the-difference-between-punishment-and-discipline-1095044.

3. "Balanced and Restorative Justice Practice: Accountability." Office of Juvenile Justice and Delinquency Prevention. n.d. https://ojjdp.ojp.gov/sites/g/files/xyckuh176/files/pubs/implementing/accountability.html.

4. "Balanced and Restorative Justice Practice: Accountability."

5. Montessori Academy Sharon Springs. "Natural Consequences vs Punishment," April 8, 2019. https://montessoriacademysharonsprings.com/natural-consequences-vs-punishment.

6. Gershoff, Elizabeth T., and Sarah A. Font. "Corporal Punishment in U.S. Public Schools: Prevalence, Disparities in Use, and Status in State and Federal Policy." *Social Policy Report* 30, no. 1 (September 2016): 1–26. https://doi.org/10.1002/j.2379-3988.2016.tb00086.x.

7. Federal Register. "Manner of Federal Executions," November 27, 2020. https://www.federalregister.gov/documents/2020/11/27/2020-25867/manner-of-federal-executions.

8. "Barbara L. Fredrickson, Ph.D." Authentic Happiness. Upenn.edu. 2009. https://www.authentichappiness.sas.upenn.edu/faculty-profile/barbara-l-fredrickson-phd.

9. Fredrickson, Barbara L. "The Role of Positive Emotions in Positive Psychology: The Broaden-and-Build Theory of Positive Emotions." *American Psychologist* 56, no. 3 (2001): 218–26. https://doi.org/10.1037/0003-066x.56.3.218.

10. Breines, Juliana G., and Serena Chen. "Self-Compassion Increases Self-Improvement Motivation." *Personality and Social Psychology Bulletin* 38, no. 9 (May 29, 2012): 1133–43. https://doi.org/10.1177/0146167212445599.

11. Neff, Kristin D. "The Role of Self-Compassion in Development: A Healthier Way to Relate to Oneself." *Human Development* 52, no. 4 (2009): 211–14. https://doi.org/10.1159/000215071.

12. Brown, Brené. *Daring Greatly: How the Courage to Be Vulnerable Transforms the Way We Live, Love, Parent, and Lead*. New York: Gotham Books, 2012.

13. Chan, David W. "Life Satisfaction, Happiness, and the Growth Mindset of Healthy and Unhealthy Perfectionists among Hong Kong Chinese Gifted Students." *Roeper Review* 34, no. 4 (October 2012): 224–33. https://doi.org/10.1080/02783193.2012.715333.

Chapter 6: You'll Enjoy the Solution about as Much as You Enjoy Getting an A−

1. Neff, Kristin. "Definition and Three Elements of Self-Compassion." Self-Compassion, 2019. https://self-compassion.org/the-three-elements-of-self-compassion-2.

2. Neff. "Definition and Three Elements of Self-Compassion."

3. Neff. "Definition and Three Elements of Self-Compassion."

4. Lamott, Anne. "12 Truths I Learned from Life and Writing." www.ted.com, April 2017. https://www.ted.com/talks/anne_lamott_12_truths_i_learned_from_life_and _writing.

5. Neff. "Definition and Three Elements of Self-Compassion."

6. Horney. *Neurosis and Human Growth.*

7. Derrick, Jaye L., Shira Gabriel, and Kurt Hugenberg. "Social Surrogacy: How Favored Television Programs Provide the Experience of Belonging." *Journal of Experimental Social Psychology* 45, no. 2 (February 2009): 352–62. https://doi.org/10.1016 /j.jesp.2008.12.003.

8. Turner, Victor. "Liminal to Limonoid in Play, Flow, and Ritual: An Essay in Comparative Symbology." *Rice University Studies* 60, no. 3 (1974): 53–92.

Chapter 7: New Thoughts to Think to Help You Stop Overthinking It

1. Roese, N. J., and M. Morrison. "The Psychology of Counterfactual Thinking." *Historical Social Research* 34, no. 2 (2009): 16–26. https://doi.org/10.12759/hsr.34.2009.2.

2. Roese and Morrison. "The Psychology of Counterfactual Thinking."

3. Roese and Morrison. "The Psychology of Counterfactual Thinking."

4. Sirois, F. M., J. Monforton, and M. Simpson. "If Only I Had Done Better: Perfectionism and the Functionality of Counterfactual Thinking." *Personality and Social Psychology Bulletin* 36, no. 12 (2010): 1675–92. https://doi.org/10.1177/0146167210387614.

5. Sirois, Monforton, and Simpson. "If Only I Had Done Better."

6. Roese and Morrison. "The Psychology of Counterfactual Thinking."

7. Sirois, Monforton, and Simpson. "If Only I Had Done Better."

8. Sirois, Monforton, and Simpson. "If Only I Had Done Better."

9. Medvec, Victoria Husted, Scott F. Madey, and Thomas Gilovich. "When Less Is More: Counterfactual Thinking and Satisfaction among Olympic Medalists." *Journal of Personality and Social Psychology* 69, no. 4 (1995): 603–10. https://doi.org/10.1037 /0022-3514.69.4.603.

10. Medvec, Madey, and Gilovich. "When Less Is More."

11. Roese and Morrison. "The Psychology of Counterfactual Thinking."

12. Medvec, Madey, and Gilovich. "When Less Is More."

13. Sirois, Monforton, and Simpson. "If Only I Had Done Better."

14. Roese and Morrison. "The Psychology of Counterfactual Thinking."

15. Roese and Morrison. "The Psychology of Counterfactual Thinking."

16. "Physical Activity for People with Disability." Centers for Disease Control and Prevention, May 21, 2020. https://www.cdc.gov/ncbddd/disabilityandhealth/features/physical-activity-for-all.html.

17. Neff, Kristin. "The Criticizer, the Criticized, and the Compassionate Observer." Self-Compassion, February 23, 2015. https://self-compassion.org/exercise-4-supportive-touch/.

18. LaMorte, Wayne. "The Transtheoretical Model (Stages of Change)." Boston University School of Public Health, September 9, 2019. https://sphweb.bumc.bu.edu/otlt/MPH-Modules/SB/BehavioralChangeTheories/BehavioralChangeTheories6.html.

19. LaMorte. "The Transtheoretical Model (Stages of Change)."

20. LaMorte. "The Transtheoretical Model (Stages of Change)."

21. Wilson, Timothy D., and Daniel T. Gilbert. "Affective Forecasting." *Current Directions in Psychological Science* 14, no. 3 (June 2005): 131–34. https://doi.org/10.1111/j.0963-7214.2005.00355.x.

22. Wu, Haijing, et al. "Anticipatory and Consummatory Pleasure and Displeasure in Major Depressive Disorder: An Experience Sampling Study." *Journal of Abnormal Psychology* 126, no. 2 (2017): 149–59. https://doi.org/10.1037/abn0000244.

23. Boehme, Stephanie, et al. "Brain Activation during Anticipatory Anxiety in Social Anxiety Disorder." *Social Cognitive and Affective Neuroscience* 9, no. 9 (August 11, 2013): 1413–18. https://doi.org/10.1093/scan/nst129.

24. Bellezza, Silvia, and Manel Baucells. "AER Model." Email message to the author, 2021.

25. "Will Smith's Red Table Takeover: Resolving Conflict." Red Table Talk, January 28, 2021. https://omny.fm/shows/red-table-talk/will-smith-s-red-table-takeover-resolving-conflict.

26. Winfrey, Oprah, and Bruce Perry. *What Happened to You?: Conversations on Trauma, Resilience, and Healing.* New York: Flatiron Books, 2021.

27. *Choiceology with Katy Milkman* podcast. "Not Quite Enough: With Guests Howard Scott Warshaw, Sendhil Mullainathan, and Anuj Shah," season 4, episode 2. Charles

Schwab, September 23, 2019. https://www.schwab.com/resource-center/insights/content/choiceology-season-4-episode-2.

28. *Choiceology with Katy Milkman* podcast. "Not Quite Enough."

Chapter 8: New Things to Do to Help You Stop Overdoing It

1. *Masters of Scale with Reid Hoffman* podcast. "BetterUp's Alexi Robichaux and Prince Harry: Scale Yourself First, and Then Your Business," episode 107. Spotify, April 26, 2022. https://open.spotify.com/episode/7zJs27PmhL8QFCeJuICfin?si=d1b5082d7ea84289&nd=1.

2. Grossmann, Igor, and Ethan Kross. "Exploring Solomon's Paradox: Self-Distancing Eliminates the Self-Other Asymmetry in Wise Reasoning about Close Relationships in Younger and Older Adults." *Psychological Science* 25, no. 8 (June 10, 2014): 1571–80. https://doi.org/10.1177/0956797614535400.

3. Grossmann and Kross. "Exploring Solomon's Paradox."

4. O'Reilly, Charles A., and Nicholas Hall. "Grandiose Narcissists and Decision Making: Impulsive, Overconfident, and Skeptical of Experts—but Seldom in Doubt." *Personality and Individual Differences* 168 (January 1, 2021): 110280. https://doi.org/10.1016/j.paid.2020.110280.

5. Rice, Kenneth G., and Clarissa M. E. Richardson. "Classification Challenges in Perfectionism." *Journal of Counseling Psychology* 61, no. 4 (October 2014): 641–48. https://doi.org/10.1037/cou0000040.

6. Yalom, Irvin D. *The Gift of Therapy: An Open Letter to a New Generation of Therapists and Their Patients.* London: Piatkus Books, 2002.

7. Horney. *Neurosis and Human Growth.*

8. Worley, S. L. "The Extraordinary Importance of Sleep: The Detrimental Effects of Inadequate Sleep on Health and Public Safety Drive an Explosion of Sleep Research." *P&T: A Peer-Reviewed Journal for Formulary Management* 43, no. 12 (2018): 758–63.

9. "Understanding the Glymphatic System." Neuronline, July 17, 2018. https://neuronline.sfn.org/scientific-research/understanding-the-glymphatic-system.

10. Benveniste, H., et al. "The Glymphatic System and Waste Clearance with Brain Aging: A Review." *Gerontology* 65 (2019): 106–19. https://doi.org/10.1159/000490349.

11. Jessen, Nadia Aalling, et al. "The Glymphatic System—A Beginner's Guide." *Neurochemical Research* 40, no. 12 (2015): 2583–99. https://doi.org/10.1007/s11064-015-1581-6.

12. Gholipour, Bahar. "Sleep Shrinks the Brain's Synapses to Make Room for New Learning." *Scientific American*, May 1, 2017. https://www.scientificamerican.com/article/sleep-shrinks-the-brain-rsquo-s-synapses-to-make-room-for-new-learning.

13. "How Does Sleep Affect Your Heart Health?" Centers for Disease Control and Prevention, January 4, 2021. https://www.cdc.gov/bloodpressure/sleep.htm.

14. Sharma, Sunil, and Mani Kavuru. "Sleep and Metabolism: An Overview." *International Journal of Endocrinology* 2010 (August 2, 2010): 1–12. https://doi.org/10.1155/2010/270832.

15. Lange, Tanja, et al. "Sleep Enhances the Human Antibody Response to Hepatitis A Vaccination." *Psychosomatic Medicine* 65, no. 5 (September 2003): 831–35. https://doi.org/10.1097/01.psy.0000091382.61178.f1.

16. Spiegel, Karine, et al. "Brief Communication: Sleep Curtailment in Healthy Young Men Is Associated with Decreased Leptin Levels, Elevated Ghrelin Levels, and Increased Hunger and Appetite." *Annals of Internal Medicine* 141, no. 11 (December 7, 2004): 846. https://doi.org/10.7326/0003-4819-141-11-200412070-00008.

17. Karine, et al. "Brief Communication."

18. "How Does Sleep Affect Your Heart Health?"

19. Lineberry, Denise. "To Sleep or Not to Sleep?" NASA, April 14, 2009. https://www.nasa.gov/centers/langley/news/researchernews/rn_sleep.html.

20. Scott, Alexander J., Thomas L. Webb, and Georgina Rowse. "Does Improving Sleep Lead to Better Mental Health? A Protocol for a Meta-Analytic Review of Randomised Controlled Trials." *BMJ Open* 7, no. 9 (September 2017): e016873. https://doi.org/10.1136/bmjopen-2017-016873.

Chapter 9: Now That You're Free

1. Maines, Rachel P. *The Technology of Orgasm: Hysteria, the Vibrator, and Women's Sexual Satisfaction.* Baltimore, MD: Johns Hopkins University Press, 2001.

2. Oswald, A. J., E. Proto, and D. Sgroi. "Happiness and Productivity." *Journal of Labor Economics* 33, no. 4 (2015): 789–822. https://doi.org/10.1086/681096.

3. Suh, Hanna, Philip B. Gnilka, and Kenneth G. Rice. "Perfectionism and Well-Being: A Positive Psychology Framework." *Personality and Individual Differences* 111 (June 2017): 25–30. https://doi.org/10.1016/j.paid.2017.01.041.

4. Lerner, Harriet. *Why Won't You Apologize?: Healing Big Betrayals and Everyday Hurts.* London: Duckworth Overlook, 2018.

5. Lerner. *Why Won't You Apologize?*

6. Lerner. *Why Won't You Apologize?*

7. Whitaker, Holly (@holly). 2021. "You ARE doing it. This is it." Instagram photo, April 23, 2021, https://www.instagram.com/p/COAYOh7H7XZ/?igshid=MDJmNz VkMjY%3D.

8. Ben-Shahar, Tal. *The Pursuit of Perfect: Stop Chasing Perfection and Find Your Path to Lasting Happiness!* New York; London: McGraw-Hill, 2009.

9. Pressfield, Steven. "Writing Wednesdays: Resistance and Self-Loathing," November 6, 2013. https://stevenpressfield.com/2013/11/resistance-and-self-loathing.

INDEX